Knitting with Beads

Knitting with Beads

FIONA MORRIS

THE CROWOOD PRESS

First published in 2018 by
The Crowood Press Ltd
Ramsbury, Marlborough
Wiltshire SN8 2HR

www.crowood.com

British Library Cataloguing-in-Publication Data
A catalogue record for this book is available from the British Library.

ISBN 978 1 78500 507 7

Frontispiece: Garter-and-Diamond Lace Shawl, knitted with Juniper Moon Farm Findley
Dappled lace-weight yarn.

Acknowledgements
There are a number of people I need to thank for their help and support while I wrote this book:
my knitting friend and tech editor, Heather Murray; another knitting friend, Joanne Cummins,
for doing some knitting; my friend Jan Wilson, who did all of the modelling; Cathy Scott of
Stitchmastery, who helped to develop some new chart symbols to represent the techniques of
knitting with beads; and Jacquie Kennedy of Liss Wools and all the knitters who visit this yarn
store, where I often teach; but most of all my husband, Dave, who not only took many of the
photographs but also did the cooking and housework so that I could work on this book.

Tech editor: Heather Murray
Photographs: Dave Morris and Fiona Morris

Typeset by Peggy & Co. Design Inc.
Printed and bound in India by Parksons Graphics

CONTENTS

INTRODUCTION

I first came across beads in knitting in the early 1990s when I was attending a textiles course. One day, the tutor brought two vintage beaded items to class: a Victorian beaded, knitted purse and a beaded, crocheted miser's purse. I had never seen this type of knitting before. When I got home, I did a search on the Internet and came across an American website called Baglady. The website (which is now defunct) had for sale booklets of patterns and materials that included the very fine needles needed for knitting amulet beaded purses. I purchased a pattern book and some needles, which started my knitting-with-beads adventures.

I found British suppliers for the fine cotton yarns and beads required and made my first amulet purse by following the instructions in the booklet. In an American knitting magazine, I found another pattern, which I knitted, and then I started to design my own purses. I designed several small amulet purses and then a couple of beaded, knitted evening bags. I also started playing around with beads and wire, and beads and nylon fishing line, to knit jewellery pieces.

Initially, I could not find much written about knitting with beads, until I was given an old copy of *Mary Thomas's Knitting Book* by a friend; this book includes a brief history of knitting with beads and explains the difference between Bead Knitting and Beaded Knitting. I realized that the purses I was making were Beaded Knitting. I subsequently did make a couple of items of Bead Knitting, where a bead is knitted or purled through every stitch, to give a solid, beaded fabric.

Around 2000, another friend came across a book called *Purls on the Pulse*, about Norwegian Beaded-Knitting cuffs. The book was written in Norwegian but contained charts for all of the included Beaded Knitting. The cuffs were worked in garter stitch, with the beads being placed according to the chart between knit stitches when working the wrong-side rows, to produce a pattern on the right side of the knitting.

In the last ten to fifteen years, there have been quite a few developments in knitting with beads, particularly in conjunction with lace, all of which has added to my knowledge and enjoyment of knitting with beads.

I have written this book to encourage knitters of all levels to explore the various methods of including beads in their knitting. The book covers a variety of different techniques, with beads being threaded on to the yarn and beads being applied as you go along with a project. Chapter 6, which covers experimentation with beads, yarn and stitch patterns, offers starting points for you to develop your own ideas of using beads in knitting, and Part 2 of this book features projects for a wide range of items, involving various techniques.

CHAPTER 1

TOOLS AND TECHNIQUES

Tools and materials

Beads

There is a large range of different types of beads available now, but not all of these beads are suitable to use in knitting. The size, shape and weight of the beads are all important factors to consider when selecting beads to knit with. Very large and heavy beads will be uncomfortable to wear, but very small beads or beads with very small holes may not be possible to thread on to the knitting yarn.

For most types of knitting with beads, glass seed beads work best. Seed beads have a rounded or cylindrical shape and a central hole. The beads come in a range of sizes; the smaller the size of the bead, the larger the bead's size number. For example, a size 6 seed bead is much larger than a size 15 seed bead. The range of sizes available does vary from manufacturer to manufacturer. Size 11 or 10 beads are usually the smallest size of seed beads to be used in Beaded Knitting. Size 8 or 7 beads are a good size for a variety of uses, and size 6 or 5 beads generally make a bolder statement.

The main factor determining how well the beads will work is the relationship between the yarn being used and the size of the bead hole. The beads often need to be threaded on to the knitting yarn before knitting. Most seed beads will go on to fine

> ### A general guide to yarn thickness and bead size
>
> Beads of size 11 or 10 will go on to fine lace-weight yarn, No. 8 Pearl Cotton yarn and fine kid-mohair yarn.
>
> Beads of size 8 or 7 will go on to most 4ply/fingering-weight and finer yarns.
>
> Beads of size 6 or 5 will go on to fine DK-, sport- and 4ply/fingering-weight yarns.

lace-weight yarn or No. 8 Pearl Cotton yarn, but large beads may not work well on very fine yarns.

The material that the beads are made from is also important. The larger the bead, the heavier the bead is, and this is especially noticeable for heavier materials such as glass. A fine yarn may not support the weight of a heavier bead.

Other types of beads can be used in knitting, such as crystals, bi-cone beads, bugle beads and metallic, wood, bone and plastic beads, to mention a few. Decorative beads can be used to embellish the knitting, but, if you want to work with the beads by using Beaded-Knitting techniques, the holes in the beads must be large enough for the beads to be threaded on to the knitting yarn.

Fig. 1.1 A selection of different types of beads: seed beads of various sizes, cube beads, triangles, bugle beads, bi-cone beads and a variety of decorative beads.

Fig. 1.2 Samples of similarly sized seed beads from four different manufactures. From the top down are Czech Preciosa size 7, Czech Matubo™ size 8, Japanese Toho size 8 and Japanese Miyuki size 8 seed beads.

Fig. 1.3 Different bead finishes, clockwise from the top left: transparent, coloured iris, metallic, silver-lined, metallic iris, frosted and opaque.

There are a number of manufacturers of seed beads. The beads used in the samples in this book come from either Japan or Czechoslovakia. The Japanese manufacturers include Miyuki, Toho Beads® and Matsuno, and the Czech manufactures include Preciosa and Matubo™. The quality of the beads with respect to the constancy of shape and size does vary depending on where the beads are produced, with the most consistently shaped beads coming from Japan.

Seed beads also come in a variety of finishes. The beads on three out of the four featured bead strings have a similar finish and are often described as metallic-iris beads. They are opaque beads with a polished finish, and there is variation in the colours of individual beads included in a particular bead colour-way. Some other bead finishes are transparent, silver-lined, gold-lined, AB (aurora borealis), opaque, frosted and matt. The colour of transparent beads is affected by the colour of the yarn that they are threaded on to. Silver-lined beads have more sparkle than opaque or metallic beads. Beads with an AB coating have a slightly iridescent look; frosted beads have less of a shine and look more like matt-finish beads.

Yarn

The main factors to consider when the selecting yarn to use for knitting with beads are whether the yarn is fine enough to go through the holes in the beads that you want to use and how robust the yarn is.

Most designs that require Beaded-Knitting techniques are made in 4ply/fingering-weight or finer yarns, as these yarns will work with the largest range of seed-bead sizes. The yarns can be made from a variety of different fibres and by a variety of different spinning methods, but, for most Beaded-Knitting techniques, the yarn does need to be robust.

For most of the techniques covered in this book, the beads are threaded on to the yarn before the knitting is started and therefore are constantly being pushed along the yarn, which can cause the yarn to wear. If the yarn is very softly spun or is a singles yarn, the yarn may break during the knitting process or require fewer beads to be threaded on to it at any one time, to avoid yarn breakage, resulting in shorter lengths of yarn being used and therefore more yarn ends having to be woven in.

Fig. 1.4 Fine enamelled craft wire (right) and monofilament nylon fishing line (left).

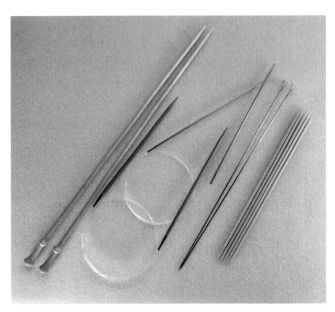

Fig. 1.5 A selection of knitting needles, including 1.25mm (US 0000) steel needles.

As well as conventional yarns, other materials such as fine knitting wire and monofilament nylon fishing line can be used for knitting with beads, to make jewellery. Wire comes in a large range of gauges and colours. Fine, 0.20mm, enamelled copper wire has been used for the samples of wire knitting featured in this book. This thickness of wire is quite flexible, making it fairly easy to knit with. If you want to use a thicker wire, the 0.20mm wire can be worked with several strands being held together, to make up a thicker wire; this approach is recommended, rather than trying to use a thicker wire, which has much less flexibility.

Monofilament nylon fishing line also comes in a range of thicknesses. A range of thicknesses between 0.17mm and 0.23mm have been used in the project samples. The nylon fishing line is fairly easy to work with, although it can be difficult to see the stitches on the needle. The nylon may be clear or it may have a tint of colour. The different colours of nylon show up better on some types of needle than on others, so you may have to experiment with using bamboo, wood and metal needles.

Fig. 1.6 Crochet hooks and dental Superfloss™, for placing beads.

Knitting needles and crochet hooks

For most Beaded-Knitting techniques, it is not necessary to have any specialist knitting needles, as long as the needle size is appropriate for the yarn being used. Knitting needles can be made from a variety of materials, including wood, bamboo, steel, coated aluminium or plastic. The type of needle, for example, straight, circular or double pointed, is more relevant to the project being knitted than the fact that beads are being included.

Bead Knitting and some fine Beaded Knitting, such as for the knitted purses, are worked with very fine yarn and small beads, so very fine needles, such as 1.25mm or 1.50mm needles (US 0000 or US 000 needles, respectively), are also required. These very fine needles are usually available only as metal or steel needles, because wood or bamboo needles this fine have a tendency to break.

Fig. 1.7   A beading mat, a piece of chamois leather and small containers are all suitable for holding beads when they need to be threaded on to the yarn or picked up with a crochet hook.

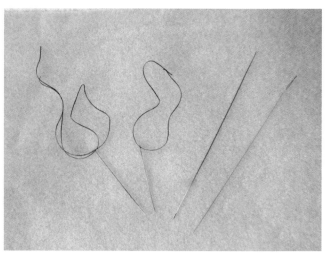

Fig. 1.8   Tools for threading beads, from left to right: a beading needle threaded with a doubled thread to create a loop at one side of the needle eye, a beading needle threaded with a thread that is tied into a loop, a Big Eye beading needle and a Beadalon® collapsible-eye needle.

When working the method that places a bead on a stitch by using a crochet hook, this method requires the use of a crochet hook that is fine enough for the bead to fit over the head of the hook. The size of the hole in the bead does vary with the size of the seed bead and with the manufacturer, but generally a crochet hook of between 0.60mm (US steel hook 14) and 1.00mm (US steel hook 12) works best. Hooks that are finer than 0.60mm may not hold on to the stitch very well and may be unable to pull the whole yarn strand through the bead, and hooks that are larger than 1.00mm (US steel hook 12) may be too thick to go through the hole in the bead.

An alternative to using a crochet hook to place beads is to use dental Superfloss. One end of the Superfloss is coated, which makes the end firm enough to go through the hole in a bead and also to pick up a stitch from the needle but flexible enough to fold back on itself when the bead is being placed.

Other beading-related tools and materials

The majority of techniques that are used when knitting with beads require the beads to be threaded on to the yarn before the process of knitting begins. To stop the beads from rolling away when being threaded, they can sit on a beading mat or be held in a shallow container. Beading mats can be made of a variety of materials, as long as the materials used will stop the beads from rolling around and will not hamper the threading

process. Mats designed specifically for beading are made with a soft, almost fur-like surface of short fibres and work very well, but other materials such as fine velvet or chamois leather can also work well. Felt does not work as well as other materials, as it tends to catch on the threading needle point, resulting in the beads flying all over the place.

Some people prefer to use a jam-jar lid or a Pringles tube lid to hold the beads. Pringles tube lids do work well, because they can be pinched together to make a funnel when returning unused beads to their storage container. Shallow bowls and containers are also good for holding beads, when working the crochet-hook method.

Yarn is too soft to be able to push the yarn end through the bead hole, when threading beads on to the yarn, so it is necessary to use another method to thread on the beads. There are a number of tools that you can use to pick up the beads and move them on to the knitting yarn. The most common method is to use a sewing or beading needle and a transition thread. The needle is threaded with the transition thread, either threaded double to make a loop at one side of the needle eye or threaded and then tied into a knot to make a loop. The knitting yarn is passed through the loop. The needle is used to pick up the beads, which are pushed down the transition thread and on to the knitting yarn.

You can also buy a Big Eye beading needle or a Beadalon® collapsible-eye needle, which allows you to thread the knitting yarn through the needle and then pick up the beads with the

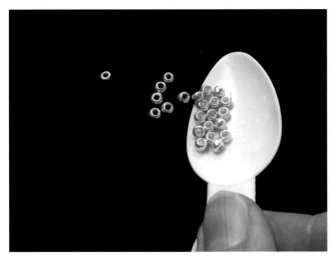

Fig. 1.9 Picking up beads with a medicine spoon to return them to their container.

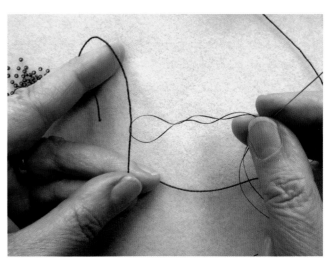

Fig. 1.10 Knitting yarn passed through the loop of Nymo® thread that is attached to the beading needle.

other end of the needle. Another alternative is to use a dental-floss threader. The yarn can be passed through the loop of the floss threader, and the end is firm enough to pick up the beads.

A bead scoop or small spoon such as a medicine spoon is very useful for picking up beads that need to be returned to their storage container.

Techniques

Threading beads on to the yarn

There are several ways to get beads on to knitting yarns. The method used may vary depending on the size of the beads to be threaded. Size 11 or 10 seed beads are about the smallest size that are used in knitting. The bead size is small, so the hole in the bead will also be small.

The method when threading beads of this size is to use a fine beading needle and Nymo® thread (a beadwork thread), threaded double through the eye of the needle.

The knitting yarn is threaded through the loop on one side of the eye of the needle. The easiest way to hold the beading needle is to hold it parallel to the surface of the beading mat and to use the point of the needle to tip the bead over so that you can push the needle through the hole in the bead. If you try to come into the bead vertically from above, it is quite difficult to pick up the bead, and you generally have to pick up the beads one at a time. By using the method of tipping the bead over,

Fig. 1.11 Beads picked up on the beading-needle point, with the needle held parallel to the surface holding the beads.

you can pick up quite a few beads on to the needle, before pushing them down the transition thread and on to the yarn.

This method of threading beads can be used for any size of bead.

If you are working with size 8 beads or larger, it is possible to use a fine sewing needle threaded with sewing thread that has been knotted into a circle to make a loop. As long as the bead hole is big enough to go over the knot, this method works well. The knitting yarn is threaded through the loop. The beads are picked up with the needle and pushed down the transition thread and on to the knitting yarn.

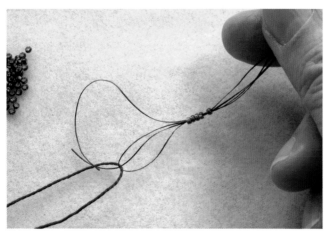

Fig. 1.12 Beads that have been pushed down the beading needle and on to the transition thread.

Fig. 1.13 Beads that have been pushed down the transition thread and on to the knitting yarn.

Fig. 1.14 Knitting yarn passed through the knotted thread loop that passes through the eye of the beading needle.

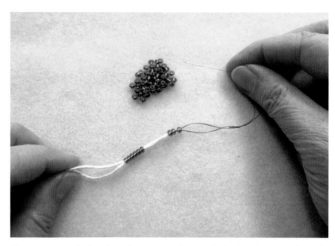

Fig. 1.15 Beads that have been picked up with the beading needle and pushed down the transition thread and on to the knitting yarn.

Fig. 1.16 Beadalon® collapsible-eye needle threaded with yarn and beads that have been pushed on to the knitting yarn.

Fig. 1.17 Green shawl edging worked with two different colours and sizes of beads.

A Big Eye beading needle is made from two thin wires that have been sealed together at each end, making a large opening along the length of the needle through which to place the knitting yarn. The Beadalon® collapsible-eye needle is very similar, but the two wires are twisted together, leaving a small loop at one end. The beads are picked up with one end of the needle and then pushed down the needle and on to the knitting yarn. The dental-floss threader works in the same way, but it is made from plastic rather than metal.

If only one colour of bead is being used for a project, the threading process is quite simple: just thread the beads on to the knitting yarn. If there are a lot of beads in the project, it is often better to try not to thread all of the beads on to the knitting yarn at the start of the project, as the beads have to be pushed along the yarn and can cause the knitting yarn to wear and become fragile. When making the small amulet beaded purses (*see* Purses and Bags), you should thread about half of the total number of beads on to the yarn at the beginning of the project.

For some projects, you may want to use more than one colour or type of bead. In this case, you will need to thread the beads in a set order, that is, in the reverse order to the order that the beads will be knitted.

In the featured green shawl, beads of two different colours were used for the edging. It was necessary to work out the bead-placement order for each repeat of the edging pattern and then thread the beads in the reverse order.

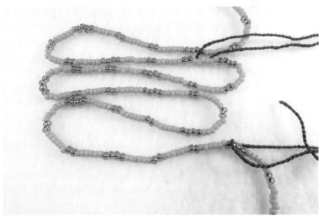

Fig. 1.18 Beads threaded in the correct sequence for working ten pattern repeats of the green shawl edging shown in Figure 1.17.

There are a lot of repeats of the edging pattern for this shawl, so, when threading the beads on to the yarn, it helps to divide the beads into groups of repeats and then to tie a piece of contrast-colour yarn around the knitting yarn after every ten repeats. This makes it easier to keep track of the number of repeats that have been threaded before you start to knit the edging. Once you start to knit the edging, these contrast-colour marker threads provide a way to double check your progress so that, when you reach a marker thread, you should also be at the end of a repeat and can then remove the marker thread, before starting on the next group of ten repeats.

Fig. 1.19 Three samples of Beaded Garter Stitch worked with the same yarn and size of needles throughout but with different sizes of seed beads.

Fig. 1.20 Three samples of Beaded Garter Stitch, for which the yarn and needle size have been changed along with the bead size used for each sample. These bead, needle-size and yarn combinations are more balanced than those of the dark-green samples with gold beads shown in Figure 1.19.

Yarn and bead combinations

It is important to ensure that the beads will go on to the yarn, but you also need to consider how well the size of the beads works with the thickness of the yarn being used and also how well the colour of the beads works with the colour of the yarn. A larger bead on a fine yarn can distort the knitting, but sometimes a small bead may be obscured by the yarn.

The dark-green yarn used for the three featured samples was a No. 8 Pearl Cotton yarn, knitted with 2.00mm (US 0) needles. The same numbers of stitches and rows were worked for each sample. The seed beads were all from the same manufacturer, Toho Beads®. The top sample was worked with size 11 seed beads, the middle sample was worked with size 8 seed beads and the bottom sample was worked with size 6 beads. As the beads get bigger, the width of the Beaded Garter Stitch gets

Fig. 1.21 This sample has been worked with four different colours of beads. From left to right are Matubo™ Crystal Full Labrador, Matubo™ Crystal Labrador, Toho Silver-Lined Crystal and Miyuki Blue/Purple Matt seed beads.

Fig. 1.22 A beaded edging worked in two different sizes of seed beads. The two beaded pattern repeats on the left were worked with Toho size 8 seed beads, and the two repeats on the right were worked with Matubo™ size 7 seed beads. The middle repeat was half worked with Matubo™ size 7 seed beads and half worked with Toho size 8 seed beads.

wider, and, with the sample showing size 6 seed beads, the beads are almost too wide for the space between stitches. For this fine yarn, the size 11 seed beads probably work best. Size 8 seed beads will create more impact, but the size 6 beads are really a bit too big.

In this second group of three samples, the same numbers of stitches and rows were worked for each sample, but the yarn and the needle size were changed with each increase of bead size, giving a more balanced fabric in relation to each bead size. The top sample shows size 11 beads on a lace-weight yarn, knitted with 2.50mm (US 1.5) needles. The middle sample shows size 8 beads on a 4ply/fingering-weight yarn, knitted with 3.25mm (US 3) needles, and the bottom sample shows size 6 beads on a DK-weight yarn, knitted with 4.00mm (US 6) needles.

Beads that may look lovely in the packet may not show up very well when knitted, particularly if the beads are used singly. The colour of the beads may be so similar to the colour of the yarn that they disappear, or a special finish on the beads may not be visible once the beads are on the yarn. It is a good idea to spend some time sampling the yarns and bead colours that you want to use for a project, before starting to make the project.

The technique being used to work the beads will also affect the way that you see the bead and yarn combination. Beads worked in Beaded Garter Stitch can look very different to beads worked in lace or placed over a stitch by using the crochet-hook method.

Fig. 1.23 The same yarn was used to knit this lace sample and Beaded-Garter-Stitch sample. The same three colours of size 6 seed beads were also used in both samples.

CHAPTER 2

BEAD KNITTING

Bead Knitting produces a solid, beaded fabric. The main feature that distinguishes Bead Knitting from Beaded Knitting is that the bead lies vertically on one leg of a stitch rather than sitting horizontally on the yarn strand between two stitches or in front of a stitch. Bead Knitting does require quite a bit of care and attention while it is being worked, and it is generally slower to work than other knitting techniques.

Bead Knitting was very popular in the nineteenth century. As people became wealthier and a middle class developed, women had more time to pursue pastimes such as embroidery, knitting and other crafts. During this period, Berlin woolwork, a form of embroidery, became very popular. The embroidery patterns were charted. Those ladies interested in decorative knitting found it was quite easy to convert these charts into charts suitable for use for knitting with beads. It became very popular to add beads to knitting, and this led to the creation of decorative Bead-Knitting bags with complicated floral images or even complete hunting scenes on them. Bead Knitting was also added to items of clothing for special occasions, such as baby bonnets for christenings, or to decorative leggings or cuffs, to embellish ordinary garments worn on special occasions.

Bead Knitting was worked in various parts of Europe, as well as Britain, and examples of these items can be found in a number of museum collections such as those of the Victoria and Albert Museum in London.

The basic fabric consists of twisted stocking stitch with a bead worked through each stitch on every row, apart from the first two and last two stitches of a row. A twisted stitch is used to tighten the stitch behind the bead, to ensure that the bead stays on the knit side of the fabric. As a result, Bead-Knitting fabric has a tendency to bias. Some of this bias can be corrected by blocking the piece of knitting, once it has been completed.

Before you start to knit, it is necessary to thread the beads on to the knitting yarn. If the fabric requires just one colour of bead, the order in which the beads are threaded does not matter. However, if the beads are being used to create a picture, the order of bead threading becomes very important. A chart is usually used to show the required bead colours and bead arrangement. The beads need to be threaded in the opposite order to the order that they will be knitted; namely, the last bead to be threaded is the first bead to be knitted.

The accompanying chart that can be used to knit a flat piece of Bead Knitting depicts a simple heart shape of red beads, surrounded by contrast-colour beads. When knitting from the chart, you would start at the bottom-right corner of the chart and read Row 1 (and all odd-number rows) from right to left and Row 2 (and all even-number rows) from left to right. To ensure that the beads are worked in the correct order for knitting and producing the charted design, you need to thread the last bead to be knitted first and work backwards through the

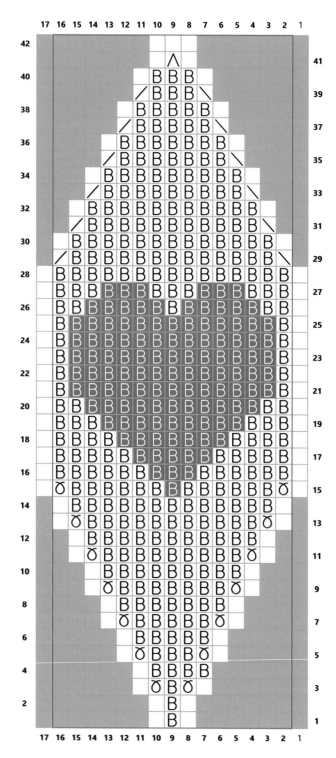

Fig. 2.1 Bead-Knitting Heart-Decoration Chart.

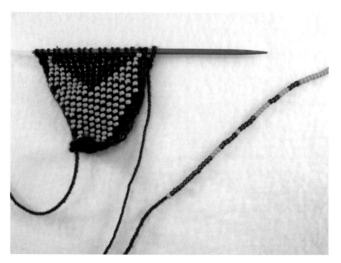

Fig. 2.2 Beads, threaded in the correct order on to the yarn, showing the next few groups of beads to be knitted.

Fig. 2.3 A piece of Bead-Knitting fabric, worked by following the Heart-Decoration Chart.

knitting sequence. Assuming that there is an even number of rows on the chart, when threading the beads on to the yarn, you need to follow the chart by starting at the top right corner of the chart, working towards the left, reading the even-number rows from right to left and the odd-number rows from left to right as previously mentioned.

It is very important to thread the beads on to the yarn in the correct order, so it is worth taking your time to thread and check the beads for each row before starting to thread the next row's beads. It is possible to correct mistakes during the knitting process by cutting the yarn to remove an extra bead or to rethread some of the beads, if necessary; however, if you take your time by checking the bead threading as you go along, you should be able to avoid the problem of having the wrong colour of bead in any particular place while knitting.

How to work bead knitting

Working a twisted, beaded knit stitch

Fig. 2.4 Insert the point of the right-hand needle through the back loop of the next stitch on the left-hand needle.

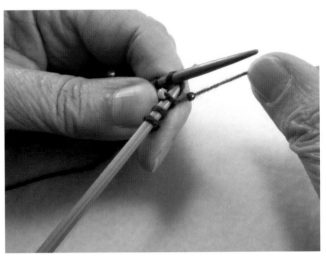

Fig. 2.5 Take the yarn with the bead on it around the point of the right-hand needle so that the bead is ready to be pushed through the stitch that is being knitted into to the knit side of the fabric.

Fig. 2.6 Knit the stitch on the left-hand needle, pushing the bead through the stitch to the knit side of the fabric as you pull the yarn through to create the new stitch on the right-hand needle.

Working a twisted, beaded purl stitch

It is quite difficult to get into the back loop of the stitch to work a twisted purl stitch. It helps to stretch the stitch slightly before putting the point of the right-hand needle into the back of this stitch.

It may be necessary to try out a couple of different sizes of needles before you get the stitch size correct for Bead Knitting. If the stitch size is a bit small, it is very difficult to get the beads through the twisted stitches, and the back of the fabric can become overstretched. In this situation, try going up by one needle size at a time, to increase the size of the stitches. You may need to increase by only one needle size, to be able to work a suitable fabric.

If the stitch size is on the large side, and the fabric is a bit loose, the beads will work through the stitches quite easily but may not stay in place on one of the vertical legs of each stitch. The stitches should allow the beads to pass through fairly easily but be able to close behind the beads once each stitch has been completed. If the fabric is loose, try going down a needle size to see whether that will fix the problem.

The sample of the Heart Decoration was worked by using a sock yarn, size 8 seed beads and 3.25mm (US 3) needles. It was initially worked with 3.00mm (US 2.5) needles, but the fabric was quite tight to work and was overstretched on the wrong side, so 3.25mm (US 3) needles were used to complete the sample.

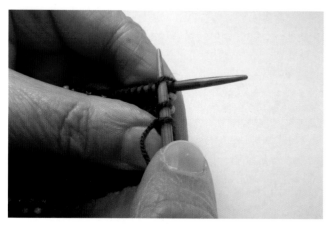

Fig. 2.7 Stretch the stitch on the left-hand needle with the point of the right-hand needle before trying to work a purl-through-the-back-loop stitch.

Fig. 2.8 The point of the right-hand needle has been inserted through the back loop of the stitch on the left-hand needle, ready for the yarn to be wrapped around the point of the right-hand needle and the purl stitch to be completed.

Fig. 2.9 Take the yarn with the bead on it over and around the point of the right-hand needle so that the bead is ready to be pushed through the stitch that is being purled into to the knit side of the fabric.

Fig. 2.10 Purl the stitch on the left-hand needle, pushing the bead through the stitch to the knit side of the fabric as you pull the yarn through to create the new stitch on the right-hand needle.

After completing each row, you need take the time to check the row, to make sure that all of the beads have been knitted correctly. Sometimes, a bead may not stay on one of the vertical legs of the stitch, but this problem is fairly easy to fix a couple of rows later, by pushing the bead back into the correct position.

If the piece of knitting is fairly small, such as for the Heart-Decoration Pattern, at the beginning of each row, push up the beads required for that row of knitting.

This method of Bead Knitting does cause the knitted fabric to bias, as all of the stitches are twisted in the same direction and each bead sits on the right leg of a stitch. Most of the time, the bias can be corrected by blocking, once the piece of knitting has been cast off. However, there is an alternative method of working Bead Knitting that does not produce a biased fabric, but the finished piece has a different, less uniform look.

Fig. 2.11 Push up the beads for you to be ready to knit the next row.

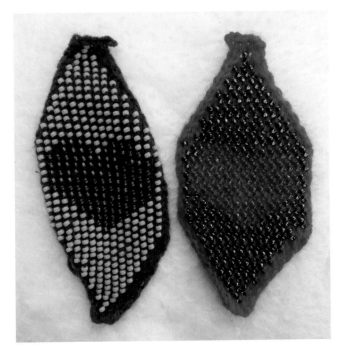

Fig. 2.12 Samples of Bead Knitting and Plaited Knitting. The left-hand sample of Bead Knitting has a bias, even though it has been blocked, but all of the beads lie in the same direction. The right-hand sample of Plaited Knitting is straight, but the beads lie in different directions on alternate rows, giving the knitting a less uniform look.

Plaited Knitting: an alternative method for working Bead Knitting, to reduce bias

The basic method of working Bead Knitting is to work a twisted stitch, but it is possible to use a technique called Plaited Knitting to work a beaded fabric. Plaited Knitting uses the Western open knit stitch and the Eastern crossed-purl stitch. A twisted-stitch fabric is still created; the stitches are twisted on the row after they are first worked, and each bead is vertical but sits on the alternate leg of a stitch on alternate rows. This produces a balanced fabric, but the beads of alternate rows lie in alternate directions, leaning to the left and right rather than all leaning to the right.

Working a Plaited-Knitting knit stitch with a bead

Fig. 2.13   The stitches on the left-hand needle are sitting with the left leg of each stitch to the front of the needle, as the stitches were worked by using the Eastern crossed-purl method for the previous row.

Fig. 2.14   A Western open knit stitch is being worked, but, because of the way the purl stitch was worked on the previous row, the right leg of the stitch is to the back of the needle. The stitch is worked by inserting the point of the right-hand needle around the left leg and into the stitch as for a normal Western open knit stitch, but, in this case, this manoeuvre twists the stitch from the previous row at the base of the stitch, turning it into a twisted knit stitch.

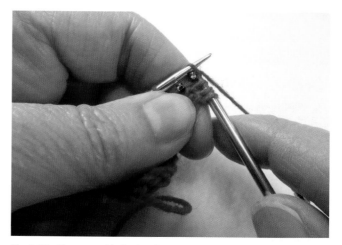

Fig. 2.15   The yarn with the bead is wrapped around the point of the right-hand needle as for working a normal Western knit stitch, and the bead is being pushed through the stitch to the knit side of the fabric.

Working a Plaited-Knitting purl stitch with a bead

Fig. 2.16 The stitches on the left-hand needle are sitting in the Western stitch orientation, with the right leg of the stitch to the front of the needle. In order to twist the stitches that were knitted on the previous row, each purl stitch is worked through the back loop of the stitch of the previous row.

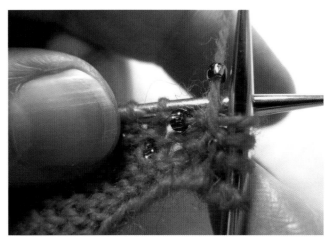

Fig. 2.17 To work an Eastern crossed-purl stitch, as well as working through the back loop of the stitch on the left-hand needle, the yarn with the bead is wrapped under the point of the right-hand needle and then taken between the points of the needles so that the strand and bead can be pushed through the stitch on the left-hand needle, making the new stitch on the right-hand needle.

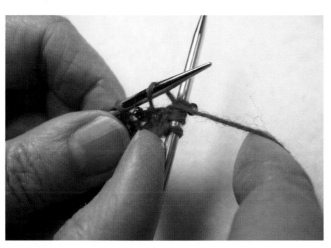

Fig. 2.18 The bead is pushed through the stitch being purled on the left-hand needle to the knit side of the fabric as the new purl stitch is worked.

Fig. 2.19 The Eastern crossed-purl stitch is completed, with the bead sitting on the knit side of the fabric. However, you can also see that the bead of the previous row is sitting on the strand between two stitches instead of on the leg of the appropriate stitch on the knit side of the fabric. This bead will need to be repositioned, but it is much easier to do this after several rows have been worked.

Again, it is important to check each row after it has been worked, to make sure that the beads have been knitted in the correct order and are positioned on one leg of the stitch, not on the strand between two adjacent stitches.

Fixing mistakes in Bead Knitting

Beads placed on previous rows can move out of position when you are manipulating the fabric on a later row. If this happens, you will need to push the beads back on to the leg of the appropriate stitch to correct the mistake. It is usually easier to do this once several rows have been worked after the row where the mistake is located.

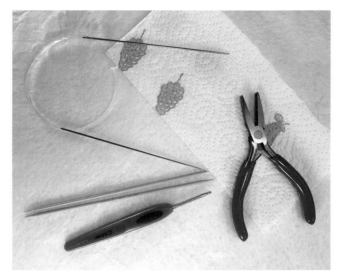

Fig. 2.20   Useful tools for fixing mistakes, anticlockwise from the bottom right: jewellery pliers, kitchen paper, a spare fine circular knitting needle or double-pointed needles, and a fine crochet hook.

Fig. 2.21   Two beads (circled in yellow) have moved out of position on the right-hand side of the fabric, three rows below the current row.

Fig. 2.22   The circled bead is sitting on the strand between two stitches.

Fig. 2.23   You can use the point of the right-hand needle to lift the leg of the stitch below the incorrectly positioned bead so that the bead can slip under this strand and on to the leg of the stitch that it should be on.

Fig. 2.24   Each of the two beads is now correctly placed on the leg of its stitch.

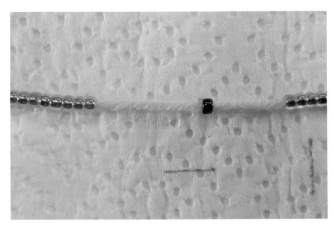

Fig. 2.25   The bead in the centre of the yarn is of the wrong colour and needs to be removed with pliers.

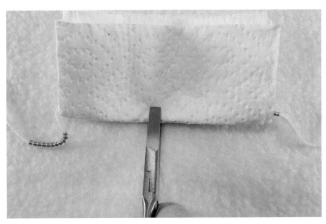

Fig. 2.26   The bead that needs to be removed is wrapped in kitchen paper and held with the pliers and then crushed.

Fig. 2.27   The bead after it has been crushed with the pliers is now only bits of glass being held in the kitchen paper.

The other main problem that occurs with Bead Knitting is the beads being incorrectly threaded. If the problem is something such as there being one bead too many, it is possible to remove the bead by breaking it with a pair of pliers.

You will need a tissue or soft cloth, a pair of jewellery pliers and a flat, hard surface in order to remove one bead safely. Place the yarn with the incorrectly threaded bead on to the tissue or soft cloth on a flat, hard surface. Wrap the tissue or soft cloth around the bead and then, with the bead and tissue/ cloth held in the pliers, rested on the surface, squeeze the pliers to crush the bead. When using the pliers, you do need to take care to make sure that you do not cut the knitting yarn when crushing the bead. Remove the tissue/cloth, and throw away the fragments of the crushed bead. You should now be able to continue knitting according to the pattern.

If there are several beads that are out of order, it will be necessary to cut the yarn and rethread the beads before continuing to knit the piece.

CHAPTER 3

BEADED KNITTING IN GARTER STITCH AND STOCKING STITCH

Beaded Knitting in garter stitch

Beaded Knitting in garter stitch requires the beads to be threaded on to the yarn before you start to knit. There are two main methods of working with beads in garter stitch. Both methods use the technique of suspending beads between knit stitches. One method adds beads on every row, whereas the other method adds beads on only alternate rows.

Beaded Garter Stitch with beads every row

This is the method that is used to make some of the Victorian-style beaded purses and jewellery. With this method, the number of beads strung between stitches can vary from one up to any number of beads that you want. However, the more beads strung between stitches, the greater the possibility of gaps appearing in the knitted fabric, so eight or nine beads is about the maximum number to string, to maintain a good fabric. The beads push the knitting apart, so it is also necessary to string beads on every row. If more than one bead is strung on one row but not on the next row, the knitting will either be pulled out of shape or there will be long strands of yarn on one side of the knitting.

The basic working method is very simple. Knit to the point where you want to add beads. Push up a bead (or the required number of beads) next to the stitch closest to the point of the right-hand needle, and knit the next stitch on the left-hand needle. The beads sit on the yarn between the previously knitted stitch and the stitch that was just knitted.

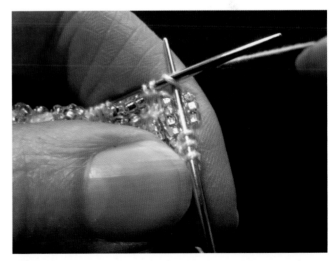

Fig. 3.1 The right-hand needle is inserted into the next stitch on the left-hand needle, and three beads are pushed up the yarn to sit next to the last stitch that was worked on the right-hand needle.

Fig. 3.2 Shades-of-Blue Amulet Purse, featuring two colours of seed beads.

Once there is more than one bead suspended between stitches, it is important to have the same number of suspended beads between stitches on both sides of the knitting. If the beads are added to only one side of the knitting, once you have three or four beads suspended between knit stitches, a long strand of yarn will be present on the other side of the knitting or the knitting will start to collapse.

When working this method of Beaded Knitting, if the knitted piece requires one colour of beads, it is possible to simply thread the beads on to the knitting yarn before you start to knit. The beads are pushed along the yarn during the knitting process, so you do have to consider the maximum number of beads that you want to be threaded on to the yarn at any one time.

When knitting a beaded amulet purse such as the featured Shades-of-Blue Amulet Purse, it is best to thread approximately half of the total number of beads required for the project before you start to knit. Initially, there will be a lot of beads to push

along the knitting yarn but not so many that it could damage the yarn, while ensuring that you do not have to deal with too many joins and yarn ends to sew in when finishing the purse.

With the small purses, it is best practice to limit the number of joins within the knitting to one join, if possible. The method of knitting these purses requires the purse to be sewn together at each side, so joining in a new end of yarn at the edge of the knitted fabric will provide some yarn for sewing up to finish the purse.

When you get to the point where you have used nearly all of the beads that are currently threaded on to the knitting yarn, you do need to make sure that you have enough beads to complete the next row, before starting to knit that row. The amulet purses and Silver Evening Bag (*see* Purses and Bags) also each have a section of short-row knitting, to create the curved shape at the bottom of the piece, so it is important to make sure that you have enough beads to complete a whole short-row sequence before you start to knit that section.

If the purse is to be knitted with more than one colour of bead, as with the Shades-of-Blue Amulet Purse, it is necessary to thread the beads on to the knitting yarn in the correct order. For the purse pattern, threading instructions are provided to help you to thread the beads correctly, to ensure that, when the purse is knitted, the beads will be worked in the correct order; namely, the first bead to be threaded is the last bead to be knitted.

The patterns for the featured purses are also written in a slightly different way to other patterns. The number of stitches cast on and knitted at the start of the purse remains the same throughout the pattern. The beginning of the pattern sets the position of the bead groups, with the number of stitches being knitted between each bead group remaining the same throughout the pattern. The number of beads strung between stitches changes, so the pattern tells you the number of beads to string in each group on each row, rather than the number of stitches to knit. It is this change in the number of beads between stitches that creates the shape of the purses.

Each purse is basically a long strip of knitting. The narrowest part of the purse is usually the cast-on and cast-off points, unless the purse is knitted to include a shaped flap. As you knit down the piece, the purse gets wider (there are more beads between stitches). At a set point, short-row shaping may be added (with the sequence being worked an even number of times) to create a rounded shape at the bottom of the purse, and then the purse gets narrower again. If a flap is added, as with the Shades-of-Blue Amulet Purse, the beading sequence from the start of the purse is repeated, and the flap is cast off with beads being strung between stitches as part of the cast-off.

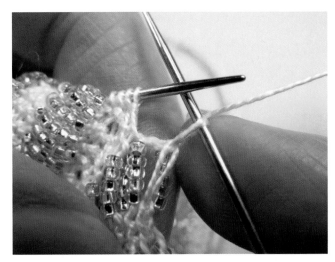

Fig. 3.3 A group of beads being pushed up next to the stitch just worked, with the stitch being kept as a large loop.

Fig. 3.4 Casting off a stitch with beads being strung between stitches.

Casting off with beads strung between stitches

The method of casting off is a variation of the basic Chain Cast-Off (*see* Chapter 7 for further details about this basic cast-off method):

Knit the next two stitches on the left-hand needle. *Lift the first stitch to be knitted on the right-hand needle over the second stitch to be knitted on the right-hand needle and off the right-hand needle. Knit the next stitch on the left-hand needle*, repeat from * to *. When you get to the point where beads are strung between the stitches closest to the points of both needles, for example, five beads are strung between these stitches, with one stitch on the right-hand needle and a line of five beads being present before the next stitch on the left-hand needle, push up the next five beads to be placed next to the stitch closest to the point of the right-hand needle, but do not pull this stitch on the right-hand needle tight. Knit the next stitch on the left-hand needle, and lift the loose first stitch to be knitted on the right-hand needle over the second stitch to be knitted, making sure that there is enough yarn in the lifted-over stitch to stretch across the gap created by the five strung beads that have just been placed. The stitch has been cast off with a string of five beads sitting behind the long chain of the cast-off stitch. Continue casting off as before.

With this type of Beaded Garter Stitch, a lot of beads are used. The small amulet purses require about 40g (1½oz) of size 10 or 11 seed beads and are knitted with a fine Pearl

Cotton yarn. The cotton yarn is strong enough to withstand the friction of the beads being pushed along it, is fine enough for the beads to be threaded on to the yarn and has enough body to help keep the shape of the bag once the purse has been knitted.

Beaded Garter Stitch with beads every other row

With this second method of working Beaded Knitting in garter stitch, only one bead is strung between stitches. This method of Beaded Garter Stitch was traditionally employed in some Scandinavian and Baltic countries, for the knitting of decorative beaded cuffs, which were used to dress up garments worn for Sundays and special occasions. The beads create a pattern similar to a stranded-colourwork pattern on the right side of the fabric. The cuffs are knitted in garter stitch, and the beads are added between stitches on wrong-side rows so that they appear on the right side of the fabric.

Occasionally, you may come across charts that are not drawn in what is now accepted as the standard way, that is, matching how the fabric will look from the right side, with the chart for flat knitting being read from right to left for right-side rows and from left to right for wrong-side rows. Working the charts for Beaded Garter Stitch is one of these occasions. The charts were originally drawn to show a black spot, representing a bead, sitting on the chart grid line between two stitches.

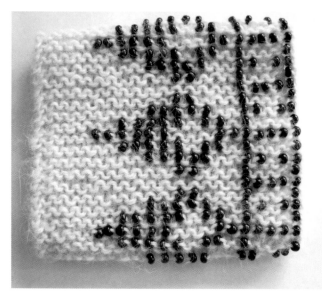

Fig. 3.5 A Beaded-Garter-Stitch cuff.

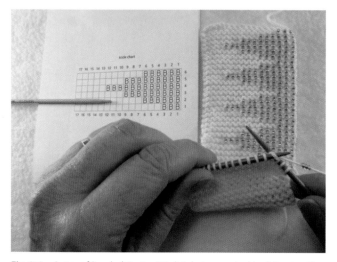

Fig. 3.7 A row of Beaded Garter Stitch is being worked by following the chart. The wrong side of the fabric is facing the knitter, but the right side of the fabric is laid next to the chart. When the knitting is turned around to be viewed from the right side, the bead pattern will be mirrored.

For flat knitting, two rows of all knit stitches produces one ridge when looked at from the right side of the fabric. The beads are placed while knitting the wrong-side rows, to give a ridge of Beaded Garter Stitch. The row numbers on the chart relate to the ridge numbers of the garter-stitch fabric rather than the number of the row that you are knitting.

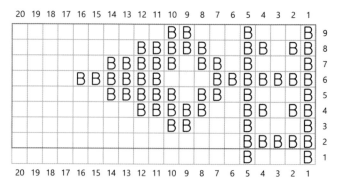

Fig. 3.6 A chart for placing beads in garter stitch, showing wrong-side rows only.

The charts in this book are drawn featuring the 'knit the stitch and push up a bead' symbol, to show the bead positions as you work the wrong-side row. Only wrong-side rows are shown on the chart, and the chart is read from right to left, giving a mirror image of the pattern when it is viewed from the right side of the fabric. The blank squares are worked as normal knit stitches. The squares with a 'B' symbol are worked as a knit stitch followed immediately by a bead being pushed up next to the stitch that was just worked.

The beads are not facing you when they are being placed in the knitted fabric, so it is important to check the row from the right side, before knitting the next row.

Beaded Knitting in stocking stitch

There are two main methods of working Beaded Knitting in stocking stitch: stringing beads between purl stitches and using the slip-stitch technique.

Beads placed between purl stitches

For Beaded Knitting generally, the bead sits on the yarn between two adjacent stitches. When working a knit stitch, the yarn comes through the stitch on the left needle from the back of the work to make a new loop on the right needle and passes through the stitch on the left needle to the back of the work again. The strand between stitches runs along the back of the knitting. As a result, when beads sit between knit stitches, the bead is visible on the purl side or wrong side of the fabric

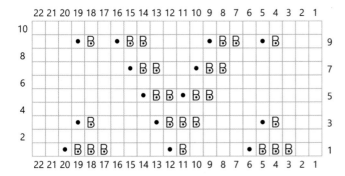

Fig. 3.8 A chart for placing beads between purl stitches in stocking-stitch fabric.

Fig. 3.9 Knit up to the position of the next stitch that will have a bead following it once the stitch has been purled.

Fig. 3.10 The purl stitch has just been worked, and two beads, which are to be placed next to the next two stitches, are on the yarn near the point of the right-hand needle.

Fig. 3.11 The first of the two beads has been placed and sits between two purl stitches. The second of the two beads is about to be placed, by working another purl stitch.

when it is worked in stocking stitch. When working garter stitch (knitting every row), if beads are worked on every row, they are visible on both sides of the fabric. If they are worked on every other row in garter stitch, the beads are visible on only one side of the fabric. When working stocking stitch, to make the beads visible on the knit side of the fabric, it is necessary to work a purl stitch on each side of the bead.

The beads can be placed to make a visual pattern on the right side of the fabric. The pattern for bead placement is usually given in the form of a chart.

The chart is drawn to represent the knitting as viewed from the right side of the fabric. Generally, for flat knitting, the odd-number rows will be read from right to left and the even-number rows from left to right. The 'B' symbol with a spot within it indicates that the stitch should be worked as a purl stitch, with a bead being pushed up against this stitch after the stitch has been worked. The final B of the group is followed by the normal symbol for a purl stitch, as the beads are always suspended between two purl stitches.

Purl one stitch, push up a bead next to this purl stitch on the right-hand needle, and then purl the next stitch.

Continue by working knit stitches until you reach the next point at which a bead is to be placed. The beads can also be placed on wrong-side rows, in which case they will sit between knit stitches. The disadvantage of placing beads on wrong-side rows is that, while you are placing the beads, you cannot see the beaded pattern as it will appear on the right side of the fabric.

Depending on the size of beads being used, if beads are placed on every row, one bead above another, they will distort the fabric. This technique works better if there is a non-beaded row worked between every beaded row.

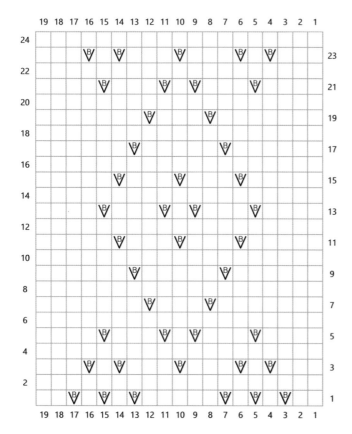

Fig. 3.12 A chart for working a beaded slip-stitch pattern.

Fig. 3.13 Bring the yarn with the bead on it between the points of the needles, ready for the next stitch on the left-hand needle to be slipped and for the bead to be placed in front of that slipped stitch.

Fig. 3.14 The stitch has been slipped purlwise to the right-hand needle.

Beads placed with the slip-stitch technique

As with other Beaded-Knitting techniques, it is necessary to thread the beads on to the yarn before you start to knit the piece. A chart is often used to show the placement of the beads. For this method, the bead sits on a strand of yarn in front of a stitch rather than in the gap between two stitches.

When working from a chart for flat knitting, odd-number rows are read from right to left and even-number rows from left to right, unless otherwise stated in the pattern. On the featured chart, on right-side rows, the blank squares indicate knit stitches, and the squares with the V symbol indicate stitches to be slipped purlwise, followed by a bead being pushed along the yarn until it is next to the stitch that was just knitted, so the bead will lie on the yarn strand in front of the slipped stitch.

Knit to the stitch that is going to be slipped. Bring the yarn forward between the points of the needles, with the next bead to be placed on the yarn that is next to the right-hand needle.

Slip the next stitch on the left-hand needle purlwise to the right-hand needle.

Fig. 3.15 The bead sits on the strand of yarn in front of the slipped stitch, after the yarn was taken from the front to the back between the points of the needles.

Fig. 3.16 The next stitch has been knitted. The beads placed within the fabric sit on the strands of yarn in front of the slipped stitches.

Take the yarn back between the points of the needles, to be ready to knit the next stitch, but make sure that the bead stays on the yarn strand in front of the slipped stitch. Try to ensure that the yarn strand holding the bead is the same width as the stitch that it is in front of. Be careful not to pull the strand tight, as a tight strand will distort the knitted fabric.

Knit the next stitch as normal.

Beads can be placed on both knit and purl rows, but it is necessary to have a stitch worked normally on each side of the slipped stitch, to hold the bead in place, and the stitch that was slipped on one row should be worked on the next row, in order not to distort the fabric.

Fixing mistakes in Beaded Knitting

When working Beaded Knitting, the size of the stitch in comparison to the size of the bead is important. If the stitch is quite large compared to the beads being used, this may result in beads not staying where they are placed. For the beads-placed-between-purl-stitches technique, the most common problem is a bead popping into a stitch rather than sitting on the yarn strand between two adjacent stitches. This can be fixed quite easily by pushing the bead along the yarn, back to the correct position, in a similar way to the repositioning of beads shown in Chapter 2, but this time the bead is being moved out of the stitch and on to the stand between stitches.

The method of removing a bead by using pliers, covered in Chapter 2, is also applicable for fixing mistakes in Beaded Knitting.

You may not notice that a bead is missing until the piece is finished. It is possible to fix this problem by sewing in a bead at the appropriate place.

CHAPTER 4

BEADS AND LACE

Along with the revival of general interest in knitting in the mid-2000s and a growing interest in knitted shawls, working beads in combination with lace has become increasingly popular. There are a variety of ways that beads can be included in lace patterns. This chapter focuses on the method of placing beads that are already threaded on to the yarn and that are worked in association with yarn overs.

A yarn over creates an eyelet hole in the knitted fabric. A bead or several beads can be pushed up to sit on the yarn over so that the bead(s) sit on one side or the other of the eyelet space. The basic method involves working to the point where the yarn over is to be made, pushing up a bead next to the stitch that was just worked on the right-hand needle, making the yarn over and continuing along the row. How the bead looks in the finished pattern is determined by the position of the bead on the yarn over when the yarn over is worked into on the next row.

In this book, the term 'to yarn over' is used to signify the common way to make the loop that will form an eyelet hole in the knitted fabric. To make a yarn over, the working yarn must pass over the right-hand needle from the front of the knitting (the side nearest to you) to the back (the side away from you). How the stitch is worked depends on the type of stitch before and after the yarn over. From a knit stitch to a knit stitch, the yarn comes forward between the points of the needles and over the right-hand needle. From a knit stitch to a purl stitch, the yarn comes forward between the points of the needles, over the right-hand needle and forward between the points of the needles again, to be available for working the purl stitch. From a purl stitch to a purl stitch, the yarn is already at the front, so it goes over the right-hand needle and then comes forward between the points of the needles, to be available for working a purl stitch. From a purl stitch to a knit stitch, the yarn simply goes from the front and then over the right-hand needle to the back, to be available for working a knit stitch.

Fig. 4.1 One bead has been pushed up near the last stitch to have been worked on the right-hand needle, ready to be included as part of the yarn over that is currently being worked. Beaded yarn overs that have been worked on previous rows can also be seen within the fabric.

Fig. 4.2 The beaded yarn over of the previous row is about to be purled, with the bead positioned at the left-hand end of the yarn-over loop.

Fig. 4.3 A purl stitch being worked, with the bead at the left-hand end of the yarn-over loop.

Fig. 4.4 The bead sits at the left-hand side of the eyelet hole, when viewed from the purl side of the fabric.

Working yarn overs holding one bead

In this sample, the beads are being worked in a stocking-stitch-based lace fabric. On a knit row, knit to the position of the yarn over, and push a bead along the yarn until it is near to the stitch that was just worked on the right-hand needle, for the bead to be available to be included in the yarn over.

Work the beaded yarn over, and continue following the lace pattern to the end of the row. The yarn overs are now worked into on the purl row. The position of the bead on the yarn-over loop as it is worked on this purl row will determine how the bead looks within the overall lace pattern.

Purl to the position of the beaded yarn over. Check the position of the bead: in this case, the bead is at the left-hand end of the yarn over. When working in stocking stitch, the bead will also be sitting to the back of the left-hand needle, on the side of the fabric away from you when working the purl row.

Purl the yarn-over stitch, keeping the bead at the left-hand end of the yarn-over loop.

Fig. 4.5 The bead is positioned at the right-hand end of the yarn-over loop on the side of the fabric nearest to you when working a purl row in stocking stitch.

Fig. 4.6 Purling the beaded yarn-over loop, with the bead at the right-hand end of the yarn-over loop.

Fig. 4.7 The bead sits at the right-hand side of the eyelet hole, when viewed from the purl side of the fabric.

Fig. 4.8 A sample of the Zigzag-Lace Pattern.

In the next example, the bead is at the right-hand end of the yarn-over loop, which in stocking stitch will put the bead to the front of the left-hand needle, on the side of the fabric nearest to you when working the purl row.

Purl the next stitch on the left-hand needle.

This completed sample of the Zigzag-Lace Pattern (*see* Chapter 6 for instructions for how to work this pattern) shows the beads sitting on the right-hand side of the eyelet holes when the lace fabric is moving to the left and on the left-hand side of the eyelet holes when the lace fabric is moving to the right, as viewed from the right side of the fabric.

When placing one bead on a yarn over, the beads can be placed on every row but are more commonly placed every other row or even several rows apart. However, when placing more than one bead on a yarn over, it is necessary to place beads on every row, in the same way as strings of beads are placed on every row when working Beaded Garter Stitch.

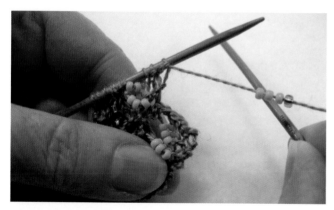

Fig. 4.9 Beads pushed up near the point of the right-hand needle, ready for the next beaded row to be worked.

Fig. 4.10 A yarn over holding three beads is about to be made.

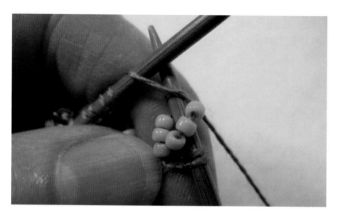

Fig. 4.11 Knit the next stitch, by reaching over the group of three beads of the yarn over made in the previous row and making a new three-bead yarn over at the same time.

Fig. 4.12 Knit the single-bead yarn-over stitch with the bead at the right-hand end of its yarn-over loop.

Working yarn overs holding several beads

The Butterfly-Lace Edging on the Rainbow-Storms Wing Shawl is knitted with some single beads and some strings of beads. Stringing several beads across a yarn over also adds quite a bit of weight to the knitting, so, although the main part of the shawl included size 6 seed beads, the edging includes size 8 seed beads or a combination of size 6 beads worked singly and size 8 beads worked in groups of three on the yarn over. The edging is also worked in garter stitch.

When you have only a few beads to place within a row, it is easy to push up all of the beads that are needed for that row to be near to the point of the right-hand needle, before you start to knit the row.

Knit the first two stitches, and bring the yarn forward, along with the three size 8 beads, to be ready to make a yarn over.

The next stitch on the left-hand needle is a three-bead yarn over from the row below. The beads must be at the right-hand end of the yarn over of the previous row before the next stitch is worked.

Continue knitting up to the position of the single-bead yarn over of the previous row. Make sure that the bead is at the right-hand end of its yarn over, and knit the stitch.

Make a single-bead yarn over as you knit two stitches together (k2tog), and then knit the last stitch (in the edging pattern, this last stitch will be worked together with one stitch of the body of the shawl, to cast off that shawl stitch.)

Beads are placed on every row, so, again, at the beginning of the next row, bring up the number of beads needed for that row. Knit to the single-bead yarn over from the previous row, making sure that the bead is in the correct position.

Make a single-bead yarn over, and continue in pattern to the three-bead yarn over made in the previous row. This time, the group of three beads needs to be at the left-hand end of the yarn over stitch before that stitch is knitted.

Fig. 4.13 The bead is at the right-hand end of its yarn-over loop, when the stitch is knitted.

Fig. 4.14 The three beads of this group are at the left-hand end of their yarn-over loop before the stitch is knitted on this row.

Fig. 4.15 A three-bead yarn over is about to be made.

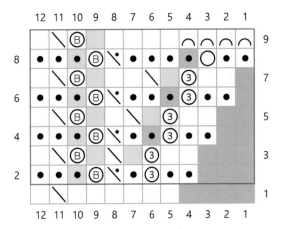

Fig. 4.16 A chart for the beaded edging of the Rainbow-Storms Wing Shawl.

Bring the yarn forward between the points of the needles, and make a three-bead yarn over. Knit the last two stitches of the row.

The edging pattern is worked by following a chart, and differently coloured squares are used to indicate how the beaded yarn over should be worked on the row after it was made.

There is a coloured square above or one stitch to the left of the yarn over made on the previous row. The yellow square on Row 2 is above the single-bead yarn over that will have been worked on the previous row (corresponding to what is shown on Row 9 of this chart). The chart key shows that, when you work a stitch corresponding to a yellow square, the bead(s) from the previous row's yarn over must be at the right-hand end of the yarn-over loop, whether you are on a right-side or wrong-side row. When you work a stitch corresponding to a blue square, the beads of the previous row's yarn over must be at the left-hand end of their yarn-over loop before you knit that stitch, whether you are on a right-side or wrong-side row.

Any other symbol in each square of the chart is read as a normal charted stitch. On Row 2, the yellow square has a black spot within it. For normal chart reading, a black spot corresponds to a purl stitch on the right side and a knit stitch on the wrong side of the fabric. The yellow square with a black spot within it therefore should be worked as a knit stitch, as Row 2 is a wrong-side row. On Row 3, each of its yellow squares is otherwise blank. For normal chart reading, a blank square corresponds to a knit stitch on the right side and a purl stitch on the wrong side of the fabric. Row 3 is a right-side row, so, for example, the stitch corresponding to the first yellow square of this row is worked as a knit stitch, which in this particular pattern will be worked into the three-bead yarn-over stitch of the previous row.

For some charts, there may be no instruction provided about how to work the beaded yarn over on the following row. In this situation, the bead will probably need to be at the left-hand end of the yarn over, as this is the easiest way to work the beaded yarn-over stitch.

CHAPTER 5

THE CROCHET-HOOK METHOD

Bead Knitting and various Beaded-Knitting techniques require the beads to be threaded on to the yarn before the knitting process starts. However, for this next technique, the beads can be added to the knitting at any time by using a crochet hook to place each bead around a stitch. The stitch passes through the hole of the bead, so the bead is visible on both sides of the fabric, making this a very useful technique to employ if you want a reversible fabric. As the beads can be placed at any time, the technique does not require as much planning as does Bead Knitting or Beaded Knitting.

This method is called the crochet-hook method, because a fine crochet hook is used to hold the bead and lift the stitch off the left-hand needle before the bead is slipped over the stitch, and the stitch, now holding the bead, is re-placed on to the left-hand needle. Other tools such as dental Superfloss or fine wire can be used to place a bead on to a stitch, instead of using a crochet hook.

The bead has to fit over the head of the crochet hook, so the size of the hole of the bead and the size of the head of the crochet hook are both important.

The smallest beads generally used for this technique are size 7 seed beads, with size 6 seed beads being the most popular size to work in this way. Decorative or accent beads can also be applied with this technique, as long as they will go over the head of the crochet hook and on to its shaft.

The head of the crochet hook needs to be fine enough to go through the hole of the bead but not so fine that the stitch will not stay hooked into it as the bead is pushed down on to the stitch. A 0.60mm or 0.75mm (US steel hook 14) crochet hook is usually about the smallest size to be used for adding beads. The beads go on to the hook quite easily, and the hook is still large enough to hold the stitch and not split the yarn. You can get finer hooks, but they tend to split the yarn when they are used to try to pick up a stitch from the left-hand needle. A 0.75mm (US steel hook 14) hook also works well, and a 1.00mm (US steel hook 12) hook can be used, but this hook size is starting to get a bit large to fit through the holes of the beads that are commonly used for this method.

Fig. 5.1 An accent bead is to be placed on the next stitch on the left-hand needle.

Fig. 5.2 The bead is on the shaft of the crochet hook.

Fig. 5.3 Using the crochet hook to lift the stitch off of the left-hand needle.

Placing a bead by using a crochet hook

As well as having the correct size of crochet hook, you also will need a container to hold the beads until you need them. You can keep them in their packet, but, when working, you may find it easier to have the beads in a shallow bowl or container, as suggested in the section 'Other beading-related tools and materials' in Chapter 1.

Knit to the stitch specified in the pattern where you want to place a bead. Slip the bead over the head of the crochet hook and on to its shaft.

Use the crochet hook to lift the next stitch on the left-hand needle off the needle.

Make sure that you are holding the crochet hook so that the hook points towards you and slightly downward. If there is a flat area on the shaft of your crochet hook, your thumb should be against the flat section, with the hook pointing towards you. It is important to have the hook at the correct angle for the next step. You need to pull the lifted stitch into the hook, with the tip of the hook extending slightly above the stitch as it is being held in the hook so that the bead can be pushed down the hook and on to the stitch.

Fig. 5.4 The bead is on the stitch, and the stitch is about to be re-placed on to the left-hand needle.

Fig. 5.5 The bead has been placed and the knitting pattern continued. In this example, the beaded stitch was knitted after being placed on the left-hand needle, because, in this pattern, the beaded stitch is preceded and followed by yarn-over stitches.

Once the bead has been transferred to the stitch, the stitch can be re-placed on to the left-hand needle.

Depending on the pattern instructions, the stitch with a bead on it is then either knitted or slipped to the right-hand needle. In the featured sample, the stitch has been knitted, because there will be a yarn over on each side of the beaded stitch.

A very important point to remember when adding beads in this way, particularly if you are working on your own design, is that the bead sits around a stitch that was made on the row below the row that you are currently working. Beads can be added in this way on both right-side and wrong-side rows, but normally you will need at least one row between the rows where the beads are placed, if the beads are being placed immediately above each other.

An alternative method of placing beads around a stitch is to use dental Superfloss or a fine, stiff thread such as Tigertail, which is used for other beading work. Dental Superfloss is a long length of fine nylon floss, with one end that has been coated to make it firm but flexible.

Fig. 5.6 An accent bead has been threaded on to the Superfloss™.

Fig. 5.7 The stiff end of the Superfloss™ has been threaded through the stitch.

Placing a bead by using dental Superfloss

One of the advantages of using Superfloss for this technique is that you can thread quite a few beads on to the floss before you start to knit, thus making the process more portable. Tie a larger bead or a button on to the far end of the Superfloss to stop the strung beads from falling off that end of the length of floss.

Knit to the stitch that you want to place the bead on. Thread the stiff end of the strung Superfloss through the next stitch on the left-hand needle so that the stitch can be lifted off that needle.

Once the stitch has been lifted off the left-hand needle, you need to fold the Superfloss to make a loop. Push the strung bead over the stiff end of the Superfloss (the Superfloss will now pass through the hole of the bead twice) and on to the loop section. The bead can now be slipped down the Superfloss and on to the stitch. Re-place the stitch, now holding the bead, on to the left-hand needle, and continue working across the row.

Sometimes, you might want to place a bead on to a stitch made with yarn that is a bit thicker than is typically used with the size of bead that you are using. For example, if you are using a DK-weight yarn with size 6 beads, you may find that, when using the crochet-hook method, the yarn is too thick to allow the stitch to be pulled through the hole of a bead. In this situation, you may want to try the Superfloss technique, as this method will often allow you to pull the thicker yarn through the hole of the bead that you want to place in the knitting.

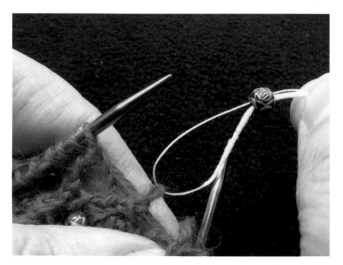

Fig. 5.8 The accent bead on the Superfloss™, which is holding the stitch.

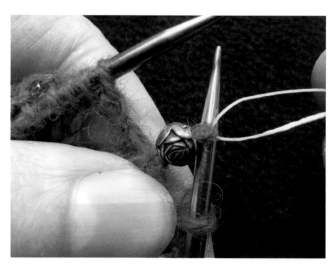

Fig. 5.9 The accent bead has been slipped over the stitch, and the stitch is to be re-placed on to the left-hand needle.

CHAPTER 6

EXPERIMENTING WITH BEADS, YARN AND STITCH PATTERNS

Experimenting with yarn

You can use a wide variety of yarns when working with beads, as long as the yarn will fit through the hole of the bead. With Bead Knitting and Beaded Knitting, the beads are typically threaded on to the yarn before the knitting process starts and are therefore constantly being moved along the yarn. The yarn needs to be fairly robust so that it can withstand the wear caused by the pushing of the beads along the yarn. When working these techniques, the construction of the yarn is often more important than the fibre that the yarn is made from. Adding beads by using the crochet-hook method causes less wear on the yarn, but the yarn must be fine enough for a stitch worked with the yarn to be pulled through the hole in the bead.

Combining yarns

Fine yarns are usually used for knitting with beads, but it is also possible to work with more than one yarn at a time, by stranding yarns together. Two fine yarns worked together are often still fine enough to be used for Beaded Knitting that is performed by threading the beads on to the yarn before the knitting process starts and by adding the beads by using a crochet hook during the knitting process. Combining more than one yarn can work particularly well for knitting beads in combination with lace.

Combining two yarns can change the overall colour of the finished fabric compared to the colour of the fabric knitted with either yarn on its own, and can also change the drape and feel of the knitting. A basic sock yarn can be made to feel much more luxurious when combined with a silk or kid-silk yarn. A luxury yarn can be made to go further when it is combined with a more basic yarn.

Fig. 6.1 Six samples of the Lacy-Diamond Pattern, worked with three different yarns either singly or with two different yarns held together. Clockwise from the top left: Rico® Design Superba Paint 4 Ply sock yarn and Juniper Moon Farm Findley lace-weight yarn, Rico® Design Superba Paint 4 Ply sock yarn and Katia Concept Silk-Mohair lace-weight yarn, Juniper Moon Farm Findley lace-weight yarn and Katia Concept Silk-Mohair lace-weight yarn, Juniper Moon Farm Findley lace-weight yarn, Katia Concept Silk-Mohair lace-weight yarn, and Rico® Design Superba Paint 4 Ply sock yarn. Toho size 6 Metallic Dragonfly seed beads were used in all six samples.

These samples were all worked with the Lacy-Diamond Pattern, with beads having been placed by using the crochet-hook method. The three yarns that were used are Juniper Moon Farm Findley lace-weight yarn, which is a merino-wool and silk mix, Rico® Design Superba Paint 4 Ply sock yarn and Katia Concept Silk-Mohair lace-weight yarn, which is a kid-mohair and silk mix. The same size 6 seed beads have been used in all of the samples. The samples show the same pattern knitted with the individual yarns and with two different yarns being worked together. The needle size used for each sample was that selected as the best size for the particular sample, based on the thickness of the yarn or yarns being knitted. The needles used ranged from 3.25mm (US 3), used for the finest yarn, up to a 6.00mm (US 10), used for the sock-yarn and mohair–silk yarn combination.

It is not always easy to tell, before knitting a sample, how the colour of the sample will change when two yarns are stranded together. Combining a kid-mohair yarn with a smooth yarn usually produces a softer, more blended colourway than when combining two smooth yarns, particularly if there is a strong tonal contrast between the two smooth yarns as well.

Experimenting with non-standard materials

Wire

Enamelled copper wire comes in a variety of thicknesses, from 0.10mm to 1.00mm, but 0.20mm enamelled copper wire works very well for knitting purposes, as it is flexible enough to be able to form the stitch shape easily but strong enough not to break. If you want to work with a thicker wire, it is better to use a number of strands of the 0.20mm wire held together rather than a thicker wire, because, by using a number of strands, you retain the flexibility of the fine wire, while making a stronger piece of knitting.

Enamelled copper wire also comes in a wide range of colours. Two different colours of wire can be worked together, to create another colour, and the wire can also be worked with a fine yarn, such as a lace-weight or 4ply/fingering-weight yarn, to create a fabric that can be shaped and manipulated after knitting.

If you are working a Beaded-Knitting project, it is typically necessary to thread the beads on to the wire before you start to knit. As the wire is fairly firm, you do not need to use a beading needle: just use the wire itself to pick up the beads. It is important to pick up enough beads to work the whole project before you start to knit.

If you find that you do not have enough beads but are nearing the end of the project, pull out enough wire to complete the project, cut the wire and thread on the extra beads from this end of the wire. Continue knitting to finish the project.

If necessary, you can cut the wire and join on the wire again at the side edge of the knitting. When you have knitted a few stitches with the new wire, twist the two wire ends around each other and, when you finish the project, wind the twisted wire end in and out of the edge of the knitting for several rows, before cutting the end and squeezing it together with the wire knitting or, if possible, burying the end in a bead hole.

When knitting wire from a reel, particularly when knitting with two or more strands of wire, push a long knitting needle through the centre of each reel and suspend and secure it over a small box or bowl, to allow the wire to reel off smoothly.

When it comes to finishing your wire-knitted projects, you can use a fine tapestry needle or ordinary needle, with an eye large enough for the wire to pass through it, to sew with the wire as you would with yarn or thread. For the Leaf-Plait Necklace, the three lengths of knitting are first plaited together and then the flat ends are sewn together. The sewn ends are then made into a loop, by sewing the ends to the plait, further down the length of knitting.

The wire knitting can be manipulated into a three-dimensional shape. The featured wire-knitted flower has been made up of several petals that were knitted with wire and a flower centre that was knitted as a ruffle and then wound around itself to achieve the necessary shape for the centre of the flower. The

petals were attached around the flower centre by being sewn on with a length of wire. The petals were knitted with wire, and the beads were added after the knitting. To add the beads, a long end of wire was left at the beginning and end of each petal. The beads were then picked up on to the wire, one at a time, and the end of wire was wrapped around the edge stitch of the petal, before the next bead was picked up and attached in the same manner. With this method, it was possible to place a bead at the edge of every row.

Knitting with wire does feel different from knitting with standard yarn, as it is a fine material with no elasticity. By using a fine wire such as the 0.20mm wire mentioned previously, it is fairly easy to form the shape of a stitch around the needle. The size of the stitch will vary according to the size of the needles being used, but, in general, size 2.00mm to 2.50mm (US 0 to 1.5) needles will produce a good wire-knitted fabric.

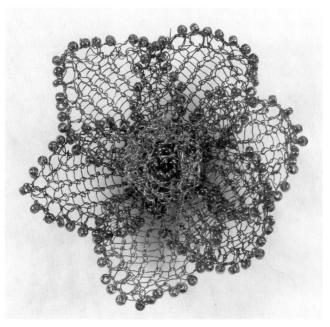

Fig. 6.2 Wire-knitted and beaded flower. (*See* Resources at the end of this book for a link to download this pattern.)

Fig. 6.3 Knitting with one strand of wire and beads on 2.00mm (US 0) needles.

Once the stitch has been formed, the wire will hold that shape, even when you remove the needle. It is possible to undo wire knitting, if necessary, but the wire will then have kinks in it, and, if knitted with again, it will not produce an even fabric. It is better to take your time when knitting with wire, to try to avoid making mistakes. If you do have to undo the wire and rework only a couple of stitches, the knitting will probably look fine, but, if you have to undo a number of rows, it would be better to cut out the section of previously knitted wire and join unworked wire at the edge of the knitting, before you resume working the pattern.

Wire can be worked in different stitch patterns. Increases and decreases can be worked, so wire can be used in lace knitting or to produce shaped pieces such as the leaf shapes at the end of the Leaf-Plait Necklace.

When working with wire, a two-needle method of casting on is probably easier to work than the Thumb/Longtail Cast-On. The normal Chain Cast-Off works quite well with wire, as the previous stitch can be lifted over the new stitch as required for this cast-off. These basic cast-on and cast-off knitting techniques are covered in Chapter 7.

The final shape of the piece of wire knitting can be modified after the piece of knitting is finished. The edges of the knitting can be pulled out or pushed in, to give a smoother, more even edge, if necessary.

Monofilament nylon fishing line

Wire is not the only non-standard material that can be used instead of yarn, particularly for knitted jewellery. Monofilament nylon fishing line comes in a range of thicknesses. On the reel label, it does give you the thickness of the nylon in millimetres, although the reels are sold according to the weight of the fish that the line is capable of holding. If the nylon is very fine, it can be almost impossible to see. The thicker the nylon fishing line, the stiffer it will be. Nylon fishing line of between about 0.15mm and 0.25mm in thickness works well for knitting purposes.

One of the main challenges of knitting with monofilament nylon fishing line is being able to see the stitches on the needles, particularly if they are metal needles. The nylon is generally clear, making it difficult to see when formed into a stitch around a needle. However, it is possible to get fishing line with a tint, for example, green or red-brown, which does make the nylon easier to see while you are knitting. When working with the clear nylon fishing line, you may find it easier to use wood or bamboo needles, to better see the stitches around the needles.

Although the fishing line itself does not have any elasticity , the fabric it makes, particularly if knitted in garter stitch, does have some stretch and flexibility. The featured Beaded Cuff was knitted in garter stitch, using the Beaded-Garter-Stitch technique, to place a bead between each stitch on wrong-side rows. When the knitting is completed, the cast-on and cast-off edges are joined to form the cuff. The garter stitch runs sideways when the cuff is worn, so the cuff has the necessary stretch to allow it to be pulled on and off over the hand.

It is possible to pick up beads with the nylon fishing line, as it is fairly stiff, but you may find it easier to use the same method for threading beads on to the nylon fishing line as for standard yarns, namely, by using a beading needle and a transition thread. A range of bead sizes can be used with the fishing line, but, for the patterns in this book, size 10 or 11 seed beads have been used.

As with knitting with wire, it is important to thread all of the beads on to the fishing line before you start to knit, because nylon fishing line is quite difficult to join midway through knitting a piece. If you have not threaded enough beads but are quite near to the end of the project, pull out enough nylon fishing line to complete the project. Cut the nylon fishing line, thread on the necessary number of beads from this end of the fishing line and then continue knitting.

Fig. 6.4 A beaded cuff worked with monofilament nylon fishing line and size 10 seed beads.

If you do have to cut the nylon fishing line and join in a new end, do so at the side edge. Start knitting with the newly joined fishing line. When you have worked a few stitches, knot the two ends of the fishing line together. Tighten the knot, and dab a spot of clear nail varnish on to the knot, to seal it and stop it from coming undone.

A standard cast-on such as one of the two-needle cast-ons or the Thumb/Longtail Cast-On can be used with nylon fishing line. The standard Chain Cast-Off can also be used, although you may find that the cast-off edge pulls in, even though this would not happen if you were casting off with a normal yarn. The nylon fishing line can be used to sew pieces together, and, in this case, the fishing line ends do need to be worked with a half-hitch knot after a few stitches when sewing in these ends, to stop the nylon fishing line from springing back out of the knitting. If the end will not stay woven into the knitting, it may be necessary to use a dab of clear nail varnish or glue to keep it in place.

Experimenting with beads

You can hold yarn and beads next to each other and think that the colour combination works well, but you cannot really tell until you have worked some knitting with the actual combination of materials. Sometimes, the beads blend so well with the yarn that they seem to almost disappear; other times the beads will stand out against the yarn very well. How well the bead and yarn combination works also depends on the stitch pattern being used in relation to the beads.

The three types of size 6 seed beads used in the featured samples are, starting at the bottom, Toho Silver-Lined Ruby, Miyuki Chartreuse Transparent and Toho Silver-Lined Teal. In the Lacy-Diamond pattern, the beads are placed around a stitch by using the crochet-hook method and create spots of colour in the lace pattern. In the samples of Beaded Garter Stitch, the beads create a block of contrasting colour.

Lined beads, such as silver-lined and gold-lined beads, catch the light more than many of the other types of beads, giving the bead colour an extra sparkle. Although the bead colour on top of the lining is transparent, the lining stops the yarn colour from being visible. In contrast, transparent beads do take on some of the colour of the yarn passing through the hole of the bead.

In the samples featuring the three different colours of beads, the Chartreuse Transparent beads in the middle section of the Lacy-Diamond-Pattern sample do look a slightly different colour to the same beads in the Beaded-Garter-Stitch sample. In the lace sample, the beads are seen as individual dots, and the colour of the bead is not strongly affected by the colour of the yarn. In the Beaded-Garter-Stitch sample, the beads and yarn are worked much more closely together, so the colour of the yarn has much more of an effect on the perceived colour of the beads.

Fig. 6.5 Three different colours of size 6 beads, used in the Lacy-Diamond Pattern and in Beaded Garter Stitch. Both samples were knitted with Rico® Design Superba Paint 4 Ply sock yarn.

In the two samples with the three different colours of beads, there was good colour and tonal contrast between the yarn and the beads. This next featured sample shows how a contrast in tone between the yarn colour and the bead colour is also important. The same beads and the same stitch pattern have been used for both samples, but the beads in the beige sample are much more difficult to see than the same beads in the lemon-yellow sample. When knitting with beads, you need to decide whether you want a very subtle effect or for the beads to make a big impact.

Most of the samples shown in this book have been made by using seed beads of a few particular sizes, but other beads can also be used. In the two featured leaf-lace panels, the same lace stitch pattern has been used, with an accent bead being placed at the centre of the leaf lace and Beaded Garter Stitch being

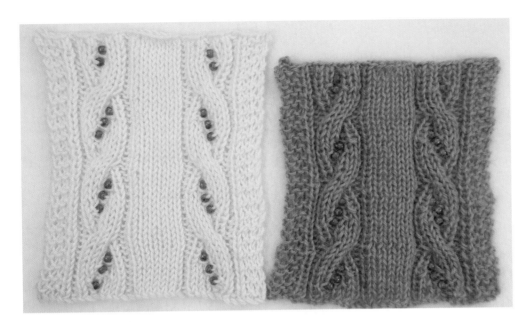

Fig. 6.6 The same beads have been used in the two samples of this cable pattern. The left-hand sample was knitted with Adriafil Genziana 4ply/fingering-weight yarn and the right-hand sample with baa ram ewe Titus 4ply/fingering-weight yarn. Both samples include Matubo™ size 6 seed beads in the colourway Aqua Picasso. The tonal contrast between the colour of the beads and of the yarn in the Titus sample is so little that the beads are very difficult to see.

Fig. 6.7 Two samples of a leaf-lace panel, worked with two different yarn-and-bead combinations, with Beaded-Garter-Stitch edges.

worked at each edge. The red sample was knitted in an alpaca 4ply/fingering-weight yarn, with size 8 Miyuki seed beads in the Beaded-Garter-Stitch sections and Metallized Antique Gold Rosebud beads in the leaf-lace section. The pale-gold sample was knitted with Katia Air Lux 4ply/fingering-weight yarn, with crystal, faceted beads in the Beaded-Garter-Stitch sections and bi-cone beads in the leaf-lace section.

Experimenting with stitch patterns

In order to offer more examples of different yarn and bead combinations for each stitch sample in this chapter, the stitch has been worked with at least two different yarns, with different bead and colour combinations. Most of the patterns are given in the form of both a chart and written instructions. The charts may show more than one repeat, both horizontally and vertically. They are provided as a starting point for your own experimentation.

Bead Knitting

The featured samples of the Bead-Knitting Heart Decoration have been worked with 4ply/fingering-weight sock yarn and size 8 seed beads. In the green sample, Toho Silver-Lined Ruby seed beads were used for the heart shape and Opaque Chartreuse seed beads were used as the background. In the red sample, the same Toho Silver-Lined Ruby seed beads were used

Fig. 6.8 Two samples of the Bead-Knitting Heart-Decoration Pattern. The left-hand sample was knitted by using the traditional twisted-stitch method of the Bead-Knitting technique. The right-hand sample was knitted by using the Plaited-Knitting technique. Both samples were worked from the same charted pattern.

for the heart, but Silver-Lined Green seed beads were used as the background. The tone and colour of the red yarn and ruby beads are very close, making the heart shape less easy to see in the second sample. The alternating direction of the beads also makes this sample look very different.

The green sample was worked with the Bead-Knitting technique, and the red sample was worked with the Plaited-Knitting technique. These techniques are both covered in Chapter 2. The same chart has been followed for both techniques, as the only difference is in the way that the stitches are worked. Both decorations are worked as flat pieces, so the chart has numbers on both the left- and right-hand sides. Odd-number rows are read from right to left, and even-number rows are read from left to right.

All of the beads required for the sample need to be threaded on to the yarn before the knitting of the sample is started. To thread the beads in the correct order for knitting, start at the top right of Row 40 on the chart, reading the pattern to the left and then move on to Row 39, reading to the right. There is a large section of one colour of bead at the top of the decoration, so it is probably easier to count the total number of beads indicated from Row 40 of the chart to Row 28, and then follow the chart

from Row 27, starting at the left-hand edge and reading from left to right, and then follow Row 26 from right to left, and so on. Once the beads for the heart section have been threaded, you can count the total number of beads of one colour that are indicated to the end of the chart.

To make the sample:
Cast on 3sts.
Purl 1 row.
Follow the Bead-Knitting Heart-Decoration Chart for 42 rows.
Cast off.

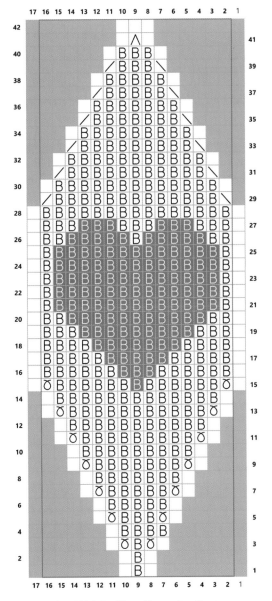

Fig. 6.9 Bead-Knitting Heart-Decoration Chart.

Beaded Garter Stitch

The two amulet purses (*see* Purses and Bags) are knitted with Beaded Garter Stitch. As well as changing the yarn and bead colours for these purses, more variations can be created by using beads of more than one colour for a particular purse. The Shades-of-Blue Amulet Purse features two different colours and types of beads, knitted on a blue yarn. The bulk of the beads are Blue Transparent seed beads, with Metallic-Iris Blue Mix seed beads as the contrast-colour beads, placed as single vertical lines of beads on the purse and as part of the edging decoration.

More complicated versions of these purses can be worked by adding more colours of beads. For example, the outer groups of beads could be of one colour, the single-bead lines of a second colour and the middle groups of beads of a third colour. Alternatively, each group or line of beads could be of a different colour. The beads could also be coloured differently horizontally, to give a shaded effect from dark to light or light to dark.

Once you move into using more than one colour of bead, the threading sequence of the beads becomes very important. The beads must be threaded in reverse order to the order that they will be knitted. For the Shades-of-Blue Amulet Purse, threading instructions are provided to help you to thread the beads in the correct order.

The purses are worked with fine yarn and size 10 or 11 seed beads. The pattern can be scaled up by using thicker yarn and larger beads, but, as beads generally get heavier as they get larger, there is a point at which the number of beads required for a larger purse would make the finished item too heavy to be of practical use.

The traditional Norwegian-style Beaded Garter Stitch also offers a lot of scope for playing around with bead colours, if you are happy to spend time planning the colours and threading the beads before you start to knit.

Fig. 6.10 Three samples of the Icicle Pattern, from left to right: four different colours of size 6 beads on a DK-weight yarn, one colour of size 8 beads on 4ply/fingering-weight yarn, and four different colours of size 8 beads on 4ply/fingering-weight yarn.

17	16	15	14	13	12	11	10	9	8	7	6	5	4	3	2	1	
											B	B	B	B	B	B	6
								B	B	B	B	B	B	B	B	B	5
					B	B	B	B	B	B	B	B	B	B	B	B	4
								B	B	B	B	B	B	B	B	B	3
											B	B	B	B	B	B	2
														B	B	B	1
17	16	15	14	13	12	11	10	9	8	7	6	5	4	3	2	1	

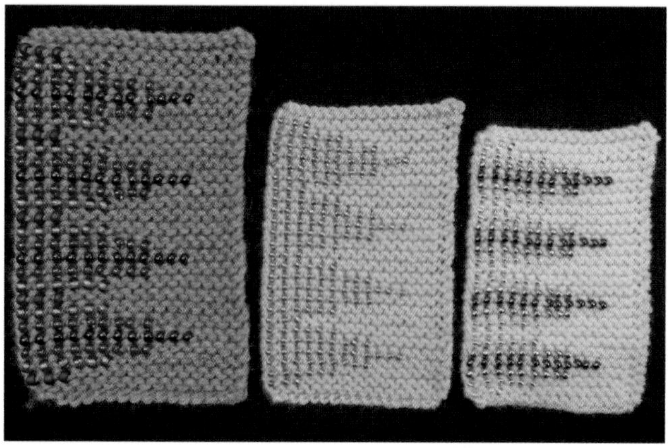

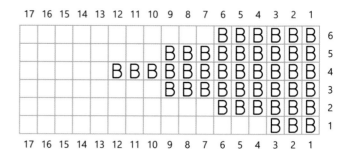

Fig. 6.11 Beaded-Garter-Stitch Icicle Chart.

In the samples of the Beaded-Garter-Stitch Icicle Pattern, the middle sample has been knitted with just one colour of bead, but the other two samples have been worked with four colours of beads. The white sample was worked with size 8 seed beads on a 4ply/fingering-weight yarn. The beads used were Toho Crystal AB, Toho Silver-Lined Crystal, Matubo™ Crystal Full Labrador and Toho Gunmetal. The green sample on the left-hand side was worked with a DK-weight yarn and size 6 seed beads. With a thicker yarn, it is necessary to use larger beads. The beads in this sample include Miyuki Matt Metallic Blue Iris Mix, Miyuki Transparent Purple, Miyuki Aqua Fuchsia Lined Lustre and Czech Purple Iris Mix beads.

Traditional stranded-knitting pattern charts can also provide a good source of inspiration for pattern design, as beads could be used in place of the contrast colour in the stitch patterns. If you use larger patterns, you may also need to consider altering the size of the beads and the thickness of the yarn. With a fine yarn, such as a lace-weight yarn, and size 10 or 11 seed beads, much larger and more complicated designs could be worked.

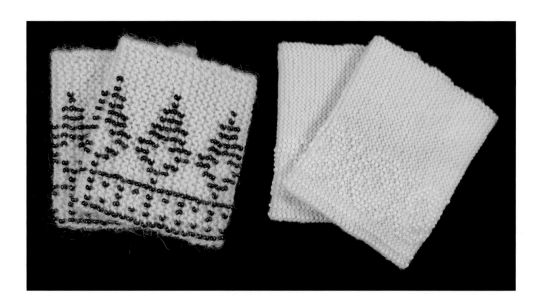

Fig. 6.12 Forest Beaded Cuffs, knitted with 4ply/fingering-weight, alpaca yarn and size 7 seed beads (left), and Scroll Beaded Cuffs, knitted with two strands of singles/fine lace-weight yarn held together and size 11 seed beads (right).

20	19	18	17	16	15	14	13	12	11	10	9	8	7	6	5	4	3	2	1	
										B	B				B				B	8
								B	B	B	B	B			B	B		B	B	7
						B	B	B	B	B		B	B		B				B	6
				B	B	B	B	B	B				B	B	B	B	B	B	B	5
						B	B	B	B	B		B	B		B				B	4
								B	B	B	B	B			B	B		B	B	3
										B	B				B				B	2
															B	B	B	B	B	1

20 19 18 17 16 15 14 13 12 11 10 9 8 7 6 5 4 3 2 1

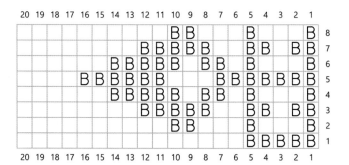

Fig. 6.13 Forest-Beaded-Cuffs Chart. *See* the section 'Beaded Garter Stitch with beads every other row' in Chapter 3 for instructions about working from charts for Beaded-Garter-Stitch patterns.

20	19	18	17	16	15	14	13	12	11	10	9	8	7	6	5	4	3	2	1	
						B	B						B	B			B		B	12
					B	B			B	B	B			B			B		B	11
				B	B			B	B	B	B	B					B		B	10
			B	B	B			B			B	B	B				B		B	9
			B	B	B	B			B			B	B	B			B		B	8
			B	B	B	B						B	B	B			B		B	7
			B	B		B	B				B	B	B	B			B		B	6
			B	B			B	B	B	B	B	B	B				B		B	5
				B	B		B	B	B	B	B	B					B		B	4
					B	B		B	B	B	B			B			B		B	3
						B	B						B	B			B		B	2
			B	B			B	B		B	B	B					B		B	1

20 19 18 17 16 15 14 13 12 11 10 9 8 7 6 5 4 3 2 1

Fig. 6.14 Scroll-Beaded-Cuffs Chart. *See* the section 'Beaded Garter Stitch with beads every other row' in Chapter 3 for instructions about working from charts for Beaded-Garter-Stitch patterns.

Beaded Stocking Stitch

In Chapter 3, the basic techniques of Beaded Stocking Stitch are explained for working both with beads placed between purl stitches and beads placed with the slip-stitch technique. Visual patterns can be created on the surface of the fabric by using either the beads-placed-between-purl-stitches technique or the slip-stitch technique.

The Double-Diamond Slip-Stitch pattern has been used in a mittens design (*see* Accessories). The beads are threaded on to the yarn before the start of the knitting process, and, once the beads are placed, they sit on the yarn in front of a slipped stitch. It is necessary to work the stitch on each side of the slipped stitch in order to keep the bead in place, so, when designing slip-stitch patterns, this requirement must be taken into consideration.

Fig. 6.15 In these two samples, one repeat of the Double-Diamond Slip-Stitch Chart has been worked. The left-hand sample has been knitted with Jenny Watson Pure Merino Double Knitting yarn, and the right-hand sample has been knitted with Lang Yarns Merino 150 4ply/fingering-weight yarn. Both samples feature Miyuki size 6 Pearl seed beads.

Please *see* Abbreviations and Chart Symbols for definitions of the abbreviations and symbols used for patterns throughout this book.

Double-Diamond Slip-Stitch Pattern
16-stitch pattern.

Special Abbreviation

slB (RS) – bring yarn forward with 1 bead, slip the next stitch purlwise from the left-hand needle to the right-hand needle, take yarn back while making sure that the bead is in front of the slipped stitch.

Row 1 (RS): (k1, slB) × 3, k4, (k1, slB) × 3.
Row 2 and all even-number rows: purl.
Row 3: k2, slB, k1, slB, k3, slB, k3, slB, k1, slB, k1.
Row 5: k3, slB, k3, slB, k1, slB, k3, slB, k2.
Row 7: k6, slB, k3, slB, k5.
Row 9: k5, slB, k5, slB, k4.
Row 11: k4, slB, k3, slB, k3, slB, k3.
Row 13: k3, slB, k3, slB, k1, slB, k3, slB, k2.
Row 15: k4, slB, k3, slB, k3, slB, k3.
Row 17: k5, slB, k5, slB, k4.
Row 19: k6, slB, k3, slB, k5.
Row 21: k3, slB, k3, slB, k1, slB, k3, slB, k2.
Row 23: k2, slB, k1, slB, k3, slB, k3, slB, k1, slB, k1.
Row 24: purl.

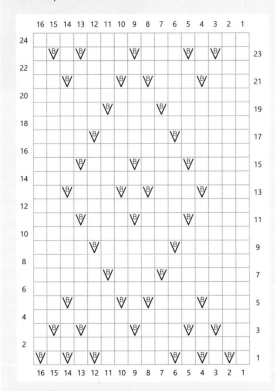

Fig. 6.16 Double-Diamond Slip-Stitch Chart, for beads to be placed on the yarn strand in front of slipped stitches.

The two featured samples of the Double-Diamond Slip-Stitch Pattern have been knitted with two different thickness of yarn but with the same size of seed beads. In the finer yarn, the pattern is more compact, but the same slip-stitch pattern worked with size 6 beads works well for both the DK- and the 4ply/fingering-weight yarns.

The next two featured samples have also been knitted with a similar large diamond pattern, but this time the beads are sitting between purl stitches. The beads sit between stitches rather than in front of a slipped stitch, so it is possible to work several beads next to each other.

Fig. 6.17 Two samples of the Beaded-Purl Diamond Pattern, worked with beads placed between purl stitches. The left-hand sample was knitted with West Yorkshire Spinners Illustrious DK yarn and Toho size 6 seed beads in the colourway Metallic Nebula. The right-hand sample was knitted with baa ram ewe Titus 4ply/fingering-weight yarn and Toho size 8 seed beads in the colourway Crystal Rainbow AB.

These two samples have also been worked in different thickness yarns, but this time each with a different size of beads. When working with beads placed between purl stitches, the bead size in relation to the yarn thickness is a bit more important. The size 6 beads work well with the DK-weight yarn but are a bit big for the 4ply/fingering-weight yarn. The beads sit between stitches, so using a larger bead on the 4ply/fingering-weight yarn can result in the overall fabric being distorted. The size 8 beads worked much better with the 4ply/fingering-weight yarn.

A large variety of stitch patterns are based on stocking stitch, which provides a rich source of patterns to play with when using both the slip-stitch and beads-placed-between-purl-stitches techniques.

Beaded-Purl Diamond Pattern
18-stitch pattern.

Special Abbreviation
p1, SB1 – purl 1st and push up 1 bead next to the stitch just purled.

Row 1 (RS): k2, p1, SB1, p1, k4, p1, SB1, p1, k4, p1, SB1, p1, k2.
Row 2 and all even-number rows: purl.
Row 3: k7, (p1, SB1) × 3, p1, k7.
Row 5: k6, (p1, SB1) × 2, p1, (p1, SB1) × 2, p1, k6.
Row 7: k5, (p1, SB1) × 2, p1, k2, (p1, SB1) × 2, p1, k5.
Row 9: k4, (p1, SB1) × 2, p1, k4, (p1, SB1) × 2, p1, k4.
Row 11: k3, (p1, SB1) × 2, p1, k2, p1, SB1, p1, k2, (p1, SB1,) × 2, p1, k3.
Row 13: k2, (p1, SB1) × 2, p1, k2, (p1, SB1) × 3, p1, k2, (p1, SB1) × 2, p1, k2.
Row 15: k3, (p1, SB1) × 2, p1, k2, p1, SB1, p1, k2, (p1, SB1,) × 2, p1, k3.
Row 17: k4, (p1, SB1) × 2, p1, k4, (p1, SB1) × 2, p1, k4.
Row 19: k5, (p1, SB1) × 2, p1, k2, (p1, SB1) × 2, p1, k5.
Row 21: k6, (p1, SB1) × 2, p1, (p1, SB1) × 2, p1, k6.
Row 23: k7, (p1, SB1) × 3, p1, k7.
Row 25: k2, p1, SB1, p1, k4, p1, SB1, p1, k4, p1, SB1, p1, k2.
Row 27: k1, (p1, SB1) × 3, p1, k8, (p1, SB1) × 3, p1, k1.
Row 28: purl.

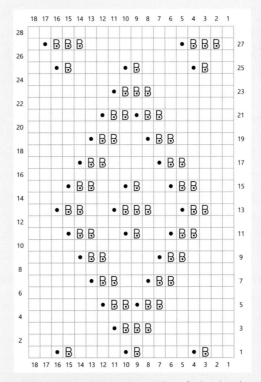

Fig. 6.18 Beaded-Purl Diamond Chart, for beads to be placed between purl stitches.

Beaded Cables

This group of pattern samples is based on basic six-stitch cable patterns.

The cream and red samples have been worked with a basic six-stitch, right-twisting cable. When beads are placed by using the slip-stitch technique, three stitches are involved in placing the bead, as you need a knit stitch on each side of the slipped stitch. The stitches can be slipped on right-side or wrong-side rows. In the samples, the slipped stitches were worked on wrong-side rows. To place a beaded slip stitch when working a wrong-side row, work to the position of the slip stitch. You should have just worked a purl stitch. Take the yarn back between the points of the needles, push up a bead near the point of the right-hand needle, slip the next stitch purlwise to the right-hand needle and bring the yarn back between the points of the needles, ready to purl the next stitch.

The beads were slipped on wrong-side purl rows to avoid working a beaded slip stitch on the same row as a cable cross. By working the beads on purl rows, it was possible to create a continuous line of beads that follows the flow of the cable.

Fig. 6.19 Right-twisting cables, featuring beads, placed with the slip-stitch technique, following the line of the cable twist. The left-hand sample was knitted with West Yorkshire Spinners Illustrious DK yarn and Toho size 6 Rosaline/Opaque Purple-Lined seed beads. The right-hand sample was knitted with Garnstudio Drops Fabel Uni Colour sock yarn and Czech size 6 Silver-Lined Gold seed beads.

Right-cross cable (C6B) with beads placed with the slip-stitch technique
8-stitch repeat.

Special Abbreviation

slB (WS) – take yarn back with 1 bead, slip the next stitch purlwise from the left-hand needle to the right-hand needle, bring yarn forward while making sure that the bead is behind the slipped stitch.

Row 1 (RS): p1, k6, p1.
Row 2: k1, p1, slB, p4, k1.
Row 3: p1, k6, p1.
Row 4: k1, p1, slB, p4, k1.
Row 5: p1, C6B, p1.
Row 6: k1, p4, slB, p1, k1.
Row 7: p1, k6, p1.
Row 8: k1, p4, slB, p1, k1.
Row 9: p1, k6, p1.
Row 10: k1, p4, slB, p1, k1.
Row 11: p1, k6, p1.
Row 12: k1, p6, k1.
Row 13: p1, C6B, p1.
Row 14: k1, p1, slB, p4, k1.
Row 15: p1, k6, p1.
Row 16: k1, p1, slB, p4, k1.

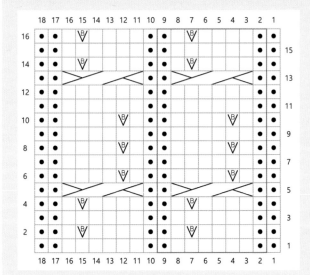

Fig. 6.20 Chart for the right-cross cable (C6B), for beads to be placed with the slip-stitch technique.

For the featured pale-green and teal samples of cables with beads, the beads are placed in the central section of the cables. In both samples, the beads sit between purl stitches. In the teal sample, the beaded cable is worked as a rib fabric, as a knit-two-stitches, purl-two-stitches, knit-two-stitches pattern, except for the cable row, where all of the stitches are worked as knit stitches. As a result, the beads tend to sink back into the knitting. In the pale-green sample, a purl stitch is used only on each side of the beads, creating a stocking-stitch fabric rather than a rib fabric. As a result, the beads remain more prominent.

Fig. 6.21 Two samples showing beads at the centre of six-stitch, left-twist cables. The pale-green sample was knitted with Stylecraft Baby 4ply/fingering-weight yarn and Miyuki size 6 seed beads in the colourway Matt Metallic Dark-Green Iris. The teal sample was knitted with Debbie Bliss Rialto 4ply/fingering-weight yarn and Matubo™ size 6 seed beads in the colourway Crystal California Gold Rush.

Left-cross cable (C6F) with beads placed between purl stitches in rib fabric
16-stitch repeat.

Special Abbreviation
p1, SB1 – purl 1st and push up 1 bead next to the stitch just purled.

Row 1 (RS): p1, k2, p1, SB1, p1, k2, p2, C6F, p1.
Row 2 and all even-number rows: k1, p6, k2, p2, k2, p2, k1.
Row 3: p1, k2, p1, SB1, p1, k2, p2, k6, p1.
Row 5: p1, k2, p2, k2, p2, k6, p1.
Row 7: p1, C6F, p2, k6, p1.
Row 9: p1, k2, p2, k2, p2, k6, p1.
Row 11: p1, k2, p1, SB1, p1, k2, p2, k6, p1.
Row 12: k1, p6, k2, p2, k2, p2, k1.

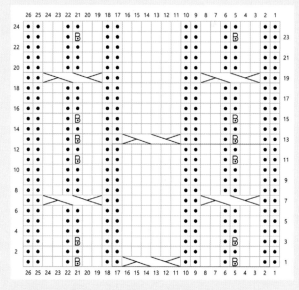

Fig. 6.22 Chart for the left-cross cable (C6F), for beads to be placed between purl stitches in rib fabric. This chart corresponds to the right-hand, teal sample shown in Figure 6.21.

Left-cross cable (C6F) with beads placed between purl stitches in stocking-stitch fabric
16-stitch repeat.

Special Abbreviation
p1, SB1 – purl 1st and push up 1 bead next to the stitch just purled.

Row 1 (RS): p1, k2, p1, SB1, p1, k2, p2, k6, p1.
Row 2 and all even-number rows: k1, p6, k2, p6, k1.
Row 3: p1, k2, p1, SB1, p1, k2, p2, C6F.
Row 5: p1, k2, p1, SB1, p1, k2, p2, k6, p1.
Row 7: p1, k6, p2, k6, p1.
Row 9: p1, C6F, p2, k6, p1.
Row 11: p1, k6, p2, k6, p1.
Row 12: k1, p6, k2, p6, k1.

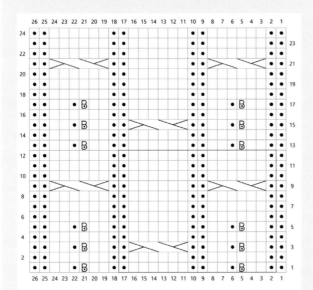

Fig. 6.23 Chart for the left-cross cable (C6F), for beads to be placed between purl stitches in stocking-stitch fabric. This chart corresponds to the left-hand, pale-green sample shown in Figure 6.21.

In the featured group of three cable samples, both right- and left-twisting cables have been worked, and the beads have been placed so that they run in diagonal lines across the cables.

In the bottom-right, beige sample, the beads were placed between purl stitches in a rib section of the cable. The beads sink back into this rib section. The colour of the beads is also tonally quite close to the colour of the yarn, so the beads have become quite difficult to see.

In the top, light-purple sample, the beads were still placed between purl stitches, but this time the fabric is of stocking stitch. As a result, the beads stand on the surface of the knitting rather than sinking into the fabric, and they are therefore easier to see.

In the bottom-left, dark-blue sample, the beads have been placed by using slip stitches. The beads could have been placed on right-side rows, but, by placing them on wrong-side rows, it was possible to create a better diagonal line of beads between each cable cross.

Fig. 6.24 Three samples of left- and right-cross cables (C6F and C6B), showing three different variations of placing the beads. The light-purple, top sample was knitted with Baby Milk 4ply/fingering-weight yarn and Czech size 6 seed beads in the colourway Metallic Purple Iris. The dark-blue, bottom-left sample was knitted with Lang Yarns Merino 150 4ply/fingering-weight yarn and Toho size 6 seed beads in the colourway Galvanized Aluminium. The beige, bottom-right sample was knitted with baa ram ewe Titus 4ply/fingering-weight yarn and Matubo™ size 6 seed beads in the colourway Aqua Picasso.

Left- and right-cross cables (C6F and C6B) with beads placed between purl stitches in rib fabric
26-stitch pattern.

Special Abbreviation
p1, SB1 – purl 1st and push up 1 bead next to the stitch just purled.

Row 1 (RS): p2, k1, p2, k3, p2, k6, p2, k3, p2, k1, p2.
Row 2: k1, p1, k2, p3, k2, p6, k2, p3, k2, p1, k2.
Row 3: p2, k1, p1, SB1, p1, k3, p2, k6, p2, k3, p1, SB1, p1, k1, p2.
Row 4: k2, p2, k2, p2, k2, p6, k2, p2, k2, p2, k2.
Row 5: p2, k2, p1, SB1, p1, k2, p2, k6, p2, k2, p1, SB1, p1, k2, p2.
Row 6: k2, p3, k2, p1, k2, p6, k2, p1, k2, p3, k2.
Row 7: p2, k3, p1, SB1, p1, k1, p2, k6, p2, k1, p1, SB1, p1, k3, p2.
Row 8: k2, p3, k2, p1, k2, p6, k2, p1, k2, p3, k2.
Row 9: p2, k3, p2, k1, p2, k6, p2, k1, p2, k3, p2.
Row 10: k2, p3, k2, p1, k2, p6, k2, p1, k2, p3, k2.
Row 11: p2, C6F, p2, k6, p2, C6B, p2.
Row 12: k2, p1, k2, p3, k2, p6, k2, p3, k2, p1, k2.

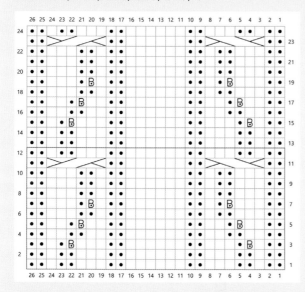

Fig. 6.25 Chart for the left- and right-cross cables (C6F and C6B), for beads to be placed between purl stitches in rib fabric, corresponding to the beige, bottom-right sample shown in Figure 6.24.

Left- and right-cross cables (C6F and C6B) with beads placed between purl stitches in stocking-stitch fabric
26-stitch pattern.

Special Abbreviation
p1, SB1 – purl 1st and push up 1 bead next to the stitch just purled.

Row 1 (RS): *p2, k6*, repeat from * to * to the last 2sts, p2.
Row 2 and all even-number rows: *k2, p6*, repeat from * to * to the last 2sts, p2.
Row 3: p2, k1, p1, SB1, p1, k3, p2, k6, p2, k3, p1, SB1, p1, k1, p2.
Row 5: p2, k2, p1, SB1, p1, k2, p2, k6, p2, k2, p1, SB1, p1, k2, p2.
Row 7: p2, k3, p1, SB1, p1, k1, p2, k6, p2, k1, p1, SB1, p1, k3, p2.
Row 9: *p2, k6*, repeat from * to * to the last 2sts, p2.
Row 11: p2, C6F, p2, k6, p2, C6B, p2.
Row 12: *k2, p6*, repeat from * to * to the last 2sts, p2.
Repeat Rows 2 to 10.

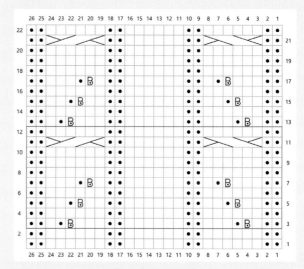

Fig. 6.26 Chart for the left- and right-cross cables (C6F and C6B), for beads to be placed between purl stitches in stocking-stitch fabric, corresponding to the light-purple, top sample shown in Figure 6.24.

Left- and right-cross cables (C6F and C6B) with beads placed with the slip-stitch technique
26-stitch pattern.

Special Abbreviation

slB (WS) – take yarn back with 1 bead, slip the next stitch purlwise from the left-hand needle to the right-hand needle, bring yarn forward while making sure that the bead is behind the slipped stitch.

Row 1 (RS): *p2, k6*, repeat from * to * to the last 2sts, p2.
Row 2: k2, p1, slB, p4, k2, p6, k2, p4, slB, p1, k2.
Row 3: *p2, k6*, repeat from * to * to the last 2sts, p2.
Row 4: k2, p2, slB, p3, k2, p6, k2, p3, slB, p2, k2.
Row 5: *p2, k6*, repeat from * to * to the last 2sts, p2.
Row 6: k2, p3, slB, p2, k2, p6, k2, p2, slB, p3, k2.
Row 7: *p2, k6*, repeat from * to * to the last 2sts, p2.
Row 8: k2, p4, slB, p1, k2, p6, k2, p1, slB, p4, k2.
Row 9: *p2, k6*, repeat from * to * to the last 2sts, p2.
Row 10: *k2, p6*, repeat from * to * to the last 2sts, k2.
Row 11: p2, C6F, p2, k6, p2, C6B, p2.
Row 12: k2, p1, slB, p4, k2, p6, k2, p4, slB, p1, k2.
Repeat Rows 2 to 10.

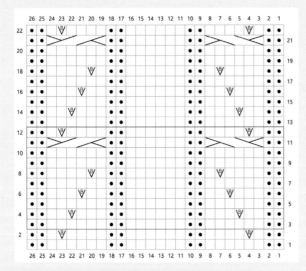

Fig. 6.27 Chart for the left- and right-cross cables (C6F and C6B), for beads to be placed with the slip-stitch technique, corresponding to the dark-blue, bottom-left sample shown in Figure 6.24.

Fig. 6.28 Two samples of Bavarian Twisted-Stitch Cables, with beads placed between purl stitches. The left-hand sample was knitted with West Yorkshire Spinners Illustrious DK yarn and Miyuki size 6 Seafoam-Lined Crystal AB seed beads. The right-hand sample was knitted with Adriafil Genziana 4ply/fingering-weight yarn and Miyuki size 8 Seafoam-Lined Crystal AB seed beads.

For the samples of Bavarian Twisted-Stitch Cables, the beads were placed between purl stitches in a section of reverse stocking stitch. Beads could also be placed in the trellis section, which would be another experiment to try.

Bavarian Twisted-Stitch Cables with beads
14-stitch pattern.

Note: On all right-side rows, each knit stitch is worked through its back loop (k1tbl).
Note: On all wrong-side rows, each purl stitch is worked through its back loop (p1tbl).

Special Abbreviations

1/1LC – 1-over-1 left-cross cable (RS). Slip the next stitch on the left-hand needle purlwise to the cable needle and hold the cable needle at the front of the knitting, knit 1st through the back loop on the left-hand needle, knit 1st through the back loop from the cable needle.

1/1RC – 1-over-1 right-cross cable (RS). Slip the next stitch on the left-hand needle purlwise to the cable needle and hold the cable needle at the back of the knitting (away from you), k1 through the back loop on the left-hand needle, knit 1 through the back loop from the cable needle.

1k/1pLC – 1-knit-over-1-purl left-cross cable (WS). Slip the next stitch purlwise from the left-hand needle to the cable needle and hold the cable needle at the front of the knitting, purl 1st through the back loop from the left-hand needle, knit 1st from the cable needle.

1k/1pRC – 1-knit-over-1-purl right-cross cable (WS). Slip the next stitch purlwise from the left-hand needle to the cable needle and hold the cable needle at the back of the knitting (away from you), knit 1st from the left-hand needle, purl 1st through the back loop from the cable needle.

p1, SB1 – purl 1st and push up 1 bead next to the stitch just purled.

Row 1 (RS): p1, k1tbl, p2, 1/1LC, p2, 1/1RC, p2, k1tbl, p1.
Row 2: k1, p1tbl, k1, 1k/1pLC, 1k/1pRC, 1k/1pLC, 1k/1pRC, k1, p1tbl, k1.
Row 3: p1, k1tbl, p1, k1tbl, p1, SB1, p1, 1/1RC, p1, SB1, p1, k1tbl, p1, k1tbl, p1.
Row 4: k1, p1tbl, k1, p1tbl, k2, p2tbl, k2, p1tbl, k1, p1tbl, k1.
Row 5 to 10: repeat Rows 3 to 4, 3 times.
Row 11: p1, k1tbl, p1, k1tbl, p1, SB1, p1, 1/1RC, p1, SB1, p1, k1tbl, p1, k1tbl, p1.
Row 12: k1, p1tbl, k1, 1k/1pRC, 1k/1pLC, 1k/1p/RC, 1k/1pLC, k1 p1tbl, k1.
Row 13: p1, k1tbl, p2, 1/1LC, p2, 1/1LC, p2, k1tbl, p1.
Row 14: k1, *1k/1pRC, 1k/1pLC*, repeat from * to * 2 times, k1.

Row 15: *p2, 1/1RC*, repeat from * to * 2 times, p2.
Row 16: k1, *1k/1pLC, 1k/1pRC*, repeat from * to * 2 times, k1.
Row 17: p1, k1tbl, p2, 1/1LC, p2, 1/1LC, p2, k1tbl, p1.
Row 18: k1, *1k/1pRC, 1k/1pLC*, repeat from * to * 2 times, k1.
Row 19: *p2, 1/1RC*, repeat from * to * 2 times, p2.
Row 20: k1, *1k/1pLC, 1k/1pRC*, repeat from * to * 2 times, k1.

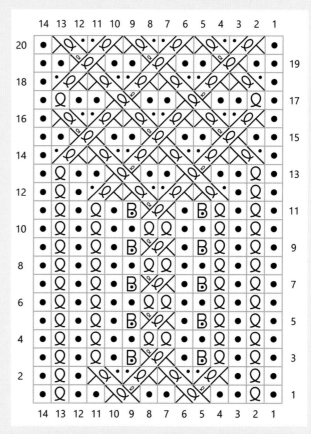

Fig. 6.29 Chart for the Bavarian Twisted-Stitch Cables, for beads to be placed between purl stitches.

In many of the other featured cable samples, size 6 seed beads have been used with 4ply/fingering-weight or DK-weight yarn, but, in the 4ply/fingering-weight yarn sample of Bavarian Twisted-Stitch Cables, size 8 beads seemed to work better.

The last samples in this cable section include single beads that hang between a right-twist cable and a left-twist cable. The stitch on each side of the gap created by the cable twists pulling away from each other has been worked as a purl stitch, to help keep the bead on the right side of the fabric.

Fig. 6.30 Two samples of the Staghorn Cable with beads. The left-hand sample was knitted with Artesano Alpaca 4ply/fingering-weight yarn and Toho size 6 Silver-Lined Dark Peridot seed beads. The right-hand sample was knitted with Adriafil Genziana 4ply/fingering-weight yarn and Toho 3mm Magatama Rainbow Light Topaz/Sea Foam beads. The hole in a Magatama bead is to one side of the bead rather than through the centre of the bead, so the bead hangs more like a drop bead.

As you can see, there is a lot of potential for adding beads to cable patterns, by using both the slip-stitch and the beads-placed-between-purl-stitches techniques.

Staghorn Cable with beads
18-stitch pattern.

Special Abbreviation
k1, SB1 – knit 1st and push up 1 bead next to the stitch just knitted.

Row 1 (RS): k1, p2, k12, p2, k1.
Row 2: p1, k2, p12, k2, p1.
Row 3: k1, p2, k12, p2, k1.
Row 4: p1, k2, p12, k2, p1.
Row 5: k1, p2, C6B, C6F, p2, k1.
Row 6: p1, k2, p5, k1, SB1, k1, p5, k2, p1.
Row 7: k1, p2, k12, p2, k1.
Row 8: p1, k2, p12, k2, p1.

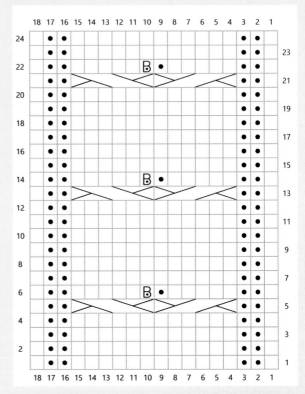

Fig. 6.31 Chart for the Staghorn Cable with beads.

Beaded Lace

The next group of samples demonstrates beads in combination with lace. When working with beads within lace patterns, the beads can be threaded on to the yarn and worked with yarn overs, they can be threaded on to the yarn and worked with the slip-stitch technique or they can be placed around stitches by using the crochet-hook method.

When a bead (or beads) is worked in combination with a yarn-over stitch, which creates an eyelet hole with a bead, the position of the bead in the design is determined by where the bead is on the yarn-over loop when that stitch is worked into on the following row. In this book, blue and yellow squares have been used on the charts to indicate where the bead should be when the yarn-over loop is worked into on the following row.

For the Zigzag-Lace Pattern, the beads are threaded on to the yarn before you start to knit the sample. The beads are placed on yarn overs, but the position of the bead, namely, on which side of the eyelet hole the bead will sit, is determined by which end of the yarn-over loop the bead is at when this stitch is worked into on the following row. For the first half of the pattern, the bead is at the left-hand end of its yarn-over loop when this stitch is worked into on the following row. The bead then sits to the right-hand side of the eyelet hole, when the fabric is viewed from the right side. For the second half of the pattern, the bead is at the right-hand end of its yarn-over loop when this stitch is worked into on the following row. The bead then sits at the left-hand side of the eyelet hole, when the fabric is viewed from the right side.

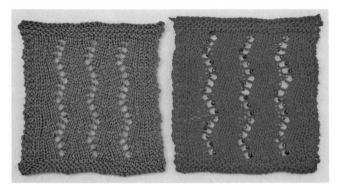

Fig. 6.32 Two samples of the Zigzag-Lace Pattern. The left-hand, blue sample was knitted with Rico® Design Bamboo sock yarn and Czech size 7 Crystal AB seed beads. The right-hand, red sample was knitted with Sirdar Cotton 4ply/fingering-weight yarn and Matubo™ size 7 Magic Red/Brown seed beads.

Zigzag-Lace Pattern
7-stitch repeat + 2 edge stitches.

Special Abbreviation

yoB – work a yarn over with 1 bead on the yarn-over loop.

Rows 1, 3 and 5 (RS): k1, *ssk, k2, yoB, k3*, repeat from * to * to the last stitch, k1.

Rows 2, 4 and 6: p1, *p3, p1 with bead at the left-hand end of the yo loop, p3*, repeat from * to * to the last stitch, p1.

Rows 7, 9 and 11: k1, *k3, yoB, k2, k2tog*, repeat from * to * to the last stitch, k1.

Rows 8, 10 and 12: p1, *p3, p1 with bead at the right-hand end of the yo loop, p3*, repeat from * to * to the last stitch, p1.

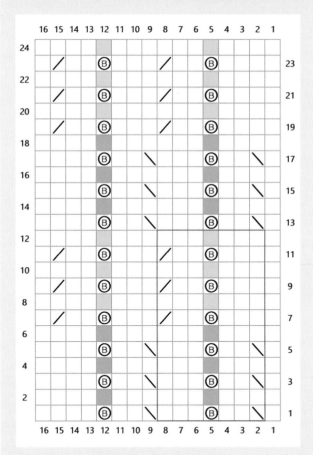

Fig. 6.33 Chart for the Zigzag-Lace Pattern.

Fig. 6.34 Two samples of the Fern-Lace Pattern with beads; the beads have been placed differently in each sample. The left-hand, light-blue sample of Fern-Lace Pattern One was knitted with Sirdar Cotton 4ply/fingering-weight yarn and Miyuki size 6 Amethyst Aqua seed beads. The right-hand, sea-green sample of Fern-Lace Pattern Two was knitted with Sirdar Cotton 4ply/fingering-weight yarn and Matubo™ size 7 Aquamarine Celsian seed beads.

Fern-Lace Pattern One with beads

9-stitch repeat + 2 edge stitches.

Special Abbreviation

yoB – work a yarn over with 1 bead on the yarn-over loop.

Row 1 (RS): k1, *k1, yoB, k2, ssk, k2tog, k2, yoB*, repeat from * to * to the last stitch, k1.

Row 2: p1, *p1 with bead at the left-hand end of the yo loop, p6, p1 with bead at the right-hand end of the yo loop, p1*, repeat from * to * to the last stitch, p1.

Row 3: k1, *yo, k2, ssk, k2tog, k2, yo, k1*, repeat from * to * to the last stitch, k1.

Row 4: purl.

Row 5: k1, *k1, yo, k2, ssk, k2tog, k2, yo*, repeat from * to * to the last stitch, k1.

Row 6: purl.

Row 7: k1, *yoB, k2, ssk, k2tog, k2, yoB, k1*, repeat from * to * to the last stitch, k1.

Row 8: p1, *p1, p1 with bead at the left-hand end of the yo loop, p6, p1 with bead at the right-hand end of the yo loop* repeat from * to * to the last stitch, p1.

Row 9: k1, *k1, yo, k2, ssk, k2tog, yo*, repeat from * to * to the last stitch, k1.

Row 10: purl.

Row 11: k1, *yo, k2, ssk, k2tog, k2, yo, k1*, repeat from * to * to the last stitch, k1.

Row 12: purl.

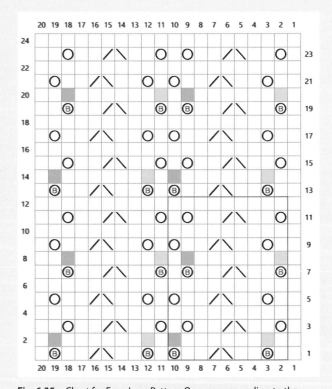

Fig. 6.35 Chart for Fern-Lace Pattern One, corresponding to the left-hand, light-blue sample shown in Figure 6.34.

The same Fern-Lace Pattern has been knitted for the two featured lace samples, but the beads have been worked at different points within the lace pattern. The basic pattern repeat is only four rows long.

For the light-blue sample, the beads were worked on every yarn over for one row, and then five rows of the pattern were worked before beads were again placed. The beads were added on every yarn over for the next row, and then five more rows were worked without the addition of beads. The pattern repeat has been extended from a four-row repeat to a twelve-row repeat. The lines of beads are also slightly staggered.

For the sea-green sample, the beads were worked in alternate horizontal repeats of the pattern. Beads were added only on alternate pattern repeats across the row. On Row 1 of the pattern, a bead was worked on the yarn over at the beginning of the repeat and at the right-hand end of the yarn-over loop on the following row. On Row 3, a bead was worked on the yarn over at the end of the repeat and at the left-hand end of the yarn-over loop on the following row. The beads, offset on each side, appear on the edges of the central stocking-stitch section.

Fern-Lace Pattern Two with beads
18-stitch repeat + 2 edge stitches.

Special Abbreviation
yoB – work a yarn over with 1 bead on the yarn-over loop.

Row 1 (RS): k1, *k1, yo, k2, ssk, k2tog, k2, yo, k1, yoB, k2, ssk, k2tog, k2, yo*, repeat from * to * to the last stitch, k1.
Row 2: p1, *p7, p1 with bead at the right-hand end of the yo loop, p10*, repeat from * to * to the last stitch, p1.
Row 3: k1, *yo, k2, ssk, k2tog, k2, yo, k1, yo, k2, ssk, k2tog, k2, yoB, k1*, repeat from * to * to the last stitch, k1.
Row 4: p1, *p1, p1 with bead at the left-hand end of the yo loop, p16*, repeat from * to * to the last stitch, p1.

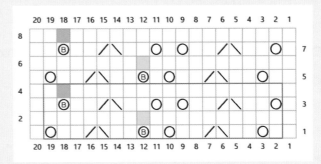

Fig. 6.36 Chart for Fern-Lace Pattern Two, corresponding to the right-hand sea-green sample shown in Figure 6.34.

The Hourglass-Lace Pattern can be worked in two versions: all in stocking stitch and in a combination of knit and purl stitches. This lace pattern is also slightly unusual, as it is worked with a double yarn over, creating a large eyelet hole. The bead has been placed at the centre of the double yarn over, so it appears to be suspended as a bead drop in the centre of the eyelet.

The first two featured samples of the Hourglass-Lace Pattern have been worked as the stocking-stitch version. They have been knitted with two different light-grey yarns, with size 6 seed beads in one sample and cube beads in the other sample. Cube beads have a central hole, so they can be threaded on to the yarn in the same manner as for any of the seed beads. They are slightly bigger than size 6 seed beads and make good accent beads, as well as being suitable to use in all-over patterns.

When knitting the pattern, only one of the two yarn overs is worked with a bead. When the double yarn overs are worked on the following row, each yarn over has to be worked as a stitch, by purling the first yarn over and dropping it from the left-hand needle, pushing the bead to the right-hand end of the remaining yarn-over loop and then knitting the second yarn over.

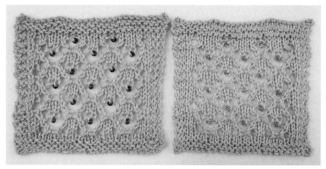

Fig. 6.37 Two samples of the Hourglass-Lace Pattern, worked in stocking stitch. The left-hand sample was knitted with Garnstudio Drops Baby Alpaca 4ply/fingering-weight yarn and Czech size 6 Silver-Lined Black Diamond seed beads. The right-hand sample was knitted with Sirdar Cotton 4ply/fingering-weight yarn and Miyuki Crystal Silver-Lined cube beads.

Hourglass-Lace Pattern with beads in stocking-stitch fabric
6-stitch repeat + 2 edge stitches.

Special Abbreviation
yoB – work a yarn over with 1 bead on the yarn-over loop.

Row 1 (RS): k1, *k1, yo, ssk, k2tog, yo, k1*, repeat from * to * to the last stitch, k1.
Row 2: purl.
Row 3: k1, *k1, k2tog, yoB, yo, ssk, k1*, repeat from * to * to the last stitch, k1.
Row 4: p1, *p2, p1 into the first of the yo loops, k1 with bead at the right-hand end of the yo loop into the second yo loop, p2*, repeat from * to * to the last stitch, p1.
Row 5: k1, *k2tog, yo, k2, yo, ssk*, repeat from * to * to the last stitch, k1.
Row 6: purl.
Row 7: k1, *yo, ssk, k2, k2tog, yoB*, repeat from * to * to the last stitch, k1. (Work the last yo of the row as a normal yo, not with a bead.)
Row 8: p1, *k1 with bead at the right-hand end of the yo loop, p4, p1 into the yo loop*, repeat from * to * to the last stitch, k1.

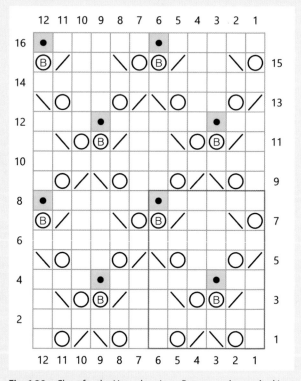

Fig. 6.38 Chart for the Hourglass-Lace Pattern, to be worked in stocking stitch.

Fig. 6.39 Two samples of the Hourglass-Lace Pattern, worked with purl stitches. The left-hand, lime-green sample was knitted with Patons Merino 4ply/fingering-weight yarn and Toho size 6 Frosted-Olive Pink-Lined seed beads. The right-hand, blue sample was knitted with Sirdar Cotton 4ply/fingering-weight yarn and Miyuki size 6 Crystal Silver-Lined seed beads.

For the lime-green and blue samples of the Hourglass-Lace Pattern, the purl-stitch version has been knitted. As well as creating a pattern with more depth, this version of the lace pattern can also be used as an edging pattern, as the fabric will lie flat. Each bead sits at the centre of a double yarn over again, and these double yarn overs are worked in the same way as for the stocking-stitch version.

Hourglass-Lace Pattern with beads and purl stitches

6-stitch repeat + 2 edge stitches.

Special Abbreviation

yoB – work a yarn over with 1 bead on the yarn-over loop.

Row 1 (RS): k1, *p1, yo, ssk, k2tog, yo, p1*, repeat from * to * to the last stitch, k1.

Row 2: p1, *k1, p4, k1*, repeat from * to * to the last stitch, p1.

Row 3: k1, *p1, k2tog, yoB, yo, ssk, p1*, repeat from * to * to the last stitch, k1.

Row 4: p1, *k1, p1, p1 into the first of the yo loops, k1 with bead at the right-hand end of the yo loop into the second yo loop, p1, k1*, repeat from * to * to the last stitch, p1.

Row 5: k1, *k2tog, yo, p2, yo, ssk*, repeat from * to * to the last stitch, k1.

Row 6: p1, *p2, k2, p2*, repeat from * to * to the last stitch, p1.

Row 7: k1, *yo, ssk, p2, k2tog, yoB*, repeat from * to * to the last stitch, k1. (Work the last yo of the row as a normal yo, not with a bead.)

Row 8: p1, *k1 with bead at the right-hand end of the yo loop, p1, k2, p1, p1 into the yo loop*, repeat from * to * to the last stitch, k1.

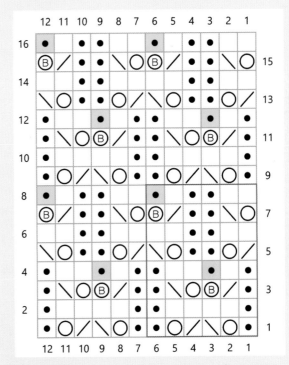

Fig. 6.40 Chart for the Hourglass-Lace Pattern, to be worked with purl stitches.

Fig. 6.41   Two samples of the Feather-Lace Pattern, with beads placed with the slip-stitch technique. The lime-green sample on the left-hand side was knitted with Sirdar Cotton 4ply/fingering-weight yarn and Miyuki Green-Lined Crystal cube beads. The light-purple sample on the right-hand side was knitted with Rowan Wool Cotton 4ply/fingering-weight yarn and Toho size 6 Purple AB seed beads.

In the lace samples shown so far, only one bead has been included on the yarn-over stitch. It is possible to include several beads when working a yarn-over. Having more beads on the yarn-over loop will make the yarn-over loop longer, so, when this technique is used, yarn overs and decreases are worked on every row to keep the fabric balanced. This is very similar to the approach used for knitting the garter-stitch purses, where beads are strung between stitches on every row. An example of using several beads on a yarn over will be covered in the section 'Edgings' at the end of this chapter.

There are a number of ways to combine beads with lace. As well as placing a bead on the yarn-over loop, beads threaded on to the yarn can also be placed by using the slip-stitch technique. You still need three knit stitches next to each other in order to place a bead with this technique, so the bead can sit in front of a slipped stitch, with a stitch on each side of it, securing it in place.

The lime-green and purple samples have been knitted with the Feather-Lace Pattern, which is a very similar lace pattern to the Lacy-Diamond Pattern. The slip stitch is placed between a left- and a right-leaning decrease stitch so that the bead sits just below the double-decrease stitch at the point of each lace repeat.

Feather-Lace Pattern with beads placed with the slip-stitch technique
6-stitch repeat + 7 stitches + 2 edge stitches.

Special Abbreviation
slB (RS) – bring yarn forward with 1 bead, slip the next stitch purlwise from the left-hand needle to the right-hand needle, take yarn back while making sure that the bead is in front of the slipped stitch.

Row 1 (RS): k2, *yo, ssk, slB, k2tog, yo, k1*, repeat from * to * to the last 7sts, yo, ssk, slB, k2tog, yo, k2.
Row 2 and all even-number rows: purl.
Row 3: k2, *yo, k1, sk2po, k1, yo, k1*, repeat from * to * to the last 7sts, yo, k1, sk2po, k1, yo, k2.
Row 5: k2, *k2tog, yo, k1, yo, ssk, slB*, repeat from * to * to the last 7sts, k2tog, yo, k1, yo, ssk, k2.
Row 7: k1, k2tog, *k1, yo, k1, yo, k1, sk2po*, repeat from * to * to the last 7sts, k1, yo, k1, yo, k1, ssk, k1.
Row 8: purl.

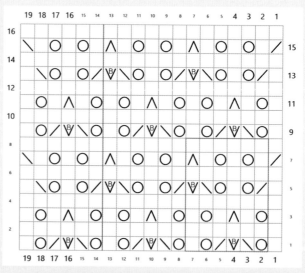

Fig. 6.42   Chart for the Feather-Lace Pattern, for beads to be placed with the slip-stitch technique.

The Lacy-Diamond Pattern has been used in the two featured shawl projects (*see* Accessories). For both shawl patterns, each bead is placed around a stitch by using the crochet-hook method, but the beads can instead be added by using the slip-stitch technique.

The slip stitch was worked on a row between a left- and a right-leaning decrease and just below the double-decrease stitch at the point of the diamond. After experimenting with the placement of the slip stitch, this seemed to give the best results.

As the left-hand sample shows, size 6 seed beads will work with DK-weight yarn when placing beads with the slip-stitch technique, as long as the beads will thread on to the yarn. However, with the crochet-hook method, it is much more difficult to use thicker yarns, as the stitch, which is a double thickness of the yarn, has to be pulled through the centre of the bead.

Fig. 6.43 Two samples of the Lacy-Diamond Pattern, worked with the slip-stitch technique. The navy-blue sample on the left-hand side was knitted with King Cole Majestic DK-weight yarn and Matubo™ size 6 Chalk-Blue Lustre seed beads. The maroon sample on the right-hand side was knitted with Patons Merino 4ply/fingering-weight yarn and Toho size 6 Silver-Lined Mauve seed beads.

Lacy-Diamond Pattern with beads placed with the slip-stitch technique
6-stitch repeat + 7 stitches + 2 edge stitches.

Special Abbreviation

slB (RS) – bring yarn forward with 1 bead, slip the next stitch purlwise from the left-hand needle to the right-hand needle, take yarn back while making sure that the bead is in front of the slipped stitch.

Row 1 (RS): k2, *ssk, yo, k1, yo, k2tog, slB*, repeat from * to * to the last 7sts, ssk, yo, k1, yo, k2tog, k2.

Row 2 and all even-number rows: purl.

Row 3: k1, k2tog, *yo, k3, yo, sk2po*, repeat from * to * to the last 7sts, yo, k3, yo, ssk, k1.

Row 5: k2, *yo, ssk, slB, k2tog, yo, k1*, repeat from * to * to the last 7sts, yo, ssk, slB, k2tog, yo, k2.

Row 7: k2, *k1, yo, sk2po, yo, k2*, repeat from * to * to the last 7sts, k1, yo, sk2po, yo, k3.

Row 8: purl.

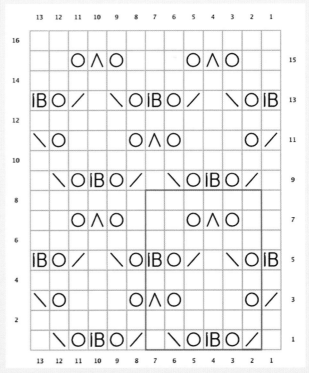

Fig. 6.44 Chart for the Lacy-Diamond Pattern, for beads to be placed with the slip-stitch technique.

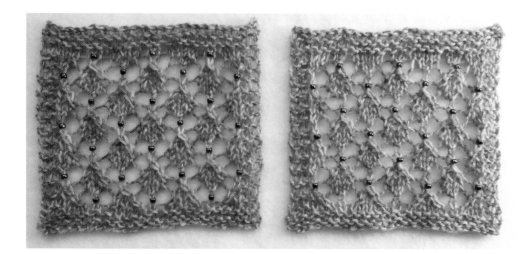

Fig. 6.45 Two samples of the Lacy-Diamond Pattern, with hooked beads. Both samples were knitted with the same yarn, Rico® Design Superba Paint 4 Ply sock yarn, and with the same beads, Toho size 6 Metallic Dragonfly seed beads, but the beads have been placed on to stitches on different rows.

The crochet-hook method of adding beads is much more frequently used when knitting lace patterns than when knitting other types of stitch pattern. The beads are added as they are required in the knitting process rather than having to be threaded before the knitting process starts, which makes it easier to add beads more spontaneously. If a bead is added to a stitch with an eyelet hole on each side of it, the bead creates a nice focal point.

The two Lacy-Diamond-Pattern samples were knitted with the same yarn and the same beads. For the left-hand sample, the beads were each added between two yarn overs on a right-side row. For the right-hand sample, the beads were each added on a wrong-side row immediately after the row in which double decreases were worked, with each bead directly above a double-decrease stitch. In the left-hand sample, the beads hang in space, whereas, in the right-hand sample, the beads sit forward, on top of the diamond points.

Lacy-Diamond Pattern One with hooked beads between yarn overs

6-stitch repeat + 7 stitches + 2 edge stitches.

Special Abbreviation

hB – place 1 bead on to the crochet hook, slip the next stitch on the left-hand needle on to the crochet hook, push the bead off of the crochet hook and over the stitch, and re-place the stitch on to the left-hand needle. Work the stitch as a knit stitch on RS rows and as a purl stitch on WS rows.

Row 1 (RS): k2, *k2tog, yo, hB, yo, ssk, k1*, repeat from * to * to the last 7sts, k2tog, yo, hB, yo, ssk, k2.

Row 2 and all even-number rows: purl.

Row 3: k1, k2tog, *yo, k3, yo, sk2po*, repeat from * to * to the last 7sts, yo, k3, yo, ssk, k1.

Row 5: k1, hB, *yo, ssk, k1, k2tog, yo, hB*, repeat from * to * to the last 7sts, yo, ssk, k1, k2tog, yo, hB, k1.

Row 7: k2, *k1, yo, sk2po, yo, k2*, repeat from * to * to the last 7sts, k1, yo, sk2po, yo, k3.

Row 8: purl.

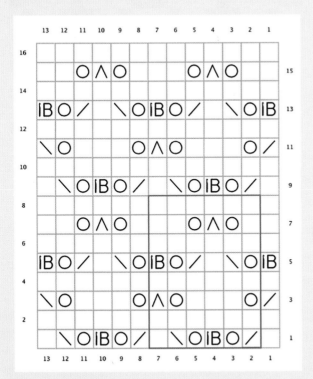

Fig. 6.46 Chart for Lacy-Diamond Pattern One, for hooked beads between yarn overs, corresponding to the left-hand sample shown in Figure 6.45.

Lacy-Diamond Pattern Two with hooked beads above double-decrease stitches

6-stitch repeat + 7 stitches + 2 edge stitches.

Special Abbreviation

hB – place 1 bead on to the crochet hook, slip the next stitch on the left-hand needle on to the crochet hook, push the bead off of the crochet hook and over the stitch, and re-place the stitch on to the left-hand needle. Work the stitch as a knit stitch on RS rows and as a purl stitch on WS row.

Row 1 (RS): k2, *k2tog, yo, k1, yo, ssk, k1*, repeat from * to * to the last 7sts, k2tog, yo, k1, yo, ssk, k2.

Row 2: purl.

Row 3: k1, k2tog, *yo, k3, yo, sk2po*, repeat from * to * to the last 7sts, yo, k3, yo, ssk, k1.

Row 4: p1, *hB, p5*, repeat from * to * to last 2sts, hB, p1.

Row 5: k2, *yo, ssk, k1, k2tog, yo, k1*, repeat from * to * to the last 7sts, yo, ssk, k1, k2tog, yo, k2.

Row 6: purl.

Row 7: k2, *k1, yo, sk2po, yo, k2*, repeat from * to * to the last 7sts, k1, yo, sk2po, yo, k3.

Row 8: p1, *p5, hB, p2*, repeat from * to * to the last 2sts, p2.

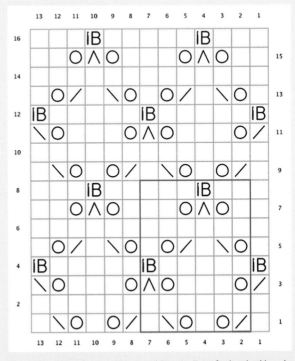

Fig. 6.47 Chart for Lacy-Diamond Pattern Two, for hooked beads above double decreases, corresponding to the right-hand sample shown in Figure 6.45.

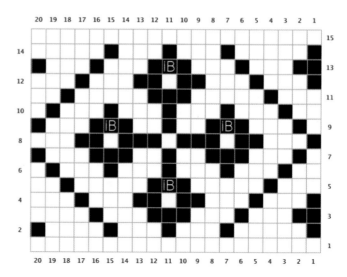

Fig. 6.49 Chart for the beaded Fair Isle pattern, corresponding to the top sample, worked in lemon-yellow and purple yarns, shown in Figure 6.48.

Fig. 6.48 Traditional stranded Fair Isle patterns featuring beads. Both samples were knitted with Adriafil Genziana 4ply/fingering-weight yarn. For the top sample, Czech size 6 Silver-Lined Gold beads were placed on a background-colour stitch that is surrounded by contrast-colour stitches. For the bottom sample, Miyuki size 6 Metallic Green Iris beads were placed on a contrast-colour stitch that is surrounded by a mix of both background- and contrast-colour stitches.

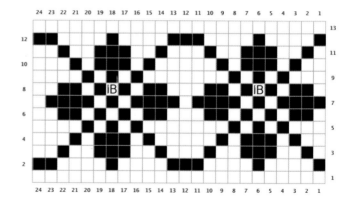

Fig. 6.50 Chart for the beaded Fair Isle pattern, corresponding to the bottom sample, worked in green and red yarns, shown in Figure 6.48.

Beaded Fair Isle

Fair Isle is another fabric that is basically all stocking stitch and that can have beads added to it. It is possible to thread the beads on to the yarn before you start to knit and then use the slip-stitch or beads-placed-between-purl-stitches technique, but this does add quite a bit more complication to the knitting process, whereas using the crochet-hook method to easily include an occasional bead can add to the overall pattern.

When looking at the possibility of adding beads to Fair Isle by using the crochet-hook method, you need to remember that the bead is placed on the row after the row that you want the bead to appear on. The bead is placed on an existing stitch when working the row after that stitch was created.

Here are a couple of samples with beads added by using the crochet-hook method, in combination with a traditional stranded Fair Isle pattern. When adding beads, you may have to try out several colours of beads on a sample, before selecting the bead colour to use for the actual knitting. Depending on where the bead is to be placed, it might be surrounded by

the background-colour yarn or it might be surrounded by the contrast-colour yarn, which may make the same colour of bead look very different.

For the Fair Isle samples, the beads do not completely cover the stitches that they sit around. For the green-and-red sample, this does not seem to make much difference to the look of the pattern: the beads just provide highlights where the diagonal contrast-colour lines cross. For the sample knitted with lemon-yellow and purple yarns, the beads sit in the middle of a group of contrast-colour stitches within a large motif. The light background colour does show through more than for the other sample.

Fig. 6.51 Samples of four methods of casting on. Working clockwise from the top left: Knit Cast-On, worked with Patons Merino 4ply/fingering-weight yarn and Toho 3mm Magatama Rainbow Light Topaz/Sea Foam beads; Picot-Point Cast-On, worked with Patons Merino 4ply/fingering-weight yarn and Toho 3mm Magatama Rainbow Light Topaz/Sea Foam beads; Cable Cast-On, worked with Stylecraft Countrylife 4ply/fingering-weight yarn and Czech size 7 Silver-Lined Purple beads; and Thumb/Longtail Cast-On, worked with Patons Merino 4ply/fingering-weight yarn and Toho size 6 Silver-Lined Mauve seed beads.

Edgings

The last group of samples in this chapter is of edgings. A very simple way to add some interest to a pattern is to use beads in the cast-on. With all of the cast-on samples shown here, the beads have been threaded on to the yarn before the knitting process was started.

For both the Knit-Cast-On sample and the Cable-Cast-On sample, the beads sit better on what is normally regarded as a wrong-side row. The Thumb/Longtail-Cast-On sample was worked by using the English method, where the yarn is held in your right hand.

Beaded-Knitting Knit Cast-On
This is a two-needle cast-on.

Place a slip knot on to the left-hand needle, and class this slip knot as a stitch. *Push up a bead next to the stitch on the left-hand needle. Put the right-hand needle into the stitch on the left-hand needle, take the yarn around the point of the right-hand needle, pull the wrapped yarn through the stitch being knitted into, to make a new stitch on the right-hand needle, and place this new stitch in a twisted orientation on to the point of the left-hand needle.* Repeat from * to * until you have cast on the required number of stitches.

These instructions will result in a bead being placed between all of the stitches along the cast-on edge. You can vary the number of beads in the cast-on by working several new stitches before pushing up a bead against the stitch that was just cast on.

Beaded-Knitting Cable Cast-On
This is a two-needle cast-on that is very similar to the Knit Cast-On.

Place a slip knot on to the left-hand needle, and class this slip knot as a stitch. Push up a bead next to the stitch on the left-hand needle. Put the right-hand needle into the stitch on the left-hand needle, take the yarn around the point of the right-hand needle, pull the wrapped yarn through the stitch being knitted into, to make a new stitch on the right-hand needle, and place this new stitch in a twisted orientation on to the point of the left-hand needle. *Push up a bead next to the stitch on the left-hand needle. Insert the point of the right-hand needle between the first two stitches on the left-hand needle, and take the yarn around the point of the right-hand needle. Pull the wrapped yarn through the space between the two stitches where the right-hand needle was inserted, to make a new stitch on the right-hand needle, and place this new stitch in a twisted orientation on to the left-hand needle.* Repeat from * to * until you have cast on the required number of stitches.

Beaded-Knitting Thumb/Longtail Cast-On (English method)
This is a one-needle cast-on.

Calculate the length that is three times the width of the required cast-on width, and pull out a length of yarn from the ball or cone that is a little bit longer than this calculated length. Make a slip knot at this point on the pulled-out yarn, as measured from the start of the yarn tail. Place the slip knot on to the right-hand needle, and class this slip knot as a stitch.

Hold the yarn tail in your left hand and the yarn attached to the ball in your right hand. *Push up a bead next to the stitch on the right-hand needle. Wrap the yarn tail clockwise around your left thumb to make a loop. Put the point of the right-hand needle under the loop (the needle point runs parallel to your thumb), and take the yarn end attached to the ball around the point of the right-hand needle, as if you were knitting a stitch. Lift the yarn-tail loop over the point of the right-hand needle with your thumb, and allow the loop to drop off your thumb. Pull the yarn tail tight, taking care to make sure that the yarn sits behind the bead.* Repeat from * to * until you have cast on the required number of stitches.

Beaded Picot-Point Cast-On

This is a beaded, decorative, two-needle cast-on and a variation of the Cable Cast-On.

Make a slip knot, place it on to the left-hand needle and class this slip knot as a stitch. Cast on five stitches as for working the Cable Cast-On. *Push up a bead next to the last stitch that was cast on. Knit and cast off the next two stitches. Slip the last stitch that was knitted (the working stitch) purlwise to the left-hand needle, and cast on four stitches as for working the Cable Cast-On.* Repeat from * to * until you have cast on the required number of stitches, finishing with the step of placing the working stitch purlwise on to the left-hand needle. If you need an even number of stitches, you will need to cast on one stitch after the last time that you place the working stitch on to the left-hand needle.

As well as placing beads within the cast-on, decorative edgings can also be worked. The simplest decorative edging would be knitting a garter-stitch edging with beads being placed between each stitch on wrong-side rows. Garter stitch will allow the edging to lie flat, and the beads will add colour and sparkle. The beads also add weight, which may or may not be an advantage.

Trellis-Stitch Border

A slightly more unusual edging is the Trellis-Stitch Border. Trellis stitch is a slip-stitch pattern that can be used as an all-over pattern. Either side of the fabric can be used as the public side, but the featured samples have been presented with the side featuring long slip-stitch floats as being the right side of the fabric. When working the stitch pattern, the long strands of yarn in front of several slipped stitches are picked up several rows later, to produce the trellis effect. These long strands seemed an ideal place to add beads.

Fig. 6.52 Two samples of the Trellis-Stitch Border. The left-hand sample was knitted with Adriafil Genziana 4ply/ fingering-weight yarn and Miyuki size 8 Crystal AB seed beads. The right-hand sample was knitted with Sirdar Cotton 4ply/fingering-weight yarn and Toho size 8 Gold-Lined Rainbow Crystal seed beads.

Trellis-Stitch-Border Pattern

6-stitch repeat + 5 stitches to balance the pattern.

Special Abbreviation

Lifted stitch – insert the point of the right-hand needle upwards under the 2 beaded strands, knit the next stitch by lifting the 2 strands over and off of the point of the right-hand needle as you finish the stitch and make sure that there are 3 beads on both strands on each side of the stitch just made before continuing

Thread the beads on to the yarn before you start to knit.

Row 1 (RS): k1, p3, *slip 3sts purlwise while keeping yarn at front of work, push up 6 beads on to the strand in front of the slipped stitches while taking care not to pull the strand tight, p3*, repeat from * to * to the last stitch, k1.

Row 2: p1, k3, *slip 3sts purlwise while keeping yarn at back of work, push up 6 beads on to the strand behind the slipped stitches while taking care not to pull the strand tight, k3*, repeat from * to * to the last stitch, p1.

Row 3: k1, p3, *k3, p3*, repeat from * to * to the last stitch, k1.

Row 4: p1, k3, *p3, k3*, repeat from * to * to the last stitch, p1.

Row 5: k5, *lifted stitch, k5*, repeat from * to * to the end of the row.

Row 6: k1, p3, *k3, p3*, repeat from * to * to the last stitch, k1.

Row 7: p1, *slip 3sts purlwise while keeping yarn at front of work, push up 6 beads on to the strand in front of the slipped stitches while taking care not to pull the strand tight, p3*, repeat from * to * to the last 4sts, slip 3sts purlwise with 6 beads as before, p1.

Row 8: k1, *slip 3sts purlwise while keeping yarn at back of work, push up 6 beads on to the strand behind the slipped stitches while taking care not to pull the strand tight, k3*, repeat from * to * to the last 4sts, slip 3sts purlwise with 6 beads as before, k1.

Row 9: p1, k3, *p3, k3*, repeat from * to * to the last stitch, p1.

Row 10: k1, p3, *k3, p3*, repeat from * to * to the last stitch, k1.

Row 11: k2, *lifted stitch, k5*, repeat from * to * to the last 3sts, lifted stitch, k2.

Row 12: p1, k3, *p3, k3*, repeat from * to * to the last stitch, p1.

Rows 1 to 12 form the pattern repeat.

The two featured samples were worked with four rows of garter stitch and two rows of stocking stitch before working the Trellis-Stitch Border Pattern. The Trellis-Stitch Border Pattern was repeated one and a half times, finishing after Row 5 of the pattern repeat, and then six rows of garter stitch were worked to finish the border.

Beads and lace work very well together, and this is also true for lace edgings. The two edgings that are included with the shawl projects are lace edgings worked in garter stitch. For both edgings, the beads are threaded on to the yarn before the edging is knitted. For one edging, the beads are visible on only one side of the fabric, whereas, for the second edging, the beads are visible on both sides of the fabric.

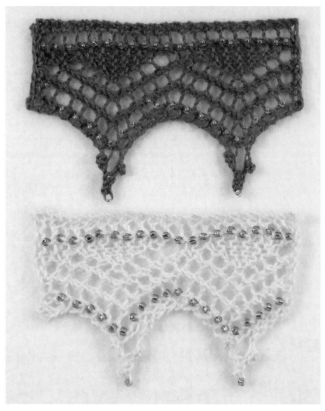

Fig. 6.53 Two samples of the Chevron-Picot Edging. The top sample was knitted with Rico® Design Bamboo sock yarn and Czech size 7 Crystal AB seed beads. The bottom sample was knitted with Artesano Alpaca 4ply/fingering-weight yarn and Toho size 6 Silver-Lined Dark Peridot seed beads.

Chevron-Picot Edging

For the Chevron-Picot Edging, the beads are placed on one row but appear on the opposite side of the fabric from the side that they were placed on. The chart shows that the beads are to be placed when working the row that is read from right to left (nominally, the right-side row), and the position of the beads is set by the way that the yarn over is worked into for the following row, which is read from left to right.

When the edging is worked on to the shawl, the edging is used to cast off the stitches of the body of the shawl at the end of every odd-number row, by working the last stitch of the edging together with the next shawl-body stitch. The edging is cast on to the same needles that hold the shawl-body stitches. The pattern gives detailed instructions about which end of the shawl to start knitting the edging at, to ensure that the beads appear on the right side of the shawl fabric.

There are twenty-one beads in each repeat of the Chevron-Picot Edging. If the same size of bead is being used throughout the edging, it is not necessary to count the number of beads that are threaded before you start to knit, other than taking into account the number of repeats required for the full length of the edging. When knitting the edging on to the shawl, it may be necessary to have a join part way along the edging so that there are not too many beads to push along the thread when you start to knit.

With this edging, it is possible to ignore the picot point on Row 9 and just work this edge stitch as a knit stitch. This will give a smoother, more scalloped edge. The sample of the Garter-and-Diamond Lace Shawl that was knitted with Katia Air Lux (*see* Accessories) was worked without the picot points within the Chevron-Picot Edging. Another variation is to use a different type of bead for the picot points. A differently coloured bead or a differently shaped bead, such as a drop bead, could be used at each picot point. If you do want to use a different type of bead for the picot points, the beads do have to be threaded on to the yarn in the correct order before the start of the knitting process for the edging.

When different beads were used on the picot points of the Findley Dappled-yarn version of the Garter-and-Diamond Lace Shawl, locking stitch markers were used to divide the shawl body into groups of ten stitches. Although the Chevron-Picot Edging is a twenty-row repeat, the edging is joined to the shawl on every other row, so one pattern repeat will join the edging to ten stitches of the shawl.

The shawl edge at the centre of the shawl has a picot point. The centre stitch of the three garter stitches will be knitted to the edging when Row 9 of the Chevron-Picot Edging Chart is being worked, so it is necessary to start counting pattern repeats in both directions from this point of the shawl edge. Once you have established the position of the pattern repeats, you will know whether there are any part repeats at each end of the shawl edging. Once you have worked out the position of the edging repeats, it is fairly easy to then work out how many beads you need for any partial repeats and to then start threading the beads for full pattern repeats, with the special picot-point bead in the correct place within the bead sequence. Remember that you will be working from the top of the chart downwards while threading the beads, so there will be twelve beads before the picot-point bead for each full pattern repeat.

Chevron-Picot-Edging Pattern with beads
15-stitch pattern.

Special Abbreviations

BP – Beaded Picot. Cast on 2sts, knit and cast off the next 2sts, slip the working stitch purlwise to the left-hand needle, cast on 3sts, push up 1 bead next to the stitch on the right-hand needle, knit and cast off the next 3sts, slip the working stitch purlwise to the left-hand needle, cast on 2sts, knit and cast off the next 2sts.

yoB – work a yarn over with 1 bead on the yarn-over loop.

Cast on 10sts.

Row 1 (RS): k2, yoB, k2tog, yo, k2tog, yo, k2tog, yoB, k2 – 11sts.

Row 2 and all even-number rows: knit and, when you come to a yo with bead, make sure that the bead is at the left-hand end of the yo loop before that stitch is knitted into.

Row 3: k2, yoB, (k2tog, yo) twice, k1, k2tog, yoB, k2 – 12sts.

Row 5: k2, yoB, (k2tog, yo) twice, k2, k2tog, yoB, k2 – 13sts.

Row 7: k2, yoB, (k2tog, yo) twice, k3, k2tog, yoB, k2 – 14sts.

Row 9: BP, k1, yoB, (k2tog, yo) twice, k4, k2tog, yoB, k2 – 15sts.

Row 11: k1, k2tog, yoB, (k2tog, yo) twice, k2tog, k2, k2tog, yoB, k2 – 14sts.

Row 13: k1, k2tog, yoB, (k2tog, yo) twice, k2tog, k1, k2tog, yoB, k2 – 13sts.

Row 15: k1, k2tog, yoB, (k2tog, yo) twice, k2tog, k2tog, yoB, k2 – 12sts.

Row 17: k1, k2tog, yoB, k2tog, yo, k2tog, k1, k2tog, yoB, k2 – 11sts.

Row 19: k1, k2tog, yoB, k2tog, yo, k2tog, k2tog, yoB, k2 – 10sts.

Row 20: knit and, when you come to a yo with bead, make sure that the bead is at the left-hand end of the yo loop before that stitch is knitted into.

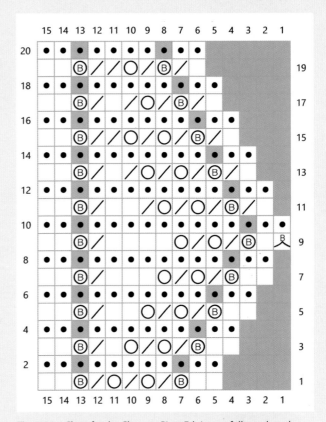

Fig. 6.54 Chart for the Chevron-Picot Edging, to follow when the edging is to be knitted on its own (not being attached to another knitted piece).

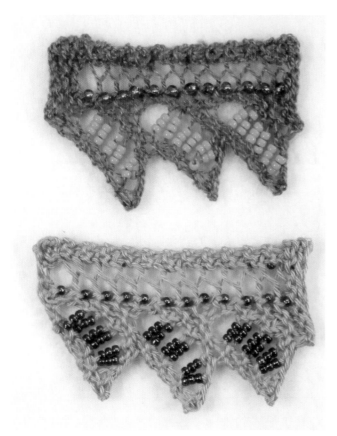

Fig. 6.55 Two samples of the Butterfly-Lace Edging, showing the front side. The top sample was knitted with Fyberspates Scrumptious Lace yarn and Czech size 7 Silver-Lined Green seed beads and Miyuki size 8 Chartreuse Opaque seed beads. The bottom sample was knitted with Sirdar Cotton 4ply/fingering-weight yarn and Miyuki size 8 Dark Amethyst seed beads.

Fig. 6.56 Two samples of the Butterfly-Lace Edging, showing the reverse side. The positioning of the singly placed beads is different on this side of the fabric compared to that shown in Figure 6.55.

Butterfly-Lace Edging

The Butterfly-Lace Edging has several beads that are strung across a large eyelet hole, as well as singly placed beads. When more than one bead is held on a yarn over, it is necessary to work the beaded yarn overs and decreases on every row. There is also a section of faggot lace, just inside the straight edge of the edging, which involves decreases and yarn overs on every row. As a result, for this edging, beads are placed on every row both for the large eyelet lace holes and on each side of the faggot-lace section. This makes the edging reversible.

A step-by-step guide of how to knit this edging is given in the section 'Working yarn overs holding several beads' in Chapter 4.

Butterfly-Lace-Edging Pattern with beads

12-stitch pattern.

Special Abbreviations

yoB – work a yarn over with 1 bead on the yarn-over loop.

yoB3 – work a yarn over with 3 beads on the yarn-over loop.

Cast on 9sts.

Row 1 (RS): k6, ssk, k1 – 8sts.

Row 2: k2, k1 with bead at the right-hand end of the yo loop, yoB, ssk, k1, yoB3, k2 – 9sts. (Note: On the first repeat, there will not be a beaded yo to knit into.)

Row 3: k2, yoB3, k1 with 3 beads at the right-hand end of the yo loop, ssk, k1 with bead at the right-hand end of the yo loop, yoB, ssk, k1.

Row 4: k2, k1 with bead at the right-hand end of the yo loop, yoB, ssk, k1, k1 with 3 beads at the left-hand end of the yo loop, yoB3, k2 – 10sts.

Row 5: k2, yoB3, k1 with 3 beads at the right-hand end of the yo loop, ssk, k1, k1 with bead at the right-hand end of the yo loop, yoB, ssk k1.

Row 6: k2, k1 with bead at the right-hand end of the yo loop, yoB, ssk, k2, k1 with 3 beads at the left-hand end of the yo loop, k2 – 11sts.

Row 7: k2, yoB3, k1 with 3 beads at the right-hand end of the yo loop, ssk, k2, k1 with bead at the right-hand end of the yo loop, yoB, ssk, k1.

Row 8: k2, k1 with bead at the right-hand end of the yo loop, yoB, ssk, k3, k1 with 3 beads at the left-hand end of the yo loop, yo, k2 – 12sts.

Row 9: cast off 4sts (1st present on right-hand needle), k3, k1 with bead at the right-hand end of the yo loop, yoB, ssk, k1 – 8sts.

Repeat Rows 2 to 9.

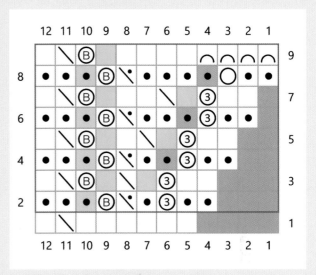

Fig. 6.57   Chart for the Butterfly-Lace Edging.

For the Butterfly-Lace Edging, there are strings of three beads that are placed on six rows. These strings need to include size 8 seed beads. The strings of beads add quite a bit of weight to the edging, so using size 6 seed beads for the strings of beads would make the edging too heavy. Size 6 seed beads can be used for the single-bead yarn overs. If you want to add more colour and variety to the edging, you can use two different sizes of beads, but the beads must then be threaded on to the yarn in the correct order for knitting.

To thread the beads, if you are using different beads for the single-bead yarn overs as described, you need to follow the chart from the top left, reading back and forth to the bottom right; therefore, you will need to thread three large beads, six small beads, two large beads, six small beads, two large beads, six small beads and one large bead, for each pattern repeat.

This chapter has covered a variety of ways of using beads. There is lots of scope for more experimentation.

CHAPTER 7

GENERAL KNITTING TECHNIQUES

Although this book is about knitting with beads, this chapter will cover some general knitting techniques to ensure that the included projects can be made and finished as intended. (*See* Resources, at the end of the book, for a link to online demonstrations.)

Methods of casting on and casting off

For some of the projects, a specific cast-on has been mentioned as the method to use when making that item, usually because a particular finish is required.

Casting on

For several projects, you are instructed to cast on by using the Knit Cast-On method. The Knit Cast-On results in loops along the cast-on edge. Sometimes, it is suggested that you knit through the back loop for each stitch of the first row following this cast-on; however, in this book, you are asked to work a Knit Cast-On so that stitches can be picked up through these loops, for example, for a garter-stitch tab, when starting the shawls, or for joining the first and last rows of the Icicle-Wristlets Pattern.

Knit Cast-On

This is a two-needle cast-on.

Place a slip knot on the left-hand needle, and class this slip knot as a stitch. *Put the right-hand needle into the stitch on the left-hand needle, take the yarn around the point of the right-hand needle, pull the wrapped yarn through the stitch being knitted into, to make a new stitch on the right-hand needle, and place this new stitch in a twisted orientation on to the point of the left-hand needle.* Repeat from * to * until you have cast on the required number of stitches.

This cast-on also works well if you need the cast-on edge to stretch; for example, this cast-on is ideal when knitting lace patterns that cause the bottom edge of the knitting to curve and scallop.

Cable Cast-On

This is a two-needle cast-on that gives a firm, hard-wearing bottom edge to a piece of knitting. It is worked in a very similar way to the Knit Cast-On.

Place a slip knot on the left-hand needle, and class this slip knot as a stitch. Put the right-hand needle into the stitch on the left-hand needle, take the yarn around the point of the right-hand needle, pull the wrapped yarn through the stitch being knitted into, to make a new stitch on the right-hand needle, and place this new stitch in a twisted orientation on to the point of the left-hand needle. *Insert the right-hand needle between the first two stitches on the left-hand needle, and take the yarn around the point of the right-hand needle. Pull the wrapped yarn through the space between the two stitches where the right-hand needle was inserted, to make a new stitch on the right-hand needle, and place this new stitch in a twisted orientation on to the point of the left-hand needle.* Repeat from * to * until you have cast on the required number of stitches.

Backward Loop/Single Thumb-twist Cast-On
This is a one-needle cast-on.

Place a slip knot on the right needle. Holding the working yarn in your left hand with the palm up, wrap the yarn clockwise around your left thumb. Put the point of the right needle into the loop created, slide the loop onto the right needle and tighten the yarn.

Take care when working the first row that you keep the needle points close to each other as you work the row. If you pull the needles apart after each stitch you may develop a long loop of yarn between the two needles.

This cast-on gives a very soft, flexible edge. It is particularly good for adding groups of stitches within a section of knitting e.g. after completing a thumb gusset when making mittens, as it allow for adding stitches without interrupting the flow of the knitting.

Thumb/Longtail Cast-On (English method)
This is a one-needle cast-on. It is a basic cast-on that can be used for general knitting. As a result of the action of working this cast-on, the bottom edge looks like a row of purl bumps. Therefore, this cast-on works very well with garter-stitch edgings, as the garter stitch appears to start straight away at the edge of the fabric. As the alternative name of Longtail Cast-On implies, it is necessary to measure off a long tail of yarn, of a length that is three to four times the width of the required cast-on width, before you start to work this cast-on.

Make a slip knot on the yarn, allowing for the necessary length of the long tail of yarn. Place the slip knot on the right-hand needle, and class this slip knot as a stitch. Hold the yarn tail in your left hand, with the yarn running over your palm, and hold the yarn attached to the ball in your right hand. *Wrap the yarn tail clockwise around your left thumb to make a loop. Put the point of the right-hand needle under the front part of the loop (the needle point runs parallel to your thumb), and take the yarn end attached to the ball around the point of the right-hand needle, as if you were knitting a stitch. Lift

the yarn-tail loop over the point of the right-hand needle with your thumb, and allow the loop to drop off your thumb. Pull on the yarn tail, to tighten any loose yarn along the bottom edge of the cast-on.* Repeat from * to * until you have cast on the required number of stitches.

A cast-on can be decorative as well as functional. For the Flying-V Mittens and Double-Diamond Mittens (see Accessories), the Picot Cast-On is used to add decoration and also to allow the cast-on edge to stretch over the widest part of the hand when the mittens are pulled on and off.

Picot Cast-On
This is a two-needle cast-on and a variation of the Cable Cast-On. It works best when an even number of stitches are required to be cast on.

Make a slip knot, place it on the left-hand needle and class this slip knot as a stitch. Cast on four more stitches as for working the Cable Cast-On, knit and cast off the next two stitches. *Slip the last stitch that was knitted (the working stitch) on to the left-hand needle, cast on four stitches as for working the Cable Cast-On, and knit and cast off the next two stitches.* Repeat from * to * until you have cast on one fewer stitch than the required number of stitches. Slip the working stitch on to the left-hand needle. For an even number of cast-on stitches, cast on one more stitch.

The stitches will be in pairs, with a gap between each pair. If you have cast on an even number of stitches and are going to work in a rib of knit two stitches, purl two stitches, work the first row after the cast-on as follows, to establish the rib pattern:

Row 1: k1, *p2, k2*, repeat from * to * to the last stitch, k1.

The rib looks better if the two knit stitches and two purl stitches are on either side of the gap, as this helps to stabilize the cast-on edge. Garter stitch also works well with this cast-on, but knit 1, purl 1 rib does not work as well.

Alternative Cable Cast-On
This is a two-needle cast-on, and, as the name implies, it is a variation of the Cable Cast-On. This cast-on is also known as the invisible k1, p1-rib cast-on. If it is used when starting a garment with a rib edging worked by alternately knitting one stitch and purling one stitch, the rib looks as though it has started already and does not have a hard line along the bottom edge. It also has quite a bit of flexibility, making it a very suitable cast-on for the top of socks or the rib edging on a beret.

Place a slip knot on the left-hand needle; this stitch will be counted as a purl stitch. Put the point of the right-hand needle into the stitch on the left-hand needle, take the yarn around the point of the right-hand needle, pull the wrapped yarn through the stitch being knitted into, to make a new stitch on the right-hand needle, and place this new stitch in a twisted orientation on to the left-hand needle. *Taking the right-hand needle around the back of the left-hand needle, insert the point of the right-hand needle between the first two stitches on the left-hand needle as if to purl and take the yarn around the point of the right-hand needle. Pull the wrapped yarn through the space between the two stitches where the right-hand needle was inserted, to make a new stitch on the right-hand needle, and place this new stitch on to the left-hand needle, with the two needle points facing each other. Bring the right-hand needle to the front of the left-hand needle as if to knit, put the needle point between the first two stitches on the left-hand needle as if to knit, take the yarn around the point of the right-hand needle, pull the wrapped yarn through the space between the two stitches where the right-hand needle was inserted, and place this new stitch in a twisted orientation on to the left-hand needle.* Repeat from * to * until you have cast on the required number of stitches.

Note: On the first row after this cast-on, you must knit into the back of the loop for the knit stitches and purl the purl stitches normally. After this first row, the knit stitches are knitted normally. The reason for knitting through the back loop is that this makes the knit stitch flat and open along the bottom edge of the fabric, so it looks as though a knit stitch has just been worked from nothing, giving an attractive edge to the knitting.

If you want to start and finish the rib with a knit stitch, you need to cast on an even number of stitches and then drop the slip knot when you reach the end of the first row of knitting.

Casting off

As with most techniques in knitting, there are many ways to work a cast-off. The cast-off used in most of the projects is the common Chain Cast-Off.

Chain Cast-Off

The Chain Cast-Off can be worked with knit stitches, as the Knit Cast-Off, or it can be worked with purl stitches, as the Purl Cast-Off.

To work the Knit Cast-Off, knit two stitches from the left-hand needle, *using the point of the left-hand needle, lift the first stitch to have been knitted on the right-hand needle over the second stitch to have been knitted on the right-hand needle and off the needle, knit one stitch from the left-hand needle.*

Repeat from * to * until there is one stitch remaining on the right-hand needle. Cut the yarn, and pull the yarn end through the last loop.

When the Chain Cast-Off is worked with knit stitches, as the Knit Cast-Off, the cast-off chain will roll to the side of the fabric facing you as you cast off. To achieve a neater finish in garter stitch, work the Knit Cast-Off on a wrong-side row. The cast-off chain will then sit on the far side of the fabric (which will often be on the inside of an accessory or garment) when viewed from the right side.

To work the Purl Cast-Off, purl two stitches from the left-hand needle, *using the point of the left-hand needle, lift the first stitch to have been purled on the right-hand needle over the second stitch to have been purled on the right-hand needle and off the needle, purl one stitch from the left-hand needle.* Repeat from * to * until there is one stitch remaining on the right-hand needle. Cut the yarn, and pull the yarn end through the last loop.

If you work a Purl Cast-Off, the cast-off chain will roll to the side of the fabric away from you. Working a purl stitch usually takes more yarn than working a knit stitch, so working a Purl Cast-Off often does give a slightly looser cast-off edge than does working a Knit Cast-Off.

The Chain Cast-Off method can also be worked in a stitch pattern. If it is worked in conjunction with a rib stitch pattern, the chain sits along the top of the cast-off edge.

Sewn Cast-Off

A cast-off that works particularly well with garter stitch and moss (seed) stitch is the Sewn Cast-Off. This cast-off is worked with a blunt sewing needle.

With all of the stitches to be cast off being held on a knitting needle, measure off a tail of yarn that is two to three times the width of the piece to be cast off, and cut the yarn. Thread the yarn tail into the eye of the sewing needle.

With the knitting needle in your left hand (assuming you are right handed), *pass the sewing needle through the first two stitches from right to left, and pull the yarn tail through these stitches until no slack remains in the yarn, but the yarn should not be pulled tight. Bringing the sewing needle around in front of the knitting, pass the sewing needle through the end stitch closest to the point of the knitting needle from left to right, pull the yarn through this stitch and drop this stitch off the knitting needle.* Repeat from * to * until there is one stitch remaining on the knitting needle. Pass the sewing needle through this stitch from right to left, and drop it off of the knitting needle.

Fig. 7.1   Pass the threaded sewing needle through the first two stitches on the needle from right to left.

Fig. 7.2   Pass the threaded sewing needle through the end stitch, closest to the point of the needle, from left to right.

Apart from for the very first stitch to be worked with this cast-off method, the yarn should go through every stitch from right to left twice. The result of casting off with this method is to give a garter ridge along the edge of the knitting. The cast-off is flexible, without being loose and untidy, and it is possible to adjust the stretchiness of the cast-off as you are working it. It is very unlikely to make a tight cast-off edge.

Three-Needle Cast-Off

The Three-Needle Cast-Off is often used to join two pieces of knitting together. Two groups of stitches may already be on knitting needles, or stitches may need to be picked up first. The Three-Needle Cast-Off is used to join the beginning and the end of the fabric pieces of the beaded Icicle Wristlets (see Accessories).

For the Icicle Wristlets, each wristlet is cast on by using the Knit Cast-On, so there are loops along the cast-on edge. When you reach the end of the pattern, the piece of knitting is still on one needle. You are instructed to use another needle of the same size or a slightly smaller size to pick up the loops from the cast-on edge. You now have two groups of stitches held on two needles: one group at the beginning of the wristlet and one at the end.

Fig. 7.3   Two sets of stitches on needles held in your left hand with right sides together.

To join the two groups of stitches, you need to bring the needle holding the stitches of the cast-on edge up to the stitches at the opposite end of the fabric, with the right sides of the fabric facing, so the beaded pattern should not be visible. Holding both of the needles with live stitches in your left hand, and with a third needle of the same size as used to knit the main piece of knitting in your right hand, cast off as follows:

Insert the point of the right-hand needle through the first stitch on each needle in your left hand, knit these two stitches

Fig. 7.4   Knit together the first stitch on the two needles in your left hand and cast off as normal the stitches on the right needle.

together and drop both stitches off of their respective needles.* Insert the point of the right-hand needle into the stitch closest to the point of each needle in your left hand, knit these two stitches together and drop both stitches off of their respective needles. There are now two stitches on the right-hand needle. With the point of one of the left-hand needles, lift the first stitch to be knitted on the right-hand needle over the second stitch to be knitted on the right-hand needle and off the right-hand needle, as for working a normal Chain Cast-Off.* Repeat from * to * until there is one stitch remaining on the right-hand needle. Cut the yarn, and pull the yarn tail through the last loop.

Methods of increasing and decreasing

Increasing

Knit front and back
One of the most common increase methods is the 'knit front and back' or 'bar' increase (kfb). As the name suggests, the increase is made by knitting into a stitch as usual but not dropping the stitch from the left-hand needle. Instead, you knit through the back loop of the same stitch and then drop the stitch from the left-hand needle. It is easy to work, but it does leave a purl bump or bar to the left-hand side of the increase stitch, which will show in a stocking-stitch fabric. However, this increase works very well in a garter-stitch fabric or when reverse stocking stitch is used as the right side of the fabric.

Make one
An alternative increase is the 'make one' increase (m1), which is less visible than is a kfb increase in a stocking-stitch fabric. The new stitch is created from the strand running between two adjacent stitches.

Work to the position of the increase. From the front to the back, lift the strand running between the stitch closest to the point of the left-hand needle and the stitch closest to the point of the right-hand needle on to the point of the left-hand needle. The strand makes what looks like a yarn-over loop. Knit this strand by working it through the back of the loop, to twist the loop shut as the new stitch is made.

When working increases for a garment, for example, when shaping a tapered sleeve, it is much better to work the increases one or two stitches in from the edge of the fabric. An m1

increase will have to be worked at least one stitch in from the edge, in order for there to be a strand to pick up between stitches, but, for a garment, this increase is better worked two stitches in from the edge. This will produce a clean column of stitches, making it much easier to sew together the pieces of a garment when the knitting is completed.

Decreases

To achieve a good finish for the shaping of a garment, it is important to use mirrored decreases and to work the decreases at least one or two stitches in from the edge of the knitting. For the garment projects in this book, mirrored decreases have been worked two stitches in from the edge for all armhole, neckline and sleeve-cap shaping. This gives a fully fashioned finish to the garments and a neat column of stitches for seaming or for picking up stitches when adding a front band or neckband.

Right-leaning decrease

Knit two stitches together
For fully fashioned shaping in stocking stitch, the right-leaning decrease is worked at the end of right-side rows. The most commonly used right-leaning decrease is the 'knit two stitches together' decrease (k2tog), which is worked as follows:

Knit to the last four stitches, knit two stitches together, knit two stitches.

This decrease leans in the same direction as the fabric is being decreased.

Left-leaning decreases

As a result of the way that knitting is constructed in rows being worked from right to left and left to right, it is very difficult to make a left-leaning decrease that exactly mirrors the k2tog right-leaning decrease. In fully fashioned shaping in stocking stitch, the left-leaning decrease is worked at the beginning of right-side rows.

Slip one stitch, knit one stitch, pass the slipped stitch over
In Britain, the most commonly used left-leaning decrease is the 'slip one stitch, knit one stitch, pass the slipped stitch over' decrease (skpo or sl1, k1, psso), which is worked as follows:

Knit two stitches, slip the next stitch on the left-hand needle to the right-hand needle knitwise, knit one stitch, pass the slipped stitch over the stitch that was just knitted and off the right-hand needle, and continue knitting across the row.

It is important to slip the stitch knitwise, as this turns the stitch so that it will lie flat when it has been passed over the next stitch. This decrease can result in a slightly uneven fabric, because the slipped stitch can be pulled, making it longer.

Slip, slip, knit

A left-leaning decrease that more closely mirrors the k2tog right-leaning decrease is the 'slip, slip, knit' decrease (ssk). This decrease is more commonly used in American patterns and is worked as follows:

Knit two stitches, slip the next two stitches, one at a time, knitwise, from the left-hand needle to the right-hand needle, put the point of the left-hand needle through these two slipped stitches from left to right, in front of the right-hand needle (as if you were going to work a k2tog through the back loops) and knit these two stitches together.

By slipping the two stitches knitwise, the stitches have been turned so that, when they are knitted together, they lie flat on the surface of the knitting, leaning towards the left.

This decrease is different to a 'k2tog through the back loop', as the stitches are not twisted when the decrease is completed.

There are occasions when you may have to work decreases on every row, which means working decreases on both right-side and wrong-side rows. The direction of a decrease worked on a knit row does not show on the purl side of stocking-stitch fabric, but the direction of a decrease worked on a purl row will be visible on the knit side of the fabric. Therefore, it is important to use left- and right-leaning decreases that match the same direction as the knit decreases worked at the corresponding end of the fabric on knit rows.

Matching decreases worked on wrong-side rows

Purl two stitches together

The 'Purl two stitches together' decrease (p2tog) worked on a purl row in stocking stitch will match the k2tog decrease made on a knit row on the right side of the fabric. It is worked at the beginning of a wrong-side row as follows:

Purl two stitches, purl the next two stitches together, and then continue working across the row.

Slip, slip, purl

The 'slip, slip, purl' decrease (ssp) matches the ssk decrease worked on a knit row on the right side of the fabric. This decrease is worked at the end of a wrong-side row as follows:

Purl to the last four stitches, slip the next two stitches, one at a time, knitwise, to the right-hand needle, slip these two stitches back to the left-hand needle and purl the two stitches together through their back loops, purl two stitches.

This decrease is very similar to the 'p2tog through the back loops', but, by slipping the stitches knitwise before purling them together through the back loops, the stitches have been turned, so they lie flat on the right side of the fabric rather than being twisted.

Double decrease

Slip one stitch, knit two stitches together, pass the slipped stitch over
This decrease, commonly referred to by its abbreviation of 'sk2po', is a left-leaning double decrease that is worked in a very similar way to the skpo decrease.

Knit to the decrease point, slip the next stitch on the left-hand needle to the right-hand needle knitwise, knit two stitches together (k2tog) on the left-hand needle and pass the slipped stitch over the stitch that was just knitted and off of the right-hand needle.

Short-row shaping in garter stitch

Short rows have been used for three of the Beaded-Knitting projects (*see* Purses and Bags), to create a rounded shape at the point where the purse or bag fabric folds, making the bottom edge of the purses. The purses are knitted in garter stitch.

The basic 'wrap and turn' (w&t) technique has been used and is worked as follows:

*Knit to the turning point of the short row, slip the next stitch purlwise from the left-hand needle to the right-hand needle.

Bring the yarn forward between the points of the needles.

Slip the slipped stitch back to the left-hand needle, and turn the work.*

Repeat from * to * until you have completed the required number of short rows to be worked. You will be knitting fewer and fewer stitches on each row.

Once you have worked the shortest row and turned the work, you will be instructed to knit to the end of the row. Work all of the stitches as normal knit stitches.

Unlike stocking stitch, garter stitch has ridges on both sides of the fabric. When working short rows, the wrap around the base of a stitch at the end of a short row disappears into the valley below the garter ridge, so, when the stitches are being brought back into work after the short rows have been completed, it is not necessary to pick up any of these wraps (whereas picking up the wraps is commonly done when working stocking-stitch fabric, in order to hide these wraps).

Picking up stitches for front bands and neckbands

An area that often causes problems for knitters is the picking up of stitches for a neckband or front band. The neatest method of picking up stitches is to hold the edge of the knitting (with the right side facing you) to which the edging is to be applied in your left hand and a knitting needle in your right hand (called a knit pick-up).

Start from the very right-hand side of the edge from which stitches are to be picked up, and work from right to left. *Insert the knitting needle straight through the knitted fabric between the edge stitch and the next stitch in from the edge of the fabric. Take the working yarn around the point of the needle and pull a loop of yarn through to the right side of the fabric, to make a new stitch on the needle.* Repeat from * to * until the required number of stitches have been picked up, ending at the very left-hand side of the edge.

If any shaping has been worked two stitches in from the edge of the fabric, you will have two neat columns of stitches at the edge, making it easier to see where to pick up stitches. It is important to try to keep the selvedge to include one stitch only, rather than one and a half stitches, which can happen, but it is also important to be consistent the whole way along or around the edge from which stitches are being picked up.

The pattern should state the number of stitches that need to be picked up, but getting an even spread of these stitches can be difficult. One approach is to divide the edge into equal sections by using locking stitch markers, and then divide the total number of stitches to pick up by the number of sections, to find out how may stitches to pick up in each section.

An alternative approach is to base the rate of pick up on what you have actually knitted. Stitches are not square; for a given square area of stocking stitch, you need more rows from the bottom to the top of the fabric than you need stitches from the right to the left of the fabric. When you are picking up stitches along the side edge of a piece of knitting, you are picking up stitches from rows, so you will pick up fewer stitches than the number of rows that have been knitted. A ratio that generally works well is to pick up three stitches from every four rows.

You will not always be picking up from a straight, vertical edge. For example, when picking up along a V-shaped neckline, the edge is sloping like a diagonal line drawn across a rectangle. You may have knitted the same number of rows for the fabric, but the sloping edge of this fabric is longer than the vertical edge. You could pick up three stitches for every four rows along this edge, but this will shorten the edge, and you may find that, once the band is completed, the knitted fabric below the neckband has been distorted, as a result of the diagonal edge being shortened. When picking up stitches for a V-shaped neckline, picking up five stitches for every six rows gives a better result.

Round necklines combine sections of straight, vertical edges and sections of curved or diagonal edges. When picking up stitches from a round neckline, you should pick up three stitches for every four rows down the vertical, straight section at the top of the front neckline and one stitch for every row along the shaped, curved section of the neckline, before picking up stitches from the stitches held on a stitch holder at the bottom of the front neckline.

Make a note of how many stitches you picked up in each section as you worked down the first side of the neckline so that you can pick up the same numbers of stitches in each corresponding section as you work up the other side of the round neckline.

If you are picking up stitches from a garter-stitch edge, the ratio of stitches to rows is different again. Garter stitch compresses the knitting lengthwise, so, in this situation, you should pick up one stitch for every two rows.

If you are picking up stitches from an edge where stitches have been cast off, you pick up one stitch below each stitch that was cast off, ensuring that all of the cast-off chain remains on the wrong side of the fabric (which will therefore be on the inside of the accessory or garment).

Working with tension swatches

Tension swatches are an important step in making a knitted item that will come out to the size specified in the pattern. For some knitted items such as shawls, scarves and other accessories, matching the gauge quoted in the pattern is not as vital as when making something such as a garment, which has to be of a specified size in order to fit as intended.

Tension swatches are worked to check your row and stitch gauges against those quoted in the pattern, but they can be viewed as an opportunity in a number of ways. Knitting a tension swatch gives you the opportunity to sample the yarn that you are going to knit with. Does it knit easily or does it keep catching on the needle points and splitting? If a yarn is hard work to use for knitting a tension swatch, will you enjoy knitting a whole garment with that yarn?

Knitting a tension swatch is an opportunity to try out the stitch pattern of the garment. Again, if you find it frustrating to work the stitch pattern as a tension swatch, you are not likely to enjoy making a larger item with that stitch pattern.

By matching the row and stitch gauges of the pattern, you should be able to make the garment to the size stated in the pattern. It is not always possible to match both the row gauge and the stitch gauge. In this situation, it is generally better to match the stitch gauge, as row measurements are often given as lengths rather than a set number of rows.

When knitting a tension swatch, it is also important to work with the needles that you are going to use to work the garment or knitted item. For example, if you are going to knit the garment on straight needles, knit the tension swatch on straight needles. If you are going to knit the garment on a circular needle then you should knit the tension swatch on a circular needle. For many knitters, their gauge when knitting on straight needles is different to their gauge when knitting on circular needles.

A tension swatch should be a piece of knitting that is about 15cm (6in) square so that the area that is to be measured is in the centre of the square and not affected by rolling or distorted edges. There are different ways to knit a tension swatch. One method that is not so frequently used but does result in accurate measurements for whatever stitch pattern is being used is to knit marker rows and marker stitches.

Fig. 7.5 A tension swatch for the Beaded Channel Jacket, showing marker rows and marker stitches that have been knitted with contrast-colour, pink yarn.

Knitting a tension swatch including marker rows and marker stitches

Before starting to knit the tension swatch, you need to decide on the number of rows and stitches that are to be measured. Refer to the gauge stated in the pattern as a guide; for example, the pattern may quote the gauge as twenty-eight stitches and thirty-seven rows in 10cm (4in). The pattern should also tell you the needle size that was used to knit the sample tension swatch and the stitch pattern that was knitted, say, stocking stitch or some other stitch pattern, for the sample tension swatch over which the gauge was measured.

You also need a contrast-colour, smooth yarn of the same or similar thickness to the yarn that you intend to use for the project. You need to cut two 15cm (6in) lengths of the contrast-colour yarn to use to knit marker stitches, before you start to knit the tension swatch.

The tension swatch needs to be larger than 10cm (4in) square, so you will need to cast on more stitches than the number of stitches of the quoted gauge over 10cm (4in); for this example, twelve more stitches would be appropriate. Therefore, to be able to measure twenty-eight stitches in the centre of the square, you should cast on forty stitches for the tension swatch.

You need to knit more than thirty-seven rows to gain an accurate row measurement, and, to help keep the tension swatch lying flat, it is a good idea to work about four rows of garter stitch and then at least four rows of the stitch pattern, all knitted with the main yarn, before working the first pair of rows knitted with the contrast-colour yarn. The two contrast-colour rows should be worked in the same stitch pattern as worked for the rest of the tension swatch. Cut the contrast-colour yarn after working these two rows.

Approximately halfway through working the number of rows to be measured, so on Row 19 for the example gauge of thirty-seven rows, work the marked stitches as follows:

Knit five stitches, knit the next stitch with one of the 15cm (6in) lengths of contrast-colour yarn, change back to the main yarn and knit twenty-eight stitches, knit the next stitch with the other 15cm (6in) length of contrast-colour yarn, change back to the main yarn and knit to the end of the row.

Continue knitting the tension swatch with the main yarn until you have completed thirty-seven rows. Change to using the contrast-colour yarn, and work two rows, still in stitch pattern. Change back to the main yarn, work several more rows in the stitch pattern, finish with some garter-stitch rows, and then cast off.

It may be necessary to refer to the pattern to check how you need to treat the tension swatch before measuring it. The pattern may quote the gauge after the tension swatch has been washed and laid flat to dry, but it may also quote a gauge before washing. Knowing the relevant tension-swatch treatment is particularly relevant for items such as shawls, which are stretched and blocked to shape, once the knitting has been finished, so the unwashed tension swatch will be quite different to the blocked tension swatch, in both character and gauge.

Having finished the tension swatch as required, you can now measure between the two marked stitches and the two marked rows. To determine whether your gauge matches that quoted in the pattern, the measurement should be 10cm (4in) from the inside of the left-hand marked stitch to the inside of the right-hand marked stitch and be 10cm (4in) from the top of the bottom pair of marker rows to the bottom of the top pair of marker rows.

If your measurements are different to those quoted in the pattern, it is quite straightforward to calculate the gauge that you have actually knitted.

For stocking-stitch fabric, it is generally quite easy to count your rows and stitches accurately, but, when working in a stitch pattern or with a very textured yarn, it can become quite difficult to identify all the stitches and rows. However, for the

How to calculate the gauge that you have knitted

For example, 28 stitches measures 9.5cm.

You need to know how many stitches you have in 1cm, so divide 28 by your measurement, which in this case is 9.5cm.

$28 \div 9.5 = 2.95$ stitches in 1cm

Do not round up any figure at this point. The gauge is quoted as the number of stitches in 10cm, so multiply your answer by 10.

$2.95 \times 10 = 29.5$ stitches in 10cm

In this example, you have knitted more stitches than are quoted for the pattern's stitch gauge, so you will need to knit another tension swatch by using a larger needle. If your tension swatch had measured more than 10cm wide between the marker stitches, your gauge was too loose, and you would need to work another tension swatch by using a slightly smaller needle.

The row gauge is calculated in a similar way. For example, if the row measurement is 11cm, you can divide 37 rows by 11cm to find out how many rows there are in 1cm.

$37 \div 11 = 3.36$ rows in 1cm

Multiply this result by 10 to get the number of rows in 10cm.

$3.36 \times 10 = 33.6$ rows in 10cm

In this example, you have fewer rows than are quoted for the pattern's row gauge, so you will need to knit another tension swatch by using a smaller needle, to give you more rows in the measured distance of 10cm. If your row measurement was less than 10cm, you would need to knit another tension swatch by using larger needles.

described tension-swatch method, it is quite easy to see the marked rows and marked stitches, even for a textured stitch pattern or textured yarn. Before starting to knit the tension swatch, you decide the numbers of stitches and rows that you are going to measure, and then add in the marker stitches and marker row in the relevant locations within the tension swatch as you are working the stitch pattern.

Once the tension swatch is finished, washed and left to relax and dry, it is easy to measure between the markers for both the stitches and the rows and then to calculate what numbers of stitches and rows you have knitted, if the measurements are not 10cm (4in).

Counting rows in garter stitch

Several of the patterns in this book, such as the purse and bag patterns, are worked in garter stitch. If you count the ridges of garter stitch within the fabric, when the right side of the knitting is facing you, and then double this number, it will give you the number of rows that have been worked.

Fig. 7.6 A mitten being knitted, with a marker thread being used to mark the beginning/end of the round.

Using marker threads when knitting in the round

When knitting large items such as garments on a circular needle, a stitch marker is used to mark the beginning/end of the round. The stitch marker can sit on the needle between stitches and does not normally fall off unless the knitting is stopped at the very beginning/end of the round. When knitting smaller items such as mittens and socks, these items are often knitted by using several double-pointed needles, or two circular needles or, if the Magic-Loop technique is being used, one long circular needle.

When working with more than one circular needle, there are at least two break points in the round: the beginning/end of the round and at least one other point where the knitting goes from one circular needle to another. When working with several double-pointed needles, there are typically three or four break points in the round, where the knitting goes from one double-pointed needle to the next. A beginning/end of the round stitch marker can be used, but it usually has to be placed to the left of the very first stitch of the round on the relevant needle (that is, one stitch in from the very beginning/end of the round). An alternative to using a beginning/end-of-the-round stitch marker is to use a marker thread.

Cut a length of smooth, contrast-colour yarn of either the same yarn weight or a slightly finer yarn than the yarn being used for knitting the project. When you reach the point in the pattern that instructs you to place a stitch marker, instead of

putting a stitch marker on to the right-hand needle, place the marker thread across the strand of yarn running between the two stitches closest to the points of the left-hand and right-hand needles, so that one end hangs down on the outside of the knitting (towards you) and the other end hangs down in the middle of the circle of knitting (away from you). Knit one round. Take the yarn end that is hanging in the middle of the circle, and bring it back between the points of the needles and over the strand of yarn running between the two stitches closest to the points of the left-hand and right-hand needles, so that it hangs down on the outside of the knitting (towards you). Keep moving this yarn end back and forth between the points of the needles at the end of each round. The thread is not firmly knitted into the fabric, but it sits within the knitting until it is gently pulled out.

The yarn end does not need to be moved after completing each round. It can be moved every other round, or every third or fourth round, so it can also be used to help keep track of where you are in the pattern. For example, in the patterns for the Flying-V Mittens and Double-Diamond Mittens, the thumb-gusset increases are worked every three rounds. By moving the thread marker on every increase round, you can count the strands between the needles, to keep track of the number of rounds from one increase round to the next.

Fig. 7.7 Rainbow-Storms Wing Shawl, knitted with Scheepjes Whirl yarn, being blocked to form a crescent shape.

Blocking items such as shawls

Blocking is a very important part of the finishing process when making shawls. The method recommended for the shawls in this book is to soak the finished knitting in a bowl of hand-hot water with a no-rinse liquid soap such as Eucalan® for about 15 minutes, to make sure that the fibres are thoroughly wet. As you take the knitting out of the bowl, gently squeeze the fabric to remove some of the water. Place the knitting into a washing-machine laundry bag or clean pillowcase, and put it into the washing machine for a short, gentle spin, to remove more water. If you prefer, the knitting can be placed on a large, clean towel, which is then rolled up and squeezed to remove excess water.

To dry and shape the shawl, you need a large, flat area that can be pinned into. You can buy blocking mats for this purpose or use several clean towels on a carpet, double bed or other flat surface. You need to use stainless-steel, non-rusting, long pins for pinning out the shawl.

Place the damp knitting on to the blocking mat or other flat surface, stretching the shawl out from the centre of the top edge to both sides and down to the point at the base of the

shawl. Pin the centre of the top edge, and then pin the centre point at the base of the shawl vertically below the first pin, having first stretched the fabric downwards. Stretch out the top edge to the left- and right-hand sides. For some shawls, the top edge may be stretched into a slight upward-turning crescent shape rather than a straight line. Stretch out the knitting further towards the bottom edge and sides of the shawl. If the shawl has a pointed edging, pin the edging through each point, keeping the points as evenly sized and spaced as possible.

Once you are happy that the shawl is pinned out as evenly as possible, leave it to dry completely. This will probably take a couple of days. Once the shawl is completely dry, it can be unpinned.

If you used a yarn with a fibre content of at least 30-per-cent acrylic, after blocking, but before unpinning the shawl, steam the shawl to permanently fix its shape. If you are using a steam iron, hold the iron just above the knitting, to allow the steam to penetrate into the knitting without flattening the surface of the fabric or discolouring or melting the fibres of the yarn. The steam will change the feel and drape of the knitting, so it is important to make sure that all of the knitting is steamed evenly.

PURSES AND BAGS

For all of the projects in this book, yarn amounts are given based on average yarn requirements and are therefore approximate.

Please *see* Abbreviations and Chart Symbols for definitions of the abbreviations and symbols used within the patterns.

The purses in this book are based on Victorian beaded purses, worked as Beaded Knitting, as explained in Chapter 3. The samples have all been worked by using No. 8 Pearl Cotton yarn, size 10 or size 11 seed beads and fine, steel knitting needles. Beads must be threaded on to the knitting yarn before you start to work a project, but you should not try to thread all of the beads required on to the yarn at the start of the project, as this may result in the yarn being worn by the beads being pushed along the yarn.

The patterns for the Leaves Amulet Purse, Shades-of-Blue Amulet Purse and Silver Evening Bag are written in a slightly different way to most knitting patterns. The purses are worked in garter stitch with beads being strung between groups of stitches. The first row of the pattern will be written out with the number of stitches to knit and the number of beads to be pushed up next to the stitch just knitted. After this first row, the pattern will simply list the number of beads to be strung between each group of stitches across the row.

The bottoms of the bags are worked with short-row shaping. Short-row knitting involves knitting across part of the row to a turning point, wrapping the next stitch with the working yarn to avoid a hole being produced and then turning the knitting to work back across the row, to the next turning point. A dart shape is formed by gradually working fewer and fewer stitches across subsequent rows. To avoid a hole forming at the turning point, it is necessary to slip the next stitch at this point purlwise to the right-hand needle, bring the yarn to the front of the work, slip the slipped stitch back on to the left-hand needle and then turn the work and continue by working the next row.

At the end of the sequence of short rows, all of the stitches are returned to being knitted again, by knitting from the turning point on the shortest short row to the very end of the row and then knitting a complete row across the entire width of the fabric. The short-row sequence is worked four times in total. The purse folds at the midway point of the fabric that was worked with short rows, so it is important for the same number of short rows to have been worked on each side of the folding point of the purse.

Leaves Amulet Purse.

Leaves Amulet Purse

Size

- Length (with purse folded) 7.5cm (3in); width at narrowest point 4.5cm (1¾in) and at widest point 7cm (2¾in)

Materials

- 1 × 10g (½oz) ball of No. 8 Pearl Cotton yarn, approx. 85m (93yd) per ball. The sample was knitted with Anchor Pearl Cotton yarn in shade no. 403 Black.
- 35–40g (1¼–1½oz) of size 10 or 11 seed beads. The sample was knitted with size 10 Czech Preciosa Ornela beads in Transparent Red.
- 16 accent beads of a mixed selection, including 5 leaves
- Pair of 1.25mm (US 0000) needles
- Tapestry needle
- Beading mat/container, for holding beads for threading
- Beading needle, threaded with a doubled, fine thread, for threading beads on to the yarn

Tension

- 22sts in 5cm (2in) by using 1.25mm (US 0000) needles, in Beaded Garter Stitch with 1 bead pushed up every 3sts. The swatch is not washed or blocked before measuring.

Knitting Notes

Thread approximately half of the required number of beads on to the yarn before you start to knit the purse.

Halfway through the length of the main body of the purse, a short-row sequence, which is worked four times, is used to shape the bottom of the purse. Before starting to work through each short-row sequence, make sure that you have sufficient beads threaded on to the yarn to work a complete short-row sequence.

Purse

Using 1.25mm (US 0000) needles, cast on 24sts.

Foundation Row: knit.

The next row sets the position of the beads between the knit stitches, so, after this row, you will be given only the number of beads between stitches, as the knit stitches remain the same throughout the pattern.

Row 1: *k3, SB1*, repeat from * to * to the last 3sts, k3.
Rows 2 to 4: (3 rows) repeat Row 1, 3 times.
Rows 5 to 8: (4 rows) SB1, SB2, SB1, SB2, SB1, SB2, SB1.
Rows 9 to 12: (4 rows) SB1, SB3, SB1, SB3, SB1, SB3, SB1.
Rows 13 to 16: (4 rows) SB2, SB2, SB2, SB2, SB2, SB2, SB2.
Rows 17 to 20: (4 rows) SB3, SB1, SB3, SB1, SB3, SB1, SB3.
Rows 21 to 24: (4 rows) SB2, SB2, SB2, SB2, SB2, SB2, SB2.
Rows 25 to 28: (4 rows) SB1, SB3, SB1, SB3, SB1, SB3, SB1.
Rows 29 to 32: (4 rows) SB1, SB4, SB1, SB4, SB1, SB4, SB1.
Rows 33 to 36: (4 rows) SB2, SB5, SB2, SB5, SB2, SB5, SB2.
Rows 37 to 40: (4 rows) SB3, SB4, SB3, SB4, SB3, SB4, SB3.
Rows 41 to 44: (4 rows) SB4, SB3, SB4, SB3, SB4, SB3, SB4.
Rows 45 to 48: (4 rows) SB5, SB2, SB5, SB2, SB5, SB2, SB5.
Rows 49 to 52: (4 rows) SB6, SB1, SB6, SB1, SB6, SB1, SB6.
Rows 53 to 60: (8 rows) SB7, SB1, SB7, SB1, SB7, SB1, SB7.

Short rows
Note: Make sure that you have enough beads threaded on to the yarn to complete a whole short-row sequence, so at least 126 beads.

Start of the short-row-shaping sequence.
Row 61: SB7, SB1, SB7, SB1, SB7, SB1, k1, w&t.
Row 62: SB1, SB7, SB1, SB7, SB1, k1, w&t.
Row 63: SB1, SB7, SB1, SB7, k1, w&t.
Row 64: SB7, SB1, SB7, k1, w&t.
Row 65: SB7, SB1, SB7, SB1, SB7 (end of row).
Row 66: SB7, SB1, SB7, SB1, SB7, SB1, SB7.
End of one short-row-shaping sequence.

Rows 67 to 84: (18 rows) repeat Rows 61 to 66, 3 times.
Rows 85 to 92: (8 rows) SB7, SB1, SB7, SB1, SB7, SB1, SB7.
Rows 93 to 96: (4 rows) SB6, SB1, SB6, SB1, SB6, SB1, SB6.
Rows 97 to 100: (4 rows) SB5, SB2, SB5, SB2, SB5, SB2, SB5.
Rows 101 to 104: (4 rows) SB4, SB3, SB4, SB3, SB4, SB3, SB4.
Rows 105 to 108: (4 rows) SB3, SB4, SB3, SB4, SB3, SB4, SB3.

Rows 109 to 112: (4 rows) SB2, SB5, SB2, SB5, SB2, SB5, SB2.
Rows 113 to 116: (4 rows) SB1, SB4, SB1, SB4, SB1, SB4, SB1.
Rows 117 to 120: (4 rows) SB1, SB3, SB1, SB3, SB1, SB3, SB1.
Rows 121 to 124: (4 rows) SB2, SB2, SB2, SB2, SB2, SB2, SB2.
Rows 125 to 128: (4 rows) SB3, SB1, SB3, SB1, SB3, SB1, SB3.
Rows 129 to 132: (4 rows) SB2, SB2, SB2, SB2, SB2, SB2, SB2.
Rows 133 to 136: (4 rows) SB1, SB3, SB1, SB3, SB1, SB3, SB1.
Rows 137 to 140: (4 rows) SB1, SB2, SB1, SB2, SB1, SB2, SB1.
Rows 141 to 144: (4 rows) SB1, SB1, SB1, SB1, SB1, SB1, SB1.
Knit 1 row of garter stitch.

Top flap

Knit 5 more rows of garter stitch.
Rows 1 to 6: (6 rows) *k3, SB1*, repeat from * to * to the last 3sts, k3.
Rows 7 to 12: (6 rows) SB1, SB2, SB1, SB2, SB1, SB2 SB1.
Rows 13 to 18: (6 rows) SB1, SB3, SB1, SB3, SB1, SB3, SB1.
Rows 19 to 24: (6 rows) SB2, SB2, SB2, SB2, SB2, SB2, SB2.
Rows 25 to 31: (8 rows) SB3, SB1, SB3, SB1, SB3, SB1, SB3.

Cast off with the wrong side facing you, working in the beading pattern, making sure that you keep a long cast-off loop across the wide sections of strung beads, as explained in Chapter 3.

Finishing

Fold the purse so that the right sides of the main purse are together, and sew the two side seams by using an oversewing stitch, to give a flat seam. Turn the purse right-side out.

To make a fringe along the bottom of the purse or the top flap, it is necessary to switch between threading beads on to the knitting yarn and sewing the knitting yarn to the knit stitches between the strung beads at the bottom/top-flap edge.

Join the Pearl Cotton yarn to the bottom/top flap of the bag. Starting just before the first group of beads:

*Thread 5 seed beads, 1 accent bead and 1 seed bead on to the yarn, take the yarn back through the accent bead and thread 5 more seed beads on to the yarn. Sew the yarn to the knit stitches on the other side of the group of beads.

Thread 5 seed beads, 1 leaf and 5 more seed beads on to the yarn. Sew the yarn to the knit stitches on the other side of the next group of beads.*

Thread 6 seed beads, 1 leaf and 6 more seed beads on to the yarn. Sew the yarn to the knit stitches on the other side of the next group of beads.

Thread 7 seed beads, 1 leaf and 7 more seed beads on to the yarn. Sew the yarn to the knit stitches on the other side of the next group of beads.

Repeat from ** to **.

Repeat from * to * 1 time *in reverse order* so that the leaf is placed before the accent bead.

To make the handle, measure off approximately 1m of the knitting yarn, fold this length in half, thread the folded yarn into a sewing needle, take the yarn through the top edge of the purse at the seam join, unthread the needle and pass the two yarn ends through the loop, to join the yarn to the top edge of one side of the purse.

Thread 1 accent bead over both yarn ends, and then thread 20 seed beads on to each end of yarn. Thread 1 accent bead over both yarn ends, and then thread 10 seed beads on to each end of yarn.

Repeat from * to * 1 time. Thread 1 accent bead over both yarn ends, 20 seed beads on to each end of yarn and then 1 accent bead over both yarn ends again.

Sew the two yarn ends to the top of the second side of the purse at the seam join, and finish off securely.

Shades-of-Blue Amulet Purse

This purse is worked with two colours of beads. As a result, it is very important to thread the beads on to the yarn in the correct order for knitting. The purse is quite small, so it is possible to thread the beads in two groups. The first group of beads that are threaded will cover the beads required for the start of the purse to the end of the short-row sequence, and the second group of beads will cover the purse from the end of the short-row sequence to the end of the flap.

To help with the threading sequence, the bead colours have been called colour 'a' and colour 'b', and instructions for the threading the beads are provided in an accompanying box.

Size

- Length (with purse folded) 7cm (2¾in); width at narrowest point 5cm (2in) and at widest point 8cm (3¼in)

Materials

- 1 × 10g (½oz) ball of No. 8 Pearl Cotton yarn, approx. 85m (93yd) per ball. The sample was knitted with Anchor Pearl Cotton yarn in shade no. 132 Royal Blue.
- 30–35g (1–1¼oz) of colour-a size 10 or 11 seed beads. The sample was knitted with size 10 Czech Preciosa Ornela seed beads in Transparent Blue.
- 5–10g (¼–½oz) of colour-b size 10 or 11 seed beads. The sample was knitted with size 10 Czech Preciosa Ornela seed beads in Metallic Blue Iris Mix.
- 16 accent beads
- Pair of 1.25mm (US 0000) needles
- Tapestry needle
- Beading mat/container, for holding beads for threading
- Beading needle, threaded with a doubled, fine thread, for threading beads on to the yarn

Shades-of-Blue Amulet Purse.

Tension

- 22sts in 5cm (2in) by using 1.25mm (US 0000) needles, in Beaded Garter Stitch with 1 bead pushed up every 3sts. The swatch is not washed or blocked before measuring.

Knitting Notes

As instructed in the accompanying box 'Threading Instructions', thread approximately half of the required number of beads on to the knitting yarn before you start to knit.

Halfway through the length of the main body of the purse, a short-row sequence, which is worked four times, is used to shape the bottom of the purse. Before starting to work through each short-row sequence, make sure that you have sufficient beads threaded on to the yarn to work a complete short-row sequence.

Threading Instructions

For the first group of beads:
*10a, 1b, 10a, 1b, 10a.
10a, 1b, 10a.
10a.
10a, 1b.
1b, 10a, 1b.
1b, 10a, 1b, 5a.
5a, 1b, 10a, 1b, 5a.
5a, 1b, 10a, 1b, 10a.*
Repeat from * to * 3 times.
(10a, 1b, 10a, 1b, 10a) 16 times.
(8a, 1b, 8a, 1b, 8a) 8 times.
(6a, 1b, 6a, 1b, 6a) 8 times.
(4a, 1b, 4a, 1b, 4a) 6 times.
(2a, 1b, 2a, 1b, 2a) 6 times.

For the second group of beads:
(10a, 1b, 10a, 1b, 10a) 12 times.
(8a, 1b, 8a, 1b, 8a) 8 times.
(6a, 1b, 6a, 1b, 6a) 8 times.
(4a, 1b, 4a, 1b, 4a) 6 times.
(2a, 1b, 2a, 1b, 2a) 6 times.
End of flap.
(2a, 1b, 2a, 1b, 2a) 6 times.
(4a, 1b, 4a, 1b, 4a) 6 times.
(6a, 1b, 6a, 1b, 6a) 8 times.
(8a, 1b, 8a, 1b, 8a) 8 times.
(10a, 1b, 10a, 1b, 10a) 16 times.

Purse

Using 1.25mm (US 0000) needles, cast on 23sts.

Foundation Row: knit.

The next row sets the position of the beads between the knit stitches, so, after this row, you will be given only the number of beads between stitches, as the knit stitches remain the same throughout the pattern.

Row 1: k3, SB1a, k3, SB1a, k2, SB1b, k2, SB1a, k3, SB1a, k2, SB1b, k2, SB1a, k3, SB1a, k3.
Rows 2 to 6: (5 rows) repeat Row 1, 5 times.
Rows 7 to 12: (6 rows) SB2a, SB2a, SB1b, SB2a, SB2a, SB1b, SB2a, SB2a.
Rows 13 to 20: (8 rows) SB3a, SB3a, SB1b, SB3a, SB3a, SB1b, SB3a, SB3a.
Rows 21 to 28: (8 rows) SB4a, SB4a, SB1b, SB4a, SB4a, SB1b, SB4a, SB4a.
Rows 29 to 44: (16 rows) SB5a, SB5a, SB1b, SB5a, SB5a, SB1b, SB5a, SB5a.

Short rows

Note: Make sure that you have enough beads threaded on to the yarn to complete a whole short-row sequence. (If you threaded the beads by following the Threading Instructions, you should have enough beads to complete all four short-row sequences.)

Start of the short-row shaping sequence.
Row 45: SB5a, SB5a, SB1b, SB5a, SB5a, SB1b, SB5a, k1, w&t.
Row 46: SB5a, SB1b, SB5a, SB5a, SB1b, SB5a, k1, w&t.
Row 47: SB5a, SB1b, SB5a, SB5a, SB1b, k1, w&t.
Row 48: SB1b, SB5a, SB5a, SB1b, k1, w&t.
Row 49: SB1b, SB5a, SB5a, k1, w&t.
Row 50: SB5a, SB5a, k1, w&t.
Row 51: SB5a, SB5a, SB1b, SB5a, SB5a.
Row 52: SB5a, SB5a, SB1b, SB5a, SB5a, SB1b, SB5a, SB5a.
End of one short-row shaping sequence.

Rows 53 to 76: (24 rows) repeat Rows 45 to 52, 3 times.
If you followed the Threading Instructions, you will now need to thread the second group of beads.

Rejoin the yarn at the edge of the knitting, and continue as follows:

Rows 77 to 92: (16 rows) SB5a, SB5a, SB1b, SB5a, SB5a, SB1b, SB5b, SB5a.

Rows 93 to 100: (8 rows) SB4a, SB4a, SB1b, SB4a, SB4a, SB1b, SB4a, SB4a.

Rows 101 to 108: (8 rows) SB3a, SB3a, SB1b, SB3a, SB3a, SB1b, SB3a, SB3a.

Rows 109 to 114: (6 rows) SB2a, SB2a, SB1b, SB2a, SB2a, SB1b, SB2a, SB2a.

Rows 115 to 120: (6 rows) SB1a, SB1a, SB1b, SB1a, SB1a, SB1b, SB1a, SB1a.

Row 121: knit.

Knit 1 row of garter stitch.

Top flap

Knit 5 more rows of garter stitch.

Repeat Rows 1 to 39 of the main purse pattern.

Cast off with the wrong side facing you, working in the beading pattern, making sure that you keep a long cast-off loop across the wide sections of strung beads, as explained in Chapter 3.

Finishing

Fold the purse so that the right sides of the main purse are together, and sew the two side seams by using an oversewing stitch, to give a flat seam. Turn the purse right-side out.

To make a fringe along the bottom of the purse or the top flap, it is necessary to switch between threading beads on to the knitting yarn and sewing the knitting yarn to the knit stitches between the strung beads at the bottom/top flap edge.

Join the Pearl Cotton yarn to the bottom/top flap of the bag. For the fringe, all of the seed beads used are of colour b.

Starting next to the first group of beads:

Thread 5 seed beads, 1 accent bead and 1 seed bead on to the yarn, take the yarn back through the accent bead and thread 5 more seed beads on to the yarn. Sew the yarn to the knit stitches the other side of the first group of beads.

Thread 6 seed beads, 1 accent bead and 1 seed bead on to the yarn, take the yarn through the accent bead and thread 6 more seed beads on to the yarn. Sew the yarn to the knit stitches the other side of the next group of beads.

Repeat from * to * 1 time.

Thread 7 seed beads, 1 accent bead and 1 seed bead on to the yarn, take the yarn back through the accent bead and thread 7 more seed beads on to the yarn. Sew the yarn to the knit stitches the other side of the next group of beads.

Repeat from ** to ** 1 time.

Repeat from * to * 2 times.

Thread 5 seed beads, 1 accent bead and 1 seed bead on to the yarn, take the yarn back through the accent bead and thread 5 more seed beads on to the yarn. Sew the yarn to the knit stitches the other side of the last group of beads, and fasten off on the wrong side.

To make the handle, measure off approximately 1m of the knitting yarn, fold this length in half, thread the folded yarn into a sewing needle, take the yarn through the top edge of the purse at the seam join, unthread the needle and pass the two yarn ends through the loop, to join the yarn to the top edge of one side of the purse.

Thread 1 accent bead over both yarn ends, and then thread 20 seed beads on to each end of yarn. Thread 1 accent bead over both yarn ends, 10 seed beads on to each end of yarn, 1 accent bead over both yarn ends, 10 seed beads on to each end of yarn and 1 accent bead over both yarn ends. Thread 20 seed beads on to each end of yarn.

Repeat from * to * *in reverse order*.

Sew the two yarn ends to the top of the second side of the purse at the seam join, and finish off securely.

Silver Evening Bag.

Silver Evening Bag

Size

- Length (with bag folded) 15.5cm (6in); width at narrowest point 14cm (5½in) and at widest point 21cm (8¼in)

Materials

- 3 × 10g (½oz) balls of No. 8 Pearl Cotton yarn, approx. 85m (93yd) per ball. The sample was knitted with Anchor Pearl Cotton yarn in shade no. 343 Silver Grey.
- 160g (5¾oz) of size 10 or 11 seed beads. The sample was knitted with size 10 Czech Preciosa Ornela seed beads in Clear Silver-Lined.
- Pair of 1.25mm (US 0000) needles
- Tapestry needle
- Beading mat/container, for holding beads for threading
- Beading needle, threaded with doubled, fine thread, for threading beads on to the yarn
- Metal handbag frame with rods to insert through the channels sewn at the top edges of the bag

- Fabric to line the bag, if you wish to add a material lining
- Machine sewing thread in a colour matching the material
- Sewing needle, for sewing the lining

Tension

- 48sts and 46 garter ridges in 10cm (4in) by using 1.25mm (US 0000) needles, over the beaded stitch pattern. The stitches were measured over the section where 1 bead sits between stitches. The swatch is not washed or blocked before measuring.

Knitting Notes

Thread approximately 20–30g (¾–1oz) of beads on to the knitting yarn before you start to knit. You will need to thread more beads of the same amount on to the yarn several times during the knitting of this project.

Halfway through the length of the main body of the purse, a short-row sequence, which is worked four times, is used to shape the bottom of the purse. Before starting to work through each short-row sequence, make sure that you have sufficient beads threaded on to the yarn to work a complete short-row sequence.

Bag

Using 1.25mm (US 0000) needles, cast on 70sts.
Row 1 (RS): knit.
Row 2: k16, *yf, sl1, yb*, k10, repeat from * to *, k14, repeat from * to *, k10, repeat from * to *, k16.
Repeat Rows 1 to 2 until 16 rows have been worked.
The next two rows set the position of the beads between the knit stitches and slip stitches, so, after these two rows, you will be given only the number of beads between stitches, as the knit and slip stitches remain the same throughout the pattern. The number of beads between stitches is the same across the whole row.

Row 1: k5, SB1, (k4, SB1) twice, k7, SB1, k4, SB1, k7, SB1, (k4, SB1) twice, k7, SB1, k4, SB1, k7, SB1, (k4, SB1) twice, k5.
Row 2: k5, SB1, (k4, SB1) twice, *k3, yf, sl1, yb, k3, SB1*, k4, SB1, repeat from * to *, (k4, SB1) twice, repeat from * to *, k4, SB1, repeat from * to *, (k4, SB1) twice, k5.

Rows 3 to 8: (6 rows) repeat Rows 1 and 2, 3 times.
Rows 9 to 16: (8 rows) SB2.
Rows 17 to 36: (20 rows) SB3.
Rows 37 to 58: (22 rows) SB4.
Rows 59 to 84: (26 rows) SB5.
Rows 85 to 112: (28 rows) SB6.

Short rows
Note: Make sure that you have enough beads threaded on to the yarn to complete a whole short-row sequence. You will need at least 696 beads for one sequence.

Start of the short-row shaping sequence.
Row 113: SB6 worked 12 times, k2, w&t.
Row 114: SB6 worked 11 times, k2, w&t.
Row 115: SB6 worked 10 times, k2, w&t.
Row 116: SB6 worked 9 times, k2, w&t.
Row 117: SB6 worked 8 times, k5, w&t.
Row 118: SB 6 worked 7 times, k3, yf, sl1, yb, k1, w&t.
Row 119: SB6 worked 7 times, k1, w&t.
Row 120: SB6 worked 7 times, k1, w&t.
Row 121: SB6 worked 6 times, k2, w&t.
Row 122: SB6 worked 5 times, k2, w&t.
Row 123: SB6 worked 4 times, k5, w&t.
Row 124: SB6 worked 3 times, k3, yf, sl1, yb, k1, w&t.
Row 125: SB6 worked 3 times, k1, w&t.
Row 126: SB6 worked 3 times, k1, w&t.
Row 127: SB6 worked 8 times, knit to the end of the row.
Row 128: SB6 worked 13 times, knit to the end of the row.
End of one short-row shaping sequence.

Rows 129 to 176: (48 rows) repeat Rows 113 to 128, 3 times.
Rows 177 to 204: (28 rows) SB6.
Rows 205 to 230: (26 rows) SB5.
Rows 231 to 252: (22 rows) SB4.
Rows 253 to 272: (20 rows) SB3.
Rows 273 to 280: (8 rows) SB2.
Rows 281 to 288: (8 rows) SB1.
This is the end of the section that is knitted with beads.

Next row (RS): knit.
Next row: k16, *yf, sl1, yb*, k10, repeat * to *, k14, repeat * to *, k10, repeat * to *, k16.
Repeat the last 2 rows until 16 rows have been worked.
Cast off.

Finishing

If you want to line the bag with fabric, you will need to make the lining before you start to sew up the knitted bag. *See* the following section 'Making a fabric lining', before beginning the finishing of your bag.

With the rights sides of the knitting together, fold the bag in half. Using a length of the Pearl Cotton yarn, slip stitch the side seams, from the bottom edge to about 5cm (2in) from the top of the bag, but *do not* sew in the yarn ends, as you may want to adjust the depth of the opening once the bag is attached to the handle. Fold each top edge of the bag towards the wrong side, so that the cast-on or cast-off edge is in line with the row of plain, unbeaded knitting that is adjacent to the first or last beaded row of knitting. Slip stitch the cast-on/cast-off edge along the appropriate plain, unbeaded row of knitting, matching stitch for stitch. Remove the metal rods from the bag frame, and push one through each of the channels that have just been created at the top edges of the bag. Fix the metal rods back into the frame, pulling the bag over the metal bracket so that the bracket sits inside the bag. Adjust the opening at the side seams, if necessary, and finish off the yarn ends.

You may prefer to line the bag with a fabric lining, if you are concerned about the bag stretching with use. You may also wish to attach a chain handle to the rings on the frame, to allow you to carry the bag over your shoulder rather than always carrying the bag by its handle.

Making a fabric lining

Fold the bag in half, remembering that the top of the bag will be made into channels to hold the rods of the bag frame, and make a paper template of the bag shape. Add a normal seam allowance to the paper pattern, and allow an extra 3cm (1¼in) of fabric at the bag's straight top edge, to form folded-over hems. With the fabric folded double, place the paper pattern on to the fabric, and cut around the pattern. With right sides together, sew around the side and bottom sections of the bag lining, leaving the top 3cm (1¼in) of fabric at the top of each side seam unsewn. Turn over the selvedge edges at the top of the bag to the wrong side, to neaten the edges and form folded-over hems. Make a few small cuts in the seam allowance at the bottom of the bag so the bottom curved edge will not be pulled out of shape.

Having sewn the side seams of the bag, place the lining into the bag, with the wrong sides of the lining fabric next to the knitted fabric. Slip stitch the folded-over hems at the top of the lining fabric to the knitting, just below the channels of knitted fabric. Insert the bag rods through the channels to hang the bag from the handle. Adjust the knitted side seams as necessary, and slip stitch the short openings at the side seams of the lining to the knitted fabric.

Miser's Purse

Miser's purses first became popular in the late eighteenth century and remained so into the middle of the nineteenth century. They were also called stocking, ring or long purses and were used for holding coins. The term miser's purse became associated with this type of purse, because it was difficult to get the coins out of the purse.

The purse is basically a long tube of knitting, with a slit for access in the undecorated middle section, and the fabric is gathered with sliding rings to close the purse and make distinct pouches at each end.

The ends of the purses were often made a different shape, for example, with one flat end and one round, gathered end.

The reason for having different shapes was to make it easier to identify different coins. The gold coins would be dropped into one end of the purse and silver coins into the other.

In the late eighteenth century, beads were being used to embellish embroidered fabrics, so it also became popular to use beads in knitting. Beads were incorporated into the knitting to decorate the purses. By the late nineteenth century, miser's purses had largely been replaced by leather purses, but patterns for making these bags continued to appear in women's magazines up until the early twentieth century.

Originally, these purses would have been knitted in the round, but the pattern in this book has been designed to be knitted as a flat piece. It includes two Beaded-Knitting techniques that are covered in Chapter 3. The ends of the purse are knitted in Beaded Garter Stitch; that is, the beads are placed on wrong-side rows and are suspended between adjacent stitches. The diamond pattern is worked in Beaded Stocking Stitch, with beads being placed between purl stitches. Charts are used to indicate the placement of the beads.

Miser's Purse.

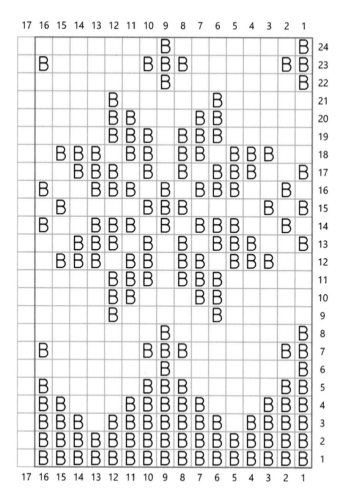

Chart A for the Beaded-Garter-Stitch section of the Miser's Purse. Beads are to be placed on wrong-side rows. Every pattern row is read from right to left, and the chart's row numbers refer to the garter-stitch ridge numbers.

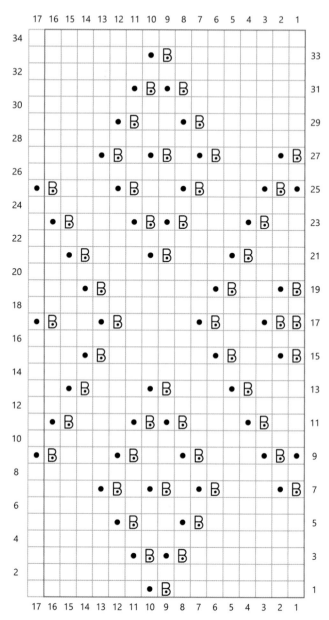

Chart B for the Beaded-Stocking-Stitch section of the Miser's Purse, for beads to be placed between purl stitches.

Size

- Approx. 31cm (12¼in) long by 12cm (4¾in) wide, when laid flat before sewing up (not including the fringing)

Materials

- 2 × 10g (½oz) balls of No. 8 Pearl Cotton yarn, approx. 85m (93yd) per ball. The sample was knitted with Anchor Pearl Cotton yarn in shade no. 339 Terracotta.
- 30g (1oz) of size 10 seed beads. The sample was knitted with size 10 Czech Preciosa Ornela seed beads in Metallic Bronze/Brown Iris Mix.
- 31 accent beads, for the fringes
- Pair of 1.25mm (US 0000) needles
- Tapestry needle
- Beading mat/container, for holding beads for threading
- Beading needle, threaded with doubled, fine thread, for threading beads on to the yarn

Tension

- 29sts and 39.5 rows in 5cm (2in) by using 1.25mm (US 0000) needles, over stocking-stitch fabric, after washing and blocking.

Knitting Notes

The fabric corresponding to Chart A is knitted in Beaded Garter Stitch. Right-side rows are knitted, and wrong-side rows are knitted with beads. The beads sit between knit stitches and are placed according to Chart A.

Note: Only wrong-side rows are shown on Chart A, and the chart is read from right to left on every row.

The fabric corresponding to Chart B is knitted in Beaded Stocking Stitch. The beads are placed on right-side rows between two purl stitches, and wrong-side rows are purled.

Note: Chart B shows all of the rows in the pattern. Odd-number (right-side) rows are read from right to left, and even-number (wrong-side) rows are read from left to right, as for normal charts for flat knitting.

Thread approximately half of the beads on to the yarn before you start to knit the purse. You will have at least one yarn join within the purse.

Purse

Using 1.25mm (US 0000) needles, cast on 65sts.
Knit 3 rows.

First Beaded-Garter-Stitch section
Next row (WS): follow Row 1 of Chart A, working the beading pattern 4 times across the row.

Continue in Beaded Garter Stitch by following Chart A on WS rows, for one vertical repeat of the chart (48 rows).
Next row: increase 1st at the beginning and the end of this row (to add a selvedge stitch at each end), and continue working in stocking stitch for 8 rows.

First of the Beaded-Stocking-Stitch section
Next row: k1, follow Row 1 of Chart B over 65sts, working the beading pattern 4 times across the row, k1.

Continue working the selvedge stitch at each end as stocking stitch and following Chart B, for one vertical repeat of the chart (34 rows).

Continue in stocking stitch until the purse fabric measures 12cm (4¾in).

Moss-stitch section
Next row: (k1, p1) twice, knit to last 4sts, (p1, k1) twice.
Next row: k1, p1, k1, purl to last 3sts, k1, p1, k1.
Repeat these 2 rows until the purse fabric measures 20cm (8in).

Continue in stocking stitch until the purse fabric measures 23cm (9in).

Second Beaded-Stocking-Stitch section
Follow Chart B as before, for 34 rows, in Beaded Stocking Stitch and working the beading pattern 4 times across each row (with a selvedge stitch at each end).

Work 8 rows of stocking stitch and, on the last row, decrease 1st at each end.
Next row: knit.

Second Beaded-Garter-Stitch section
Continue in Beaded Garter Stitch by following Chart A on WS rows, only from Row 8 to Row 1.

Continuing in Beaded Garter Stitch from now on, place 1 bead between each stitch on WS rows.

Knit 2 rows of Beaded Garter Stitch (one knit row and one row with 1 bead being placed between each stitch).

Rounded end
Row 1 (RS): knit.
Row 2 (decrease row): *(k1, SB1) 6 times, k2tog, SB1*, repeat from * to * 7 times, k1 – 57sts.
Row 3: knit.
Row 4: *k1, SB1*, repeat from * to * to the last stitch, k1.
Row 5: knit.
Row 6 (decrease row): *(k1, SB1) 5 times, k2tog, SB1*, repeat from * to * 7 times, k1 – 49sts.
Rows 7 to 9: repeat Rows 3 to 5.
Row 10 (decrease row): *(k1, SB1) 4 times, k2tog, SB1*, repeat from * to * 7 times, k1 – 41sts.
Rows 11 to 13: repeat Rows 3 to 5.
Row 14 (decrease row): *(k1, SB1) 3 times, k2tog, SB1*, repeat from * to * 7 times, k1 – 33sts.
Rows 15 to 17: repeat Rows 3 to 5.
Row 18 (decrease row): *(k1, SB1) 2 times, k2tog, SB1*, repeat from * to * 7 times, k1 – 25sts.
Rows 19 to 21: repeat Rows 3 to 5.
Row 22 (decrease row): *k1, SB1, k2tog, SB1*, repeat from * to * 7 times, k1 – 17sts.
Rows 23 to 25: repeat Rows 3 to 5.

Row 26 (decrease row): *k2tog, SB1*, repeat from * to * 7 times, k1 – 9sts.
Row 27: knit.
Row 28: k2tog (without beads) 4 times, k1.
Cut yarn, and pull the yarn end through the last 5sts to finish.

Finishing
Soak the purse fabric in water to get it thoroughly wet. Roll the fabric in a towel, to remove excess water, and then lay the fabric out flat on a dry towel. The rounded end will curl in, but block the rest of the purse fabric so that the edges are straight. Leave the fabric to dry.

Fold the purse fabric with the wrong sides together and one of the right sides facing you. With a length of Pearl Cotton yarn, slip stitch the flat end together. Slip stitch together the sides of the garter-stitch section, and mattress stitch together the selvedges of the stocking-stitch section, up to the start of the moss-stitch section.

At the rounded end, secure the yarn that was pulled through the last 5sts. With another length of Pearl Cotton yarn, slip stitch the other garter-stitch section, and mattress stitch the other stocking-stitch section, up to the start of the moss-stitch section. The moss-stitch section forms an opening at the centre of the purse.

Fringing
Using a beading needle threaded with a length of Nymo®/beading thread, attach the thread to the inside of the bag at the flat end, and bring the needle through to the right side. Sew a bead to each stitch along the seamed flat edge; this provides 32 foundation beads for attaching the fringe.

Fringe 1
Take the needle through the end/next foundation bead, and pick up 4 seed beads, 1 accent bead, 16 seed beads, 1 accent bead and 1 seed bead. Take the needle back through the closest accent bead, 16 seed beads and the other accent bead. Pick up 4 seed beads, and take the needle through the foundation bead sewn to the flat edge that is one bead away from the foundation bead that you previously brought the needle out from. Skip one bead and go through the next bead on the foundation bead row.

Take the beading needle through the knitted edge and out through the next bead so that the needle is pointing away from the knitted edge, ready to work the next fringe.

Fringe 2

Take the needle through the next foundation bead, and pick up 23 seed beads, 1 accent bead and 1 seed bead. Take the needle back through the accent bead, 23 seed beads and the foundation bead attached to the flat edge.

Take the beading needle through the knitted edge and out through the next bead.

Fringe 3

Work as for Fringe 1, but, when attaching the strung beads to a foundation bead attached to the flat edge, go through the foundation bead that is two beads away from the foundation bead that you previously brought the needle out from. Go through one foundation bead.

Repeat working Fringes 2 and 3, 2 times, going through a foundation bead between each fringe.

Repeat working Fringes 2 and 1, 2 times.

Tassel

Bring 4 ends of Nymo®/beading thread through the knitted fabric, from the inside to the outside of the purse, at the centre of the round end and through a large accent bead. Each end of Nymo®/beading thread will make 3 fringes in the tassel.

Using a beading needle threaded with 1 end of the 4 ends of Nymo®/beading thread, *pick up 23 seed beads, 1 accent bead and 1 seed bead. Take the needle back through the accent bead and 23 seed beads.* Take the needle through the large accent bead, through the knitted fabric and back through the large accent bead. **Repeat from * to *, and take the needle through the top seed bead of completed fringe.**

Repeat from ** to **, 1 time, and then go back through the large accent bead and through the knitted fabric so that the end can be tied off.

For each of the remaining 3 ends of Nymo®/beading thread, repeat the creation of the 3 fringes as detailed previously.

Turn the round end inside out, and tie the ends of Nymo®/beading thread in pairs, to secure the ends, and cut of the excess thread. You can use a dab of nail varnish to seal the Nymo®/beading thread knots.

Sliding Ring (knit two)

The rings are knitted with Beaded Garter Stitch being worked on every row, as follows:

Cast on 6sts, and knit 1 row.

Rows 1 to 4: (4 rows) k2, SB2, k2, SB2, k2.
Row 5: k2, SB1, k2, SB3, k2.
Row 6: k2, SB3, k2, SB1, k2.
Rows 7 to 8: (2 rows) repeat Rows 5 to 6.
Row 9: k2, SB1, k2, SB4, k2.
Row 10: k2, SB4, k2, SB1, k2.
Rows 11 to 12: (2 rows) repeat Rows 9 to 10.
Row 13: k2, SB2, k2, SB3, k2.
Row 14: k2, SB3, k2, SB2, k2.
Rows 15 to 16: (2 rows) repeat Rows 13 to 14.
Row 17: k2, SB3, k2, SB2, k2.
Row 18: k2, SB2, k2, SB3, k2.
Rows 19 to 20: (2 rows) repeat Rows 17 to 18.
Row 21: k2, SB4, k2, SB1, k2.
Row 22: k2, SB1, k2, SB4, k2.
Rows 23 to 24: (2 rows) repeat Rows 21 to 22.
Rows 25 to 28: (4 rows) repeat Rows 17 to 20.
Rows 29 to 32: (4 rows) repeat Rows 13 to 16.
Rows 33 to 36: (4 rows) repeat Rows 9 to 12.
Rows 37 to 40: (4 rows) repeat Rows 13 to 16.
Rows 41 to 44: (4 rows) repeat Rows 17 to 20.
Rows 45 to 48: (4 rows) repeat Rows 21 to 24.
Rows 49 to 52: (4 rows) repeat Rows 17 to 20.
Rows 53 to 56: (4 rows) repeat Rows 13 to 16.
Rows 57 to 60: (4 rows) k2, SB2, k2, SB2, k2.
Knit 1 row without beads.
Cast off.

Place the ring around the stocking-stitch sections of the purse, and, with a length of Pearl Cotton yarn, slip stitch the cast-on edge to the cast-off edge to close the ring.

Work the second Sliding Ring as for the first ring, but place the second ring around the stocking-stitch section of the purse before slip stitching the cast-on and cast-off edges as described previously.

KNITTED JEWELLERY
AND DECORATIONS

Christmas Baubles

The Christmas Baubles are knitted with a band of Bead Knitting as the decorative feature around the centre of each bauble. Using a 4ply/fingering-weight wool yarn, such as the yarn mentioned in the materials list, will make it easier to work the Bead-Knitting stitches, as such yarn has a lot of elasticity.

The patterns have been knitted with the twisted-stitch method of working the Bead-Knitting technique. Before starting to knit a particular bauble, you will need to thread the required beads on to the knitting yarn in reverse order. For detailed information about how to work Bead Knitting, *see* Chapter 2.

There may be a small amount of bias to the fabric, but, once the knitting is positioned around a polystyrene ball, the bias will not really be visible.

Diamond-Pattern Christmas Bauble, worked in Bead Knitting.

Star-Pattern Christmas Bauble, worked in Bead Knitting.

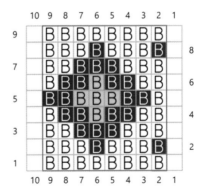

Chart for the Bead-Knitting Diamond-Pattern Christmas Bauble.

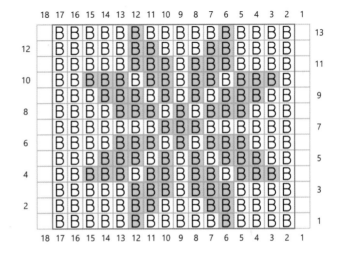

Chart for the Bead-Knitting Star-Pattern Christmas Bauble.

Size

- To fit a 20cm (8in)-circumference polystyrene ball, when the knitted fabric is stretched

Materials

- 1 × 50g (1¾oz) ball of 4ply/fingering-weight yarn, which is enough for making several baubles. The featured baubles were knitted with Adriafil Genziana 4ply/fingering-weight yarn, 100-per-cent wool, approx. 185m (202yd) per 50g ball, in shade no. 02 White.
- Size 8 seed beads: at least 270 beads of Colour 1, 132 beads of Colour 2 and 24 beads of Colour 3, for the Diamond-Pattern Christmas Bauble
- Note: If you work the pattern with two colours only, as shown for the featured sample, you will need at least 294 beads of Colour 1 and 132 beads of Colour 2.
- Size 8 seed beads: at least 393 beads of Colour 1 and 231 beads of Colour 2, for the Star-Pattern Christmas Bauble

- Pair of 3.00mm (US 2.5) needles
- 3.00mm (US D) crochet hook, for making the loop
- Tapestry needle
- Beading mat/container, for holding beads for threading
- Fine needle, threaded with a fine yarn that is tied into a loop, for threading beads on to yarn
- Two 20cm (8in)-circumference polystyrene balls or polyester stuffing

Tension

- 29sts and 38 rows in 10cm (4in) by using 3mm (US 2.5) needles, over stocking stitch. The tension swatch that was measured to determine the gauge was not washed.

Knitting Notes

Thread the beads on to the yarn in the correct order before you start to knit a particular bauble.

The chart for the Bead-Knitting Diamond-Pattern Christmas Bauble shows one repeat of the pattern, with a selvedge stitch at each side. The pattern repeat is worked six times within each row that is worked according to the chart. As the pattern starts on a wrong-side row, the beads must be threaded by starting with the top right-hand bead (on Row 9 of the chart), working to the left, and including the pattern-repeat bead sequence six times, before moving on to Row 8 of the chart and threading the corresponding beads by working from left to right, and so on.

The chart has been drawn to represent three colours of beads, but the charted pattern can be worked with two colours of beads, by placing the same colour of bead when working the yellow squares as the bead colour being placed when working the white squares.

The chart for the Bead-Knitting Star-Pattern Christmas Bauble shows one repeat of the pattern, with a selvedge stitch at each side. The pattern repeat is worked three times within each row that is worked according to the chart. The pattern starts on a right-side row and finishes after a right-side row. To thread the beads in the correct order, you need to start threading from the top left-hand corner (Row 13), working from left to right, including the pattern-repeat bead sequence three times. Row 12 will be threaded from right to left, including the pattern-repeat bead sequence three times, and so on.

For both baubles

Using 3.00mm (US 2.5) needles, leaving a long yarn tail to later close up the bottom of the knitted fabric, cast on 10sts.

Row 1 (RS): k1, *kfb*, repeat from * to * to the last stitch, k1 – 18sts.
Row 2 and all even-number rows: purl.
Row 3: k1, *kfb, k1*, repeat from * to * to the last stitch, k1 – 26sts.
Row 5: k1, *kfb, k2*, repeat from * to * to the last stitch, k1 – 34sts.
Row 7: k1, *kfb, k3*, repeat from * to * to the last stitch, k1 – 42sts.
Row 9: k1, *kfb, k4*, repeat from * to * to the last stitch, k1 – 50sts.
Row 10: purl.

For the Diamond-Pattern Christmas Bauble

Row 11: k1, *k1tbl*, repeat from * to * to the last stitch, k1. Work the Bead-Knitting Diamond-Pattern Christmas-Bauble Chart for one vertical repeat (9 rows), working the pattern repeat 6 times across each row. All stitches, apart from the first and last stitches, are worked as twisted Bead-Knitting stitches. Note: The chart starts with a WS row.
Next row: k1, *k1tbl*, repeat from * to * to the last stitch, k1.
Next row: purl.

For the Star-Pattern Christmas Bauble

Work the Bead-Knitting Star-Christmas-Bauble Chart for one vertical repeat (13 rows), working the pattern repeat 3 times across each row. All stitches, apart from the first and last stitches, are worked as twisted Bead-Knitting stitches.
Next row: p1, *p1tbl*, repeat from * to * to the last stitch, p1.

For both baubles

Decrease to shape the top of the bauble as follows:
Decrease Row 1 (RS): k1, *skpo, k4*, repeat from * to * to the last stitch, k1 – 42sts.
Decrease Row 2 and all even-number rows: purl.
Decrease Row 3: k1, *skpo, k3*, repeat from * to * to the last stitch, k1 – 34sts.
Decrease Row 5: k1, *skpo, k2*, repeat from * to * to the last stitch, k1 – 26sts.
Decrease Row 9: k1, *skpo, k1*, repeat from * to * to the last stitch, k1 – 18sts.
Decrease Row 11: k1, *skpo*, repeat from * to * to the last stitch, k1 – 10sts.
Next row: p1, *p2tog*, repeat from * to * to the last stitch, p1 – 5sts.
Cut the yarn, leaving a long yarn tail. With a sewing needle threaded with the yarn tail, pass the yarn tail through the open stitches, and pull the yarn tight, to close up the top of the knitting.

Finishing

With a sewing needle threaded with the yarn tail left at the start of the cast-on edge, draw the cast-on stitches together and then, using mattress stitch to form the start of the side seam, sew a few stitches. Insert a polystyrene ball into the fabric. Continue to sew the side seam, with the ball in place, so that the ball is evenly covered by the knitting.

If you are going to use polyester stuffing rather than a polystyrene ball to fill the centre of the bauble, before you start to insert the stuffing, you need to sew most of the side seam but still be able to get to the inside of the knitted bauble. Stuff the centre of the bauble as firmly as you can, and continue to sew the last few stitches, adding more stuffing as you go, until the bauble is firmly stuffed and the seam completed.

With a few stitches, secure the yarn tail that was used to draw together the stitches at the top of the knitting, to firmly close the top of the bauble.

If you still have a long yarn tail remaining after drawing together the cast-on edge and sewing the side seam, tie a slip knot as close to the top of the bauble as possible. Put this slip knot on to the crochet hook, and work approximately 30 chains. Fold the chain in half to make a loop, and secure the yarn tail to the top of the bauble, to form a hanging loop.

Run the two yarn tails along the side seam of the bauble, and cut off the ends so that they are not visible.

Alternatively, a hanging loop can be made from a length of ribbon that is passed through the top of the bauble and tied into a loop.

Necklaces

The three following necklace patterns are presented to be worked with No. 8 Pearl Cotton yarn. However, the patterns can also be knitted with fine yarns such as lace-weight silk and lace-weight silk-mix yarns. The silk yarns will provide drape, but the Pearl Cotton yarn provides more structure, to help maintain the shape of the necklaces.

For the featured samples, size 7 or size 8 seed beads were used with the Pearl Cotton yarn or lace-weight silk yarn, with the beads being threaded on to the yarn before the knitting of each necklace was started. The Wishbone Necklace also includes some accent beads, which are included on the cast-on row, so the beads must be threaded in the correct order before you start to knit this necklace.

Knitting Notes

The necklaces require the Knit Cast-On or a beaded variation.

The Beaded-Knitting Knit Cast-On is worked as follows. Place a slip knot on the left-hand needle, and class this slip knot as a stitch. *Push up a bead next to the stitch on the left-hand needle, knit into the stitch on the left-hand needle with the right-hand needle, pull the yarn through the stitch being knitted into, to make a new stitch on the right-hand needle, and place this new stitch in a twisted orientation on to the point of the left-hand needle.* Repeat from * to * until you have cast on the required number of stitches.

For each of the three necklaces, leave a long yarn end when casting on and off, to use when attaching the clasp.

The Scallop-Shell-Edging Necklace can be made longer by casting on more stitches in groups of five stitches at a time.

Both the Scallop-Shell-Edging Necklace and the Eyelet-Points Necklace can be made longer by adjusting the length of the bead strings between the ends of the knitted edging and the clasp.

The Wishbone Necklace includes short-row shaping.

Special Abbreviations
SB1 – slip up 1 bead next to the stitch just worked.
SB(number) – slip up the number of beads stated next to the stitch just worked.
w&t – wrap and turn. Knit to the turning point of the short row, slip the next stitch purlwise from the left-hand needle to the right-hand needle, bring the yarn forward between the points of the needles, slip the slipped stitch purlwise back to the left-hand needle, and turn the work.

Scallop-Shell-Edging Necklace

This necklace was developed as a result of swatching with some edging patterns. The whole length of the necklace is cast on, so it is important to be aware of the number of stitches in each pattern repeat, if you want to adjust the length of this necklace. The pattern repeat is a multiple of five stitches plus two stitches to balance the pattern.

Size

- Length of knitted edging approx. 36.5cm (14in), worked with Pearl Cotton yarn and size 7 seed beads
- Length of knitted edging approx. 27cm (10½in), worked with 2ply/lace-weight silk yarn and size 8 seed beads
- Note: The length of the necklace can be adjusted to the required finished length by adjusting the length of the bead strings between the ends of the edging and the clasp.

Materials

- 1 × 10g (½oz) ball of No. 8 Pearl Cotton yarn, approx. 85m (93yd) per ball, which will be enough for making at least two necklaces
  Or
  Approx. 40m (44yd) of lace-weight yarn
- Approx. 20g (¾oz) of size 7 or 8 seed beads, for one necklace
- Pair of 2.00mm (US 0) needles
- Clasp or other closure
- Tapestry needle
- Beading mat/container, for holding beads for threading
- Fine needle, threaded with a fine yarn that is tied into a loop, for threading beads on to yarn

Scallop-Shell-Edging Necklace, knitted with a 2ply/lace-weight silk yarn and size 8 seed beads.

Tension

- 24sts in 10cm (4in) by using 2.00mm (US 0) needles, with Pearl Cotton yarn and size 7 seed beads, in Beaded Garter Stitch with 1 bead placed between each stitch.
- 31sts in 10cm (4in) by using 2.00mm (US 0) needles, with 2ply/lace-weight silk yarn and size 8 seed beads, in Beaded Garter Stitch with 1 bead placed between each stitch.
- The samples were washed and blocked before measuring gauge.

Knitting Notes

Thread the beads on to the yarn before you start to knit the necklace.
  This necklace requires the Beaded-Knitting Knit Cast-On.

Necklace

Using Pearl Cotton yarn, threaded with beads, and 2.00mm (US 0) needles, cast on 132sts with the Beaded-Knitting Knit Cast-On.

Row 1 (RS): knit.

Row 2 (WS): k1, yo, *k5, slip successively the 4th, 3rd, 2nd, and 1st stitch just worked over the 5th stitch and off the right-hand needle, yo*, repeat from * to * to the last stitch, k1 – 55sts.

Row 3: p1, *(p1, yo, k1tbl) into the next stitch, p1*, repeat from * to * to the end of the row – 109sts.

Row 4: k2, k1tbl, *k3, k1tbl*, repeat from * to * to the last 2sts, k2.

Row 5: *k1, SB1*, repeat from * to * to the last stitch, k1.

Row 6: cast off by purling and slipping up a bead next to every stitch as you work across the row, and purl the last stitch to complete the cast off.

Finishing

Thread beads on to the yarn end to adjust the length of the necklace. Take the yarn end through the ring on one side of the clasp/closure a couple of times, and tie a half-hitch knot, to secure the yarn. Thread some more beads (the same number as included on the first section between the necklace and the clasp/closure), and attach the yarn end to the edge of the knitting. Sew in the yarn end securely.

Repeat from * to * for the other end of the necklace.

Put the necklace in lukewarm water, and squeeze the fabric gently to make sure that the yarn has thoroughly absorbed the water. Lay the necklace on a dry towel, and roll it in the towel to remove excess water. Lay the damp necklace on a flat surface, smoothing it into shape and, if necessary, pinning it to hold this shape. Leave it to dry completely.

Eyelet-Points Necklace

This necklace was also developed as a result of swatching with a number of edging patterns. The beads need to be threaded on to the yarn before you start to knit the necklace. The necklace is knitted sideways in Beaded Garter Stitch, so the necklace can be tried around the neck and adjusted for length, as required, while you are knitting, but remember to allow for the width of the clasp when adjusting the length of the necklace.

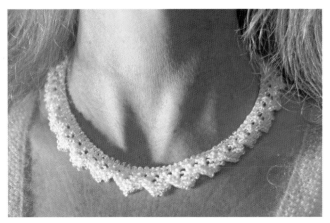

Eyelet-Points Necklace, knitted with No. 8 Pearl Cotton yarn and size 7 seed beads.

Size

- Length of knitted edging approx. 38cm (15in), worked with Pearl Cotton yarn and size 7 seed beads, measured over 23 repeats of the edging pattern
- Length of knitted edging approx. 37cm (14½in), worked with 2ply/lace-weight silk yarn and size 8 seed beads, measured over 20 repeats of the edging pattern

Materials

- 1 × 10g (½oz) ball of No. 8 Pearl Cotton yarn, approx. 85m (93yd) per ball, which will be enough for making at least two necklaces
  Or
  Approx. 40m (44yd) of lace-weight yarn
- Approx. 20g (¾oz) of size 7 or 8 seed beads, for one necklace
- Pair of 2.00mm (US 0) needles
- Clasp or other closure
- Tapestry needle
- Beading mat/container, for holding beads for threading
- Fine needle, threaded with a fine yarn that is tied into a loop, for threading beads on to yarn

Tension

- 48 rows in 10cm (4in) by using 2.00mm (US 0) needles, with Pearl Cotton yarn and size 7 seed beads, in the beaded edging pattern.
- 44 rows in 10cm (4in) by using 2.00mm (US 0) needles, with 2ply/lace-weight silk yarn and size 8 seed beads, in the beaded edging pattern.
- The samples were washed and blocked before measuring gauge.

Knitting Notes

Thread the beads on to the yarn before you start to knit the necklace.

This necklace requires the Knit Cast-On.

Note: On even-number rows, a bead is slipped up against the first stitch before that stitch is knitted.

Necklace

Using Pearl Cotton yarn, threaded with beads, and 2.00mm (US 0) needles, cast on 5sts with the Knit Cast-On.

Row 1 (RS): sl1, k1, yo twice, k2tog, k1 (on the first row after casting on, you may find it easier to knit the first 2sts rather than sl1, k1) – 6sts.
Row 2: *(SB1, k1) twice*, k1, p1, repeat from * to *.
Row 3: sl1, k3, yo twice, k2 – 8sts.
Row 4: *(SB1, k1) twice*, k1, p1, k2, repeat from * to *.
Row 5: sl1, k1, yo twice, k2tog, k4 – 9sts.
Row 6: *(SB1, k1) twice*, k4, p1, repeat from * to *.
Row 7: sl1, k8.
Row 8: slipping a bead up next to each stitch before it is knitted, cast off 4sts (5 beads), k2, (SB1, k1) twice.

Repeat Rows 1 to 8 for the required length of the necklace. Finish after a complete repeat (ending with Row 8).

Finishing

If necessary, the length of the necklace can be adjusted by adding beads to the yarn ends that are used to attach the clasp to the necklace.

Thread beads on to the yarn end to adjust the length of the necklace. Take the yarn end through the ring on one side of the clasp/closure a couple of times, and tie a half-hitch knot, to secure the yarn. Thread some more beads (the same number as included on the first section between the necklace and the clasp/closure), and attach the yarn end to the edge of the knitting. Sew in the yarn end securely.

Repeat from * to * for the other end of the necklace.

Put the necklace in lukewarm water, and squeeze the fabric gently to make sure that the yarn has thoroughly absorbed the water. Lay the necklace on a dry towel, and roll it in the towel to remove excess water. Lay the damp necklace on a flat surface, smoothing it into shape and, if necessary, pinning it to hold this shape. Leave it to dry completely.

Wishbone Necklace

For the Wishbone Necklace, beads are strung between stitches at the centre of the necklace on every row, as well as beads being placed between stitches in Beaded Garter Stitch on each side of the centre section. Accent beads are used to add detail within the cast-on row, so it is important to string the beads in the correct order before you start to knit the necklace.

Accent beads, such as drop beads or metallic antique-finish plastic beads, are generally larger beads than seed beads. If you chose to work with just accent beads for the centre section of the cast-on row, you will need nine beads, but, if you instead wish to use seed beads as spacers between the accent beads, you will need to string thirteen beads in total for this centre section (seven accent beads and six seed beads). The accent beads are the last beads to be threaded, as they are the first beads to be placed as part of the cast-on. If you want to use the combination of accent beads and seed beads, you require thirteen beads to be threaded alternately, as one accent bead and then one seed bead, finishing with an accent bead.

The shape of the necklace is also created by working short-row knitting around the centre section of the necklace. The necklace is worked in garter stitch, and the short rows are worked using the wrap-and-turn technique. The approach of using garter stitch with this short-row technique makes it much easier to work the short rows, as it is not necessary to pick up the wraps around the bases of wrapped stitches, as the garter stitch effectively hides the wraps. When you come to a wrapped stitch, simply continue knitting to the next wrap-and-turn point.

The featured modelled necklace was worked with No. 8 Pearl Cotton yarn, size 7 seed beads and antique-finish silver accent beads, but the necklace can be knitted with a wide range of yarns, including fine lace-weight, sock- and 4ply/fingering-weight yarns. The pattern is offered in two sizes.

Wishbone Necklace, knitted with No. 8 Pearl Cotton yarn and size 7 seed beads.

Details of samples of the Wishbone Necklace, showing different arrangements of accent beads and different yarns. From left to right, the necklaces were knitted with No. 8 Pearl Cotton yarn, two strands of a fine, lace-weight, wool yarn, and Katia Air Lux 4ply/fingering-weight yarn.

Size

- The inner circumference of the Pearl Cotton necklace, not including the clasp, is 42cm (16½in).
- The inner circumference of the 4ply/fingering-weight-yarn necklace, not including the clasp, is 38cm (15in).

Materials

- 1 × 10g (½oz) ball of No. 8 Pearl Cotton yarn, approx. 85m (93yd) per ball. The modelled sample was knitted with Anchor Pearl Cotton yarn in shade no. 343 Silver.
  Or
  Approx. 85m (93yd) of lace-weight or 4ply/fingering-weight yarn
- Pair of 2.00mm (US 0) needles, if working with Pearl Cotton yarn or fine lace-weight yarn
  Or
  Pair of 3.00mm (US 2.5) needles, if working with 4ply/fingering-weight yarn
- Size 8 seed beads: at least 370 beads, if working with Pearl Cotton yarn or fine lace-weight yarn
- Size 6 seed beads: at least 340 beads, if working with 4ply/fingering-weight yarn
- 9 accent beads (metallic antique-finish plastic beads)
  Or
  7 accent/drop beads and 6 seed beads
- Clasp or other closure
- Tapestry needle
- Beading mat/container, for holding beads for threading
- Fine needle, threaded with a fine yarn that is tied into a loop, for threading beads on to yarn

Tension

- 29sts in 10cm (4in) by using 2.00mm (US 0) needles and Pearl Cotton yarn, in garter stitch.
- 24sts in 10cm (4in) by using 3.00mm (US 2.5) needles and 4ply/fingering-weight yarn, in garter stitch.
- The samples were washed and blocked before measuring gauge.

Knitting Notes

Before you start to knit, you will need to thread on all of the seed beads followed by the nine accent beads or thirteen accent beads and seed beads.

This necklace requires the Knit Cast-On and includes short-row shaping.

Necklace

Using Pearl Cotton yarn[4ply/fingering-weight yarn], threaded with beads, and 2.00[3.00]mm (US 0[2.5]) needles, cast on 70[55]sts with the Knit Cast-On, slip up 9 (or 13) accent beads next to the last stitch that was cast on, work 1 Backward-Loop/Single-Thumb-Twist Cast-On and then cast on 69[54]sts with the Knit Cast-On – 140[110]sts.

Row 1 (RS): k70[55], SB15, k70[55].
Row 2: k10[3], *SB1, k1*, repeat from * to * to 4sts before the centre section, SB1, k2tog, (SB1, k1) twice, SB14, (k1, SB1) twice, k2tog, repeat from * to * to the last 9[2] sts, k9[2] – 138[108]sts.
Row 3: k69[54], SB13, k7, w&t.
Row 4: k3, k2tog, SB1, k2, SB12, k2, SB1, k2tog, k3, w&t.
Row 5: k6, SB11, k12, w&t.
Row 6: k8, k2tog, SB1, k2, SB10, k2, SB1, k2tog, k8, w&t.
Row 7: k11, SB9, k17, w&t.
Row 8: k13, k2tog, SB1, k2, SB8, k2, SB1, k2tog, k13, w&t.
Row 9: k16, SB7, k22, w&t.
Row 10: k18, k2tog, SB1, k2, SB6, k2, SB1, k2tog, k18, w&t.
Row 11: k21, SB5, k27, w&t.
Row 12: k23, k2tog, SB1, k2, SB4, k2, SB1, k2tog, k23, w&t.
Row 13: k26, SB3, knit to the end of the row.
Row 14: knit to 4sts before the centre section, k2tog, SB1, k2, SB2, k2, SB1, k2tog, knit to the end of the row – 126[96]sts.
Row 15: knit to the centre section, SB1, knit to the end of the row.
Row 16: k10[3], *SB1, k1*, repeat from * to * to 2sts before the centre section, SB1, k2tog, k2tog, repeat from * to * to the last 9[2]sts, k9[2] – 124[94]sts.

Cast off by using the Sewn Cast-Off, or knit 1 more row and then cast off.

Finishing

Sew on the clasp/closure, and sew in the yarn ends (*see* the section 'Finishing' for the Scallop-Shell-Edging Necklace or the Eyelet-Points Necklace for additional instructions to complete this step).

Put the necklace in lukewarm water, and squeeze the fabric gently to make sure that the yarn has thoroughly absorbed the water. Lay the necklace on a dry towel, and roll it in the towel to remove excess water. Lay the damp necklace on a flat surface, smoothing it into shape and, if necessary, pinning it to hold this shape. Leave it to dry completely.

JEWELLERY KNITTED WITH WIRE

Knitted jewellery can also be made by using less traditional materials, such as coloured enamelled copper wire, silver wire or even gold wire if you can afford it. A detailed explanation of knitting with wire is covered in Chapter 6.

Bead-and-Wire Bracelet

This is a very easy introduction to knitting with beads and wire. The bracelet is knitted in Beaded Garter Stitch, with a bead being placed between stitches on every other row. The beads must be threaded on to the wire before you start to knit. A mixture of beads was used for the sample bracelet, including size 10, size 8 and size 6 seed beads and 3mm bugle beads, in a variety of colours.

As wire-knitted fabric does not generally change in width following the cast-on edge (it neither flares out or pulls in above the cast-on edge), you can adjust the width of the bracelet fairly easily by casting on more stitches until the cast-on is of the required width.

Bead-and-Wire Bracelet, knitted with 0.20mm enamelled copper wire and a mixture of size 10, size 8 and size 6 seed beads and 3mm bugle beads.

Size

- Length 15cm (6in); width 3cm (1¼in)

Materials

- 1 × 35g (1¼oz) reel of 0.20mm enamelled copper wire, approx. 125m (136yd) per reel
- 20g (¾oz) of mixed-colour beads
- Pair of 2.00mm (US 0) needles
- Barrel clasp or other closure
- Jewellery pliers, for finishing
- Beading mat/container, for holding beads for threading

Tension

- 15sts and 26 rows in 5cm (2in) by using 2.00mm (US 0) needles, in Beaded Garter Stitch with 1 bead placed between each stitch on wrong-side rows.

Knitting Notes

Thread the beads on to the wire before you start to knit the bracelet. Thread enough beads to work the whole bracelet. The beads will slip down the wire quite easily, so it is better to thread more beads than not enough.

If you have not threaded enough beads at the start but are near the end of the bracelet, reel off enough wire to finish the knitting, cut the wire and thread beads on to this cut end, then complete the knitting of the bracelet.

This bracelet requires the Knit Cast-On.

Special Abbreviation
SB1 – slip up 1 bead next to the stitch just worked.

Bracelet

Using 2.00mm (US 0) needles, leaving a long end of wire to use to connect the clasp/closure to the beginning of the bracelet, cast on 15sts with the Knit Cast-On.

Row 1 (RS): knit.
Row 2: k1, *SB1, k1*, repeat from * to * to the end of the row.
Repeat Rows 1 and 2 for the desired length of the cuff.

Knit 1 more row.
Cast off, and leave a long end of wire to connect the clasp/closure to the end of the bracelet.

Finishing

The clasp/closure should have loops on each side by which the clasp/closure can be attached to the knitting. Pass one long end of wire through the edge of the knitting, one stitch at a time, until it is at the appropriate position to join one end of the closure. Pass the wire through a loop on the closure and through the knitted edge several times. If there are several loops on one side of the closure, move on to the next loop, as before, and join it to the knitting, and so on, until the closure is firmly joined to the knitting along the full length of the closure. Repeat this joining process at the other end of the bracelet, with the other long end of wire and the other side of the closure. Use jewellery pliers to twist and pinch each wire end to the knitted fabric. Cut the wire, and, if possible, try to bury the ends of the wires in a bead hole.

Leaf-Plait Necklace

This necklace is made up of three lengths of knitting that are plaited together to make the finished necklace. Each length is made by using a different combination of wire and yarn. One length is worked by using two strands of wire, each of a different colour, one length is worked by using one strand of wire and beads, and one length is worked by using one strand each of wire and a lace-weight yarn. All three lengths could be made the same, if you prefer. The accent beads at the ends of each leaf add some weight, to make the necklace hang better.

Size

- The 3 strips of knitting are between 84cm (33 in) and 89cm (35in) in length after plaiting but before being made into the lariat syle necklace. The plait is 2cm (¾ in) wide.

Materials

- 1 × 35g (1¼oz) reel of 0.20mm enamelled copper wire in Colour 1, approx. 125m (136yd) per reel
- 1 × 35g (1¼oz) reel of 0.20mm enamelled copper wire in Colour 2, approx. 125m (136yd) per reel
- Approx. 125m (136yd) of fine lace-weight yarn; for example, Rowan Fine Lace or Garnstudio Drops Lace Alpaca
- Approx. 15g (½oz) of mixed-size beads, including size 10, 8 and 6 seed beads and small bugle beads
- 3 accent beads, such as tear-drop beads
- Pair of 2.00mm (US 0) needles
- Pair of 2.50mm (US 1.5) needles
- Tapestry needle
- Beading mat/container, for holding beads for threading
- Jewellery pliers

Tension

- 15sts and 26 rows in 5cm (2in) by using 2.00mm (US 0) needles, in Beaded Garter Stitch with 1 bead placed between each stitch on wrong-side rows.

Leaf-Plait Necklace.

Knitting Notes

When making the Beaded Leaf Length, you will need to thread the beads on to the wire before you start to knit the piece.

The Two-Wire-Strands Leaf Length is worked with two slightly different colours of 0.20mm wire. To help the wire from each reel to wind off at the same rate, put a long knitting needle or thin dowel through the centre of each reel, and suspend the needle horizontally across a bowl or old shoe box. The reels then can turn more smoothly as you draw on the wires.

Special Abbreviation
SB1 – slip up 1 bead next to the stitch just worked.

Beaded Leaf Length

Thread approx. 540 beads on to 1 reel of wire.

Using 2.00mm (US 0) needles, leaving a tail end of approx. 20cm (8in), cast on 4sts.

Row 1 (RS): knit.
Row 2: *k1, SB1*, repeat from * to * to the last stitch, k1.
Repeat Rows 1 and 2 of Beaded Garter Stitch until the piece is between 95cm and 100cm (37in and 39in) in length.
Next row: k1, k2tog, k1 – 3sts.
Next row: purl.
Next row: knit.
Repeat these last 2 rows, 2 times, and then purl 1 row.

Leaf

Row 1: k1, yo, k1, yo, k1 – 5sts.
All even-number rows: *k1, SB1*, repeat from * to * to the last stitch, k1.
Row 3: k2, yo, k1, yo, k2 – 7sts.
Row 5: k3, yo, k1, yo, k3 – 9sts.
Row 7: k4, yo, k1, yo, k4 – 11sts.
Row 9: knit.
Row 11: k2tog, knit to the last 2sts, ssk – 9sts.
Row 13: k2tog, knit to the last 2sts, ssk – 7sts.
Row 15: k2tog, knit to the last 2sts, ssk – 5sts.
Row 17: k2tog, knit to the last 2sts, ssk – 3sts.
Row 19: sk2po.
Cut the wire, leaving a tail end of 15cm to 20cm (6in to 8in), and pull this end through the last stitch.

Two-Wire-Strands Leaf Length

Using 2.50mm (US 1.5) needles and 2 strands of wire held together, cast on 3sts.

Knit every row until the length measures between 95cm and 100cm (37in and 39in). The length of this piece can be slightly different to the length of the Beaded-Garter-Stitch piece.

Work 6 rows of stocking stitch.

Leaf

Row 1 (RS): k1, yo, k1, yo, k1 – 5sts.
All even-number rows: purl.
Row 3: k2, yo, k1, yo, k2 – 7sts.
Row 5: k3, yo, k1, yo, k3 – 9sts.
Row 7: k4, yo, k1, yo, k4 – 11sts.
Row 9: knit.
Row 11: k2tog, knit to the last 2sts, ssk – 9sts.

Row 13: k2tog, knit to the last 2sts, ssk – 7sts.
Row 15: k2tog, knit to the last 2sts, ssk – 5sts.
Row 17: k2tog, knit to the last 2sts, ssk – 3sts.
Row 19: sk2po.
Cut the wires, leaving tail ends of 15cm to 20cm (6in to 8in), and pull these ends through the last stitch.

Lace-Weight-Yarn-and-Wire Leaf Length

Using 2.50mm (US 1.5) needles and 1 strand of wire and 1 strand of lace-weight yarn held together, cast on 3sts.

Work in stocking stitch (knit 1 row, purl 1 row, alternately) until the length measures between 95cm and 100cm (37in and 39in). Again, this can be a slightly different length to the other two pieces of knitting.

Leaf

Row 1 (RS): k1, yo, k1, yo, k1 – 5sts.
All even-number rows: purl.
Row 3: k2, yo, k1, yo, k2 – 7sts.
Row 5: k3, yo, k1, yo, k3 – 9sts.
Row 7: k4, yo, k1, yo, k4 – 11sts.
Row 9: knit.
Row 11: k2tog, knit to last the 2sts, ssk – 9sts.
Row 13: k2tog, knit to last the 2sts, ssk – 7sts.
Row 15: k2tog, knit to last the 2sts, ssk – 5sts.
Row 17: k2tog, knit to last the 2sts, ssk – 3sts.
Row 19: sk2po.
Cut the yarn and wire, leaving tail ends of 15cm to 20cm (6in to 8 in), and pull these ends through the last stitch.

Finishing

Holding the 3 cast-on ends together, plait the 3 lengths together for about 88cm (35in). Pinch the 3 lengths together at this point, and, using 2 lengths of wire, wrap the pinched point several times, to keep the 3 lengths plaited together. Sew in the wire ends. At the cast-on end, twist all of the yarn/ wire ends together. Fold over the cast-on end to make a loop that is approximately 5cm (2in) in height, so large enough to allow the leaves to fit through, and wrap the yarn/wire ends around the plait to close the loop. Sew in the yarn/wire ends.

Add an accent bead to the end of each leaf, by threading one accent bead on to one tail end, then threading a small seed bead on to the same tail end and passing the tail end back through the accent bead. Sew in and secure all of the remaining yarn/wire ends.

Lace-and-Beads Bracelet

This design has been worked in Pearl Cotton yarn and in wire, to show how one design can be worked with different materials. For both bracelets, size 6 seed beads were threaded on to the wire or yarn before the knitting was started, to be included in edge sections of each bracelet, and accent beads were added to the centre of the lace pattern by using the crochet-hook method.

For the wire version, two strands of slightly differently coloured wires were used for knitting. The knitting process is the same for both bracelets.

As well as by using wire, the bracelet can also be knitted with a fine lace-weight yarn or a 4ply/fingering-weight yarn. A size 6 bead will fit on to a wide range of yarns, as well as being able to fit over a stitch when added by using a crochet hook. Details of how to add a bead with a crochet hook are covered in Chapter 5.

The bracelet can be finished with a clasp/closure, but, if you prefer, you can work some buttonholes, as instructed at the end of the pattern, and add decorative buttons with which to fasten the bracelet. If you are making a wire bracelet, it would be better to use a barrel clasp or other closure.

Size

- Bracelet knitted with No. 8 Pearl Cotton yarn on 2.00mm (US 0) needles, 4cm (1½in) wide by 15.5cm (6in) long, not including the clasp – 9 repeats of the pattern.
- Bracelet knitted with 2 strands of wire on 2.00mm (US 0) needles, 5.5cm (2¼in) wide by 16cm (6¼in) long, not including the clasp – 7 repeats of the pattern.
- Bracelet knitted with 4ply/fingering-weight yarn on 3.25mm (US 3) needles, 5.5cm (2¼in) wide by 17cm (6¾in) long, not including the clasp – 7 repeats of the pattern.

Lace-and-Beads Bracelet, worked in Pearl Cotton yarn with Czech Silver-Lined Clear size 6 seed beads and silver antique-finish plastic rosebud accent beads.

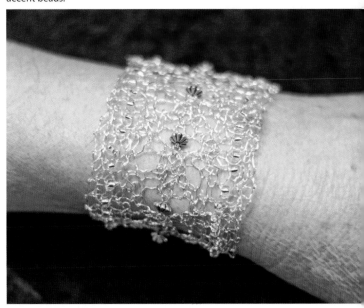

Lace-and-Beads Bracelet, worked in two strands of fine craft wire with Czech Silver-Lined Clear size 6 seed beads and silver antique-finish plastic rosebud accent beads.

Materials

- 1 × 10g (½oz) ball of No. 8 Pearl Cotton yarn, approx. 85m (93yd) per ball. The featured sample was knitted with Anchor Pearl Cotton yarn in shade no. 403 Black.
Or
Approx. 85m (93yd) of lace-weight yarn or 4ply/fingering-weight yarn that will allow the knitted fabric to drape
Or
- 1 × 35g (1¼oz) reel of 0.20mm enamelled copper wire in Colour 1, approx. 125m (136yd) per reel and 1 × 35g (1¼oz) reel of 0.20mm enamelled copper wire in Colour 2, approx. 125m (136yd) per reel, with 1 strand of each wire to be held together for knitting
- Pair of 2.00mm (US 0) needles, for working with wire and lace-weight yarn
Or
Pair of 3.25mm (US 3) needles, for working with 4ply/fingering-weight yarn
- 0.60mm or 0.75mm (US steel hook 14) crochet hook, for placing beads
- Approx. 100 size 8 or 6 seed beads
- 7 to 9 accent beads (with a hole large enough for the end of the crochet hook to pass through), depending on the yarn thickness used and the bracelet length required
- Barrel clasp or other closure
Or
Buttons
- Beading mat/container, for holding beads for threading
- Beading needle, threaded with doubled, fine thread, for threading beads on to the yarn

Tension

- 48 rows/6 pattern repeats in 10cm (4in) by using 2.00mm (US 0) needles and No. 8 Pearl Cotton yarn, over the bead-and-lace stitch pattern.
- 40 rows/5 pattern repeats in 10cm (4in) by using 2.00mm (US 0) needles and 2 strands of 0.20mm wire held together, over the bead-and-lace stitch pattern.
- 36 rows/4.5 pattern repeats in 10cm (4in) by using 3.25mm (US 3) needles and 4ply/fingering-weight wool yarn, over the bead-and-lace stitch pattern.

Knitting Notes

Thread the seed beads on to the wire or yarn before you start to knit the bracelet.

The seed beads are pushed up next to a stitch on wrong-side rows.

If making the wire version of the bracelet, to help the wire wind off each reel at the same rate, put a long knitting needle or thin dowel through the centre of each reel, and suspend the needle horizontally across a bowl or old shoe box. The reels then can turn more smoothly as you draw on the wires.

Use a small container to hold the beads that will be added by using the crochet-hook method.

To adjust the length of the bracelet, work complete repeats of the lace pattern, and then work some extra rows of garter stitch, if necessary.

Three-stitch buttonholes worked over two rows
Knit to the position of the first buttonhole. Cast off the next 3sts on the left-hand needle. *Knit to the position of the next buttonhole. Cast off the next 3sts on the left-hand needle.* Repeat from * to * until you have cast off the required number of groups of 3sts to correspond to the desired number of buttonholes. Knit to the end of the row.

Knit to the first group of cast-off stitches. *Turn the knitting. Using the Cable Cast-On, cast on 3sts, but, before placing the third new stitch on to the left-hand needle, bring the yarn between the points of the needles and then place the third stitch on to the left-hand needle as normal. Turn the knitting, and knit to the next group of cast-off stitches.* Repeat from * to * until all groups of cast-off stitches have been worked over by casting on 3sts. Knit to the end of the row.

Special Abbreviations
hB – place 1 accent bead on to the crochet hook, slip the next stitch on the left-hand needle on to the crochet hook, push the bead off of the crochet hook and over the stitch, and re-place the stitch on to the left-hand needle. Work the stitch as a knit stitch.
SB1 – slip up 1 bead next to the stitch just worked.

Bracelet

Using your chosen wire or yarn and needles, cast on 13sts. Knit 3 rows.

Next row (WS): k2, SB1, k9, SB1, k2 (this sets the position of the placement of seed beads on every WS row).

Lace Pattern

Row 1 (RS): k4, yo, ssk, k1, k2tog, yo, k4.

Row 2 and all even-number rows: k2, SB1, k1, p7, k1, SB1, k2.

Row 3: k4, yo, k1, sk2po, k1, yo, k4.

Row 5: k4, k2tog, yo, hB, yo, ssk, k4.

Row 7: k3, k2tog, k1, yo, k1, yo, k1, ssk, k3.

Row 8: k2, SB1, k1, p7, k1, SB1, k2.

Repeat Rows 1 to 8 of the Lace Pattern the number of times needed to achieve the length of knitting that you require for your bracelet (between 7 and 9 repeats).

Knit 1 row.

Next row: k2, *SB1, k1*, repeat from * to * to the last stitch, k1.

Next row: knit.

If you want to fasten the bracelet with buttons rather than a clasp:

Next row: k2, SB1, k9, SB1, k2.

Buttonhole Row: k2, make a 3st buttonhole (*see* the Knitting-Notes box), k3, make a 3st buttonhole, k2.

And/or continue to the end of the pattern as follows:

Next row: k2, SB1, k9, SB1, k2.

Next row: knit.

Next row: k2, *SB1, k1*, repeat from * to * to the last stitch, k1.

Next row: knit.

Cast off.

Finishing

Sew on a clasp/closure to both ends of the bracelet, or, on the end of the bracelet opposite the buttonholes, sew on the required number of buttons to match the number of buttonholes, with 1 button in line with each buttonhole. Sew in and secure the yarn or wire ends.

For a yarn-knitted bracelet, wet the bracelet, then place it on a clean towel. Roll it in the towel to remove excess water. Smooth out the fabric until it is flat and pin it in position, if necessary, to open out the lace pattern. Leave it to dry completely.

JEWELLERY KNITTED WITH MONOFILAMENT NYLON FISHING LINE

Beaded Cuff

The Beaded Cuff is worked in Beaded Garter Stitch with a bead being placed between each stitch on wrong-side rows. The cuff is worn with the knitting running sideways, as garter stitch adds vertical flexibility to the fabric, allowing the cuff to be pulled on over the hand.

Using a clear monofilament nylon fishing line makes the beads look as though they are suspended in air. A mixture of colours of size 10 beads has been used, adding interest and making this cuff a good project for using up lots of leftover beads.

Size

* Length (before seaming) 15cm (6in); width 4cm (1½in)
* Note: The length of the cuff can easily be modified to match your wrist circumference.

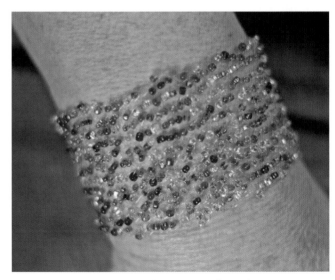

Beaded Cuff, worked with monofilament nylon fishing line.

Materials

- 1 reel of 0.18mm to 0.20mm monofilament nylon fishing line, approx. 100m (109yd) per reel
- Pair of 2.00mm (US 0) needles
- Spare 2.00mm (US 0) needle, or one size smaller, for working the Three-Needle Cast-Off
- 20g (¾oz) of size 10 or 11 seed beads, in a mixture of colours
- Beading mat/container, for holding beads for threading
- Beading needle, threaded with doubled, fine thread, for threading beads on to the yarn
- Clear nail vanish

Tension

- 16sts and 23 rows in 5cm (2in) by using 2.00mm (US 0) needles and 0.18mm monofilament nylon fishing line, over Beaded Garter Stitch with 1 bead placed between each stitch on wrong-side rows.

Knitting Notes

Thread the beads on to the monofilament nylon fishing line before you start to knit the cuff. Thread more beads than you think you may need, as it is easy to push the beads along the nylon fishing line.

If you have not threaded enough beads but are near the end of the bracelet, reel off enough nylon fishing line to finish the knitting. Cut the nylon fishing line, thread on the extra beads from this cut end and then complete the knitting of the bracelet.

This cuff requires the Knit Cast-On.

Measure your wrist to allow you to decide on the required length of the cuff, which needs to be approximately the circumference of your wrist.

For detailed information about how to join the cast-on and cast-off edges to finish the cuff, *see* the section 'Three-Needle Cast-Off' in Chapter 7.

Special Abbreviation
SB1 – slip up 1 bead next to the stitch just worked.

Cuff

Using 2.00mm (US 0) needles, cast on 13sts with the Knit Cast-On.

Row 1 (RS): knit.

Row 2: k1, *SB1, k1*, repeat from * to * to the end of the row.

Repeat Rows 1 and 2 until the strip of knitting is of the required length, finishing after Row 1.

Finishing

Using a spare needle of the same size as the main needles (or one size smaller), pick up the 13 loops from the cast-on edge.

Fold the strip in half, with right sides together, and position the needle holding the cast-on edge at the front and the needle holding the open stitches at the back. With both main needles in your left hand and the spare needle in your right hand, work a Three-Needle Cast-Off, to join the beginning and end of the strip.

Weave in the ends of the nylon fishing line, working a half-hitch knot a couple of times as part of the weaving-in process. Dab a spot of clear nail varnish on to the half-hitch knots, to keep them from coming undone.

Shell Necklace

The Shell Necklace uses a technique that was originally developed for a machine-knitted edging. It is worked in Beaded Garter Stitch with clear monofilament nylon fishing line and size 10 seed beads. A strip of knitting is worked first, and then the necklace shape is formed by manipulation of this strip, once the knitting is completed.

Size

- Length 40cm (15¾in), not including the clasp

Materials

- 1 reel of 0.18mm or 0.20mm monofilament nylon fishing line, approx. 100m (109yd) per reel
- Pair of 2.00mm (US 0) needles
- 20g (¾oz) of size 10 or 11 seed beads
- Clasp or other closure
- Beading mat/container, for holding beads for threading
- Beading needle, threaded with doubled, fine thread, for threading beads on to the yarn
- Clear nail vanish

Tension

- 16sts and 23 rows in 5cm (2in) by using 2.00mm (US 0) needles and 0.18mm monofilament nylon fishing line, over Beaded Garter Stitch with 1 bead placed between each stitch on wrong-side rows.

Knitting Notes

Thread the beads on to the monofilament nylon fishing line before you start to knit the necklace. Thread all of the beads. The beads will slide along the nylon without wearing the fishing line, and it is better to have too many beads when knitting with nylon fishing line than not enough.

If you run out of beads and are near the end of the necklace, reel off enough nylon fishing line to finish the knitting. Cut the nylon fishing line, thread more beads on to the fishing line from the cut end and then complete the knitting of the necklace.

This necklace requires the Knit Cast-On.

Be aware that the necklace will shorten in length once the knitting has been threaded through on itself, as it is passed through the eyelet holes to make the shell shapes of the necklace.

Special Abbreviation
SB1 – slip up 1 bead next to the stitch just worked.

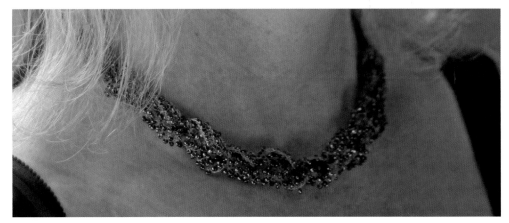

Shell Necklace, worked with monofilament nylon fishing line and Czech size 10 seed beads.

Necklace

Using 2.00mm (US 0) needles, leaving a long tail for attaching the clasp, cast on 10sts with the Knit Cast-On.

Rows 1, 3, 5, 7, 9, 11, 13, 15 and 17 (RS): knit.

Rows 2, 4, 6, 8, 10, 12, 14, 16 and 18: k1, *SB1, k1*, repeat from * to * to the end of the row.

Row 19: k3, k2tog, yo twice, skpo, k3.

Row 20: still slipping 1 bead up between each stitch (as for all WS rows), k4, knit the first yarn-over loop normally, knit into the back loop of the second yarn-over loop, k4.

Repeat Rows 1 to 20 until the necklace measures 41cm (16in), or the required length of the necklace, finishing after a RS row.

Cast off, and leave a long tail for attaching the clasp.

Finishing

The knitted strip has to be manipulated to make the shell shapes of the necklace. With the beaded side facing you and starting with the eyelet hole nearest the end of the strip, *take the cast-on edge and push it through the eyelet hole from the non-beaded side to the beaded side of the strip, pulling the rest of the strip through the hole to make a twist in the knitting at this point.*

Moving to the next eyelet hole along the strip, repeat from * to *, and keep repeating this process until the strip has been pulled through every eyelet hole. As you progress along the strip, there will be less knitting to pull through the eyelet hole each time.

Using the two nylon tails, attach the clasp to each end of the knitted strip, and weave in the ends of these nylon tails. If necessary, use a dab of clear nail vanish to seal the ends of the nylon tails in place.

The cast-on edge is being pulled through an eyelet hole, to create a twist in the knitting at this point.

ACCESSORIES

Icicle Wristlets

These wristlets are based on the Norwegian beaded cuffs that are traditionally used to dress up everyday wear for special occasions. They can be worn on their own as decorative wristlets or used as cuffs for garments, gloves and mittens.

The wristlets include Beaded Garter Stitch, with the beads forming the decorative pattern being placed when knitting wrong-side rows. This technique is covered in Chapter 3. The placement of the beads is presented in the Icicle Chart.

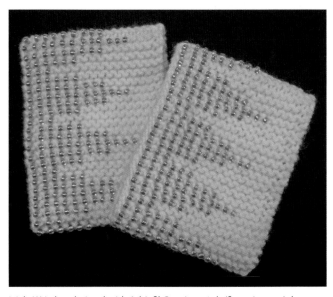

Icicle Wristlets, knitted with Adriafil Genziana 4ply/fingering-weight yarn and Miyuki size 8 Seafoam-Lined Crystal AB seed beads.

Size

- Length (before seaming) approx. 17cm (6¾in), measured over 8 vertical repeats of the beaded pattern; width 6.5cm (2½in)
- Note: Measure your wrist before starting the project, to allow you to determine the required number of repeats of the Icicle Chart to achieve the necessary wristlet circumference. The height of 1 pattern repeat in 4ply/fingering-weight yarn measures approximately 2cm (¾in).

Materials

- 1 × 50g (1¾oz) ball of 4ply/fingering-weight yarn. The yarn used in the sample was Adriafil Genziana 4ply/fingering-weight yarn, 100-per-cent wool, approx. 185m (202yd) per ball, in shade no. 02 White.
- 20g (¾oz) of size 7 or 8 seed beads. The beads used in the sample were Miyuki size 8 Seafoam-Lined Crystal AB seed beads.
- Pair of 3.00mm (US 2.5) needles
- Spare 3.00mm (US 2.5) needle, or one size smaller, for working the Three-Needle Cast-Off
- Tapestry needle
- Beading mat/container, for holding beads for threading
- Big Eye beading needle, or beading needle threaded with transition thread, for threading beads on to yarn

Tension

- 13.5sts and 14 ridges in 5cm (2in) by using 3.00mm (US 2.5) needles and 4ply/fingering-weight yarn, over Beaded Garter Stitch.

Knitting Notes

Thread the beads on to the yarn before you start to knit each wristlet.

These wristlets require the Knit Cast-On.

The Icicle Wristlets are knitted with Beaded Garter Stitch. The beads are placed on wrong-side rows.

On the chart, only the wrong-side rows are shown, and the row numbers relate to the ridge numbers of the garter-stitch fabric The chart is read from right to left for every wrong-side row.

The bead pattern on the chart will be mirrored when viewed from the right side of the knitted fabric.

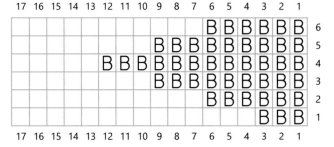

Beaded-Garter-Stitch Icicle Chart

Wristlet (knit two)

Using 3.00mm (US 2.5) needles, cast on 17sts with the Knit Cast-On.

Row 1 (RS): knit.

Row 2: knit a beaded-pattern row by following Row 1 of the Icicle Chart and, as indicated on the chart, pushing up a bead against the stitch just knitted.

Continue knitting the wristlet, working RS rows as knit only and WS rows as Beaded Knitting, by following the Icicle Chart.

Repeat the beaded pattern according to the chart until the fabric fits snugly around the wrist, finishing after Row 6 of the chart.

Finishing

Using a spare needle of the same size as the main needles, or one size smaller, pick up the 17 loops from the cast-on edge.

Fold the fabric in half, with right sides together, and position the needle holding the cast-on edge at the front and the needle holding the open stitches at the back. With both main needles in your left hand and the spare needle in your right hand, work a Three-Needle Cast-Off, to join the beginning and end of the wristlet.

If you prefer, cast off after the required number of repeats, and sew the cast-on and cast-off edges together, with the seam to be located on the inside of each wristlet.

Sew in the yarn ends.

Flying-V Mittens

These mittens are knitted by using one of the Beaded-Stocking-Stitch techniques covered in Chapter 3. Beads are strung between purl stitches in the knit two purl two rib and again between purl stitches in the stocking-stitch section on the upper part of each mitten.

The mittens are knitted in the round with a set of four double-pointed needles, two circular needles or, if the Magic-Loop technique is being used, one long circular needle. The Flying-V Chart is presented for knitting in the round. Every round is shown on the chart, and every row of the chart is read from right to left.

You will knit a right and a left mitten, and the position of the beaded pattern on the mitten is set by using stitch markers, as the chart shows only the beaded-pattern stitches. Two versions of the pattern are provided: the first is for when you are working with double-pointed needles, and the second is for when you are working with two circular needles or, if the Magic-Loop technique is being used, one long circular needle.

Flying-V Mittens, knitted with Debbie Bliss Rialto 4ply/fingering-weight yarn and Matubo™ size 7 Magic Yellow/Brown seed beads.

Sizes

	Women's Small	Women's Medium	Women's Large
Hand circumference	17cm (6¾in)	19cm (7½in)	20.5cm (8in)
Finished circumference	16.5cm (6½in)	18cm (7in)	19cm (7½in)
Cuff length	6cm (2½in)	6cm (2½in)	6cm (2½in)
Hand length (including top rib)	11.5cm (4½in)	12.5cm (5in)	14cm (5½in)

Materials

- 1 × 50g (1¾oz) ball of 4ply/fingering-weight yarn. The featured mittens were knitted with Debbie Bliss Rialto 4ply/fingering-weight yarn, 100-per-cent merino wool, approx. 180m (197yd) per ball, in shade no. 028 Tangerine.
- Four 3.00mm (US 2.5) double-pointed needles
  Or
  Two 3.00mm × 60cm (US 2.5 × 24in) circular needles
  Or
  One 3.00mm × 80cm (US 2.5 × 32in) circular needle
- 30g (1oz) of size 7 or 8 seed beads. The featured mittens include Matubo™ size 7 Magic Yellow Brown seed beads.
- 1 stitch/thread marker, for marking the beginning/end of the round

- 1 or 2 stitch marker(s) of another colour, for marking the beaded pattern
- 2 stitch markers of a third colour, for marking the thumb gusset
- Stitch-holder thread, for holding stitches
- Tapestry needle
- Beading mat/container, for holding beads for threading
- Big Eye beading needle, or beading needle threaded with transition thread, for threading beads on to yarn

Tension

- 29sts and 42 rows in 10cm (4in) by using 3.00mm (US 2.5) needles, in stocking stitch worked in the round.

Knitting Notes

Thread the beads on to the yarn before you start to knit each mitten.

The mittens are worked in Beaded Stocking Stitch, with the beads placed between purl stitches. The placement of beads for the upper part of each mitten is presented in the Flying-V Chart. The mittens are knitted in the round, so every row of the chart is read from right to left.

Two versions of the pattern are provided: the first is for when you are working with double-pointed needles, and the second is for when you are working with two circular needles or, if the Magic-Loop technique is being used, one long circular needle.

These mittens require the Picot Cast-On, which is a decorative variation of the Cable Cast-On. Detailed instructions of how to work the Picot Cast-On can be found in Chapter 7.

When working the pattern version to be worked with double-pointed needles, 'N1' signifies the first needle of the round (to the left of the beginning/end-of-the-round marker), 'N2' signifies the second needle of the round and 'N3' signifies the third needle of the round (to the right of the beginning/end-of-the-round marker), and the remaining, fourth needle is held in the right hand, for working the stitches.

Beads are also placed within the cuff of each mitten.

Special Abbreviation
SB1 – slip up 1 bead next to the stitch just worked.

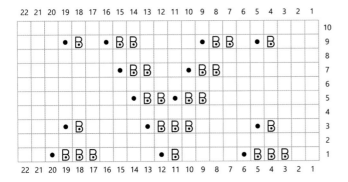

Flying-V Chart.

Mittens pattern worked with double-pointed needles

Right-Hand Mitten
Using 2 × 3.00mm (US 2.5) double-pointed needles, cast on 48[52: 56]sts with the Picot Cast-On as follows:

Cast on 5sts, *knit and cast off the next 2sts, slip the working stitch purlwise to the left-hand needle, cast on 4sts*, repeat from * to * until 47[51: 55]sts are present on the right-hand needle, cast on 1st.

Join the cast-on stitches into a circle, by slipping 16sts on to N1, 16sts on to N2 and leaving 16[20: 24]sts on N3.

When joining, take care not to twist the cast-on edge.

Cuff
Work in rib as follows: k1, *p2, k2*, repeat from * to * to the last 3sts, p2, k1.

Place a stitch marker/thread, to mark the beginning/end of the round.

Work a second round in rib.

Beaded-Rib Pattern
Round 1: k1, *p1, SB1, p1, k2*, repeat from * to * to the last 3sts, p1, SB1, p1, k1.

Round 2: k1, *p2, k2*, repeat from * to * to the last 3sts, p2, k1.

Repeat Rounds 1 and 2, 10 times in total.

Repeat Round 2 once more.

Lower hand
Change to working in stocking stitch. Reorganize your stitches as follows: 11[12: 14]sts on N1, 12[13: 15]sts on N2 and 25[27: 27]sts on N3.

Work 1[1: 3] round(s) of stocking stitch.

Beaded-Stocking-Stitch section
Next round: knit over N1 and N2; on N3, start working the beaded pattern by following the Flying-V Chart over the next 22sts, pm to mark the end of the stitch pattern, remembering to slip this marker when reached on subsequent rows, and knit to the end of the round.

Work 5[7: 7] more rounds (to the end of Row 6[8: 8] of the Flying-V Chart).

Thumb gusset

Increase to shape the thumb gusset, while continuing to place beads according to the Flying-V Chart, as follows:

Increase Round: k1, m1, pm for thumb, work to the last stitch of the round as established, pm for thumb, m1, k1.

Next 2 rounds: work the round, without increases, by following the chart for bead placement.

Increase Round: knit to thumb stitch marker, m1, sm, work to thumb stitch marker, sm, m1, knit to the end of the round.

Next 2 rounds: work the round, without increases, by following the chart for bead placement.

Repeat these last 3 rounds 5[5: 6] times in total – 60[64: 70]sts.

Work 4 rounds, without increases, by following the chart for bead placement.

Next round: k6[6: 7]sts and then slip these 6[6: 7]sts and the 6[6: 7]sts increased at the end of the round (on N3) on to a stitch-holder thread. Remove the thumb stitch markers as you continue knitting to the end of the round, and cast on 2sts with the Backward-Loop/Single-Thumb-Twist Cast-On to fill the gap above the thumb gusset and to join the mitten into the round again – 50[54: 58]sts.

Upper hand

Continue working straight (without increases) on these stitches, until you have completed 4[4: 5] repeats of the charted bead pattern but, please note, on the last repeat of Row 9 of the chart, work stitches 4 and 5 and 18 and 19 as knit stitches and do not include beads.

Work 1 round of stocking stitch, Working a k2tog decrease on the 12th[13th: 13th]st and 37th[40th: 42nd]st, decreasing 1st in the middle of each side of the mitten – 48[52: 56]sts.

Change to working in rib pattern, without beads, as given for the cuff, and work 8 rounds of rib.

Cast off in rib pattern.

Thumb

With the RS and the 2sts that were cast on to fill the gap facing you, knit pick up 1st from the ladder between the cast-on stitches and the stitches on the stitch holder (to the right), 2sts from the cast-on for the 2 sts to fill the gap, and 1st from the ladder between the cast-on stitches and the stitches on the stitch holder (to the left) on to N1, knit 6[6: 7] sts from the stitch holder on to N2 and knit the other 6[6: 7] sts from the stitch holder on to N3 – 16[16: 18]sts.

Work 4 rounds of stocking stitch.

Large size only: work one more round of stocking stitch, decreasing 1st at the centre of N2 and 1st at the centre of N3 – 16sts.

Change to working in k2, p2 rib as follows: k1, *p2, k2*, repeat from * to * to the last 3sts, p2, k1.

Work 4 rounds of rib in total.

Cast off in rib.

Left-Hand Mitten

Cast on 48[52: 56]sts by using the Picot Cast-On (as for the Right-Hand Mitten).

Join the cast-on stitches into a circle, by slipping 16[20: 24]sts on to N1, 16sts on to N2 and leaving 16sts on N3.

When joining, take care not to twist the cast-on edge.

Cuff

Work the cuff as for the Right-Hand Mitten.

Lower hand

Change to working in stocking stitch. Reorganize your stitches as follows: 25[27: 27]sts on N1, 12[13: 15]sts on N2 and 11[12: 14]sts on N3.

Work 1[1: 3] round(s) of stocking stitch.

Beaded-Stocking-Stitch section

Next round: k3[5: 5], pm, start working the beaded pattern by following the Flying-V Chart over the next 22sts and knit across N2 and N3 to the end of the round.

Complete the lower hand of the Left-Hand Mitten as for the Right-Hand Mitten, but with the beaded pattern being worked at the beginning of the round (as established on the previous round) rather than at the end of the round.

Thumb gusset

Work the thumb gusset as for the Right-Hand Mitten.

Upper hand

Work the upper hand as for the Right-Hand Mitten.

Thumb

Work the thumb as for the Right-Hand Mitten.

Finishing

Sew in the yarn ends on the WS of the fabric. Wash the mittens, and leave them lying flat to dry.

Mittens pattern worked with two circular needles or one long circular needle

Right-Hand Mitten

Using 3.00mm (US 2.5) circular needle, cast on 48[52: 56]sts with the Picot Cast-On as follows:

Cast on 5sts, *knit and cast off the next 2sts, slip the working stitch purlwise to the left-hand needle, cast on 4sts*, repeat from * to * until 47[51: 55]sts are present on the right-hand needle, cast on 1st.

Join the cast-on stitches into a circle: if you are using 2 circular needles, slip the first 24[24: 28]sts that were cast on to N1, and leave the remaining 24[28: 28]sts on N2; if you are using the Magic-Loop technique, split the stitches so that 24[28: 28]sts are on the cord at the back and 24[24: 28]sts are on the needle, with the first stitch at the point of the needle, ready to be knitted.

When joining, take care not to twist the cast-on edge.

Cuff

Work in rib as follows: k1, *p2, k2*, repeat from * to * to the last 3sts, p2, k1.

Place a stitch marker/thread to mark the beginning/end of the round.

Work a second round in rib.

Beaded-Rib Pattern

Round 1: k1, *p1, SB1, p1, k2*, repeat from * to * to the last 3sts, p1, SB1, p1, k1.

Round 2: k1, *p2, k2*, repeat from * to * to the last 3sts, p2, k1.

Repeat Rounds 1 to 2, 10 times in total.

Repeat Round 2 once more.

Lower hand

Change to working in stocking stitch, and work 1[1:3] round(s).

Beaded-Stocking-Stitch section

Next round: k23[24: 28]sts on N1/first group of stitches on Magic Loop (Small size only: slip the extra stitch to N2/second group of stitches on Magic Loop); N2/second group of stitches on Magic Loop k0[1: 1] pm, start working the beaded pattern by following the Flying-V Chart over the next 22sts, pm and knit to the end of the round.

Work 5[7: 7] more rounds as established (to the end of Row 6[8: 8] of the Flying-V Chart).

Thumb gusset

Increase to shape the thumb gusset, while continuing to place beads according to the Flying-V Chart, as follows:

Increase Round: k1, m1, pm for thumb, work to the last stitch of the round, pm for thumb, m1, k1.

Next 2 rounds: work the round, without increases, by following the chart for bead placement.

Increase Round: knit to thumb stitch marker, m1, sm, work to thumb stitch marker, sm, m1, knit to the end of the round.

Next 2 rounds: work the round, without increases, by following the chart for bead placement.

Repeat these last 3 rounds 5[5: 6] times in total – 60[64: 70]sts.

Work 4 rounds, without increases, by following the chart for bead placement.

Next round: k6[6: 7]sts and then slip these 6[6: 7]sts and the 6[6: 7]sts that were increased at the end of the round (on N2 the second group) on to a stitch-holder thread. Remove the thumb stitch markers as you continue knitting to the end of the round, and cast on 2sts with the Backward-Loop/Single-Thumb-Twist Cast-On to fill the gap above the thumb gusset and to join the mitten into the round again – 50[54: 58]sts.

Upper hand

Continue working straight on these stitches, until you have completed 4[4: 5] repeats of the charted bead pattern, but, please note, on the last repeat of Row 9 of the chart, work stitches 4 and 5 and 18 and 19 as knit stitches and do not include beads.

Work 1 round of stocking stitch, working a k2tog decrease on the 12th[13th: 13th]st and 37th[40th: 42nd]st, decreasing 1st in the middle of each side of the mitten – 48[52: 56]sts.

Change to working in rib pattern, without beads, as given for the cuff, and work 8 rounds of rib.

Cast off in rib pattern.

Thumb worked with two circular needles

With the RS and the 2sts that were cast on to fill the gap facing you, knit pick up 1st from the ladder between the cast-on stitches and the stitches on the stitch holder (to the right), 2sts from the cast-on for the 2sts to fill the gap, and 1st from the ladder between the cast-on stitches and the stitches on the stitch holder (to the left) and knit 4sts from the stitch holder on to the first circular needle. Knit the next 8[8: 10]sts from the stitch holder on to the second circular needle – 16[16: 18]sts.

Thumb worked with one long circular needle

With the RS and the 2sts that were cast on to fill the gap facing you, knit pick up 1st from the ladder between the cast-on stitches and the stitches on the stitch holder (to the right), 2sts from the cast-on for the 2sts to fill the gap, and 1st from the ladder between the cast-on stitches and the stitches on the stitch holder (to the left) and knit 4sts from the stitch holder on to the circular needle, push these stitches on to the cord (forming the first group of stitches), and then knit 8[8: 10]sts from the stitch holder on to the circular needle (forming the second group of stitches) – 16[16: 18]sts.

Work 4 rounds of stocking stitch.

Large size only: work one more round of stocking stitch, decreasing 1st at the centre of each needle/group of stitches – 16sts.

Change to working in k2, p2 rib as follows: k1, *p2, k2*, repeat from * to * to the last 3sts, p2, k1.

Work 4 rounds of rib in total.

Cast off in rib.

Left-Hand Mitten

Cast on 48[52: 56]sts by using the Picot Cast-On (as for the Right-Hand Mitten).

Join the cast-on stitches into a circle: if you are using 2 circular needles, slip the first 24[28: 28]sts that were cast on to N1, and leave the remaining 24[24: 28]sts on N2; if you are using the Magic-Loop technique, split the stitches so that 24[24: 28] sts are on the cord at the back and 24[28: 28]sts are on the needle, with the first stitch at the point of the needle, ready to be knitted.

When joining take care not to twist the cast-on edge.

Cuff

Work the cuff as for the Right-Hand Mitten.

Lower hand

Change to working in stocking stitch, and work 1[1:3] round(s).

Beaded-Stocking-Stitch section

Next round: k3[5: 5], pm (Small size only: slip 1st from N2/the second group to N1/the first group), start working the beaded pattern by following the Flying-V Chart over the next 22sts, pm, k0[1: 1] and N2/the second group knit to the end of the round.

Complete the lower hand of the Left-Hand Mitten as for the Right-Hand Mitten, but with the beaded pattern being worked at the beginning of the round (as established on the previous round) rather than at the end of the round.

Thumb gusset

Work the thumb gusset as for the Right-Hand Mitten.

Upper hand

Work the upper hand as for the Right-Hand Mitten.

Thumb

Work the thumb as for the Right-Hand Mitten.

Finishing

Sew in the yarn ends on the WS of the fabric. Wash the mittens, and leave them lying flat to dry.

Double-Diamond Mittens

The Double-Diamond Mittens are knitted by using one of the Beaded-Stocking-Stitch techniques covered in Chapter 3. Beads are strung between purl stitches in the knit two, purl two rib and on strands in front of slipped stitches in the stocking-stitch section on the upper part of each mitten.

The mittens are knitted in the round with a set of four double-pointed needles, two circular needles or, if the Magic-Loop technique is being used, one long circular needle. The Double-Diamond Chart is presented for knitting in the round. Every round is shown on the chart, and every row of the chart is read from right to left.

You will knit a right and a left mitten, and the position of the beaded pattern on the mitten is set by using stitch markers, as the chart shows only the beaded-pattern stitches. Two versions of the pattern are provided: the first is for when you are working with double-pointed needles, and the second is for when you are working with two circular needles or, if the Magic-Loop technique is being used, one long circular needle.

Double-Diamond Mittens, knitted with In the Wool Shed 4ply/fingering-weight yarn and Toho size 8 Metallic-Iris Green/Brown seed beads.

Sizes

	Women's Small	Women's Medium	Women's Large
Hand circumference	17cm (6¾in)	19cm (7½in)	20.5cm (8in)
Finished circumference	16.5cm (6½in)	18cm (7in)	19cm (7½in)
Cuff length	6cm (2½in)	6cm (2½in)	6cm (2½in)
Hand length (including top rib)	11.5cm (4½in)	12.5cm (5in)	14cm (5½in)

Materials

- 1 × 50g (1¾oz) ball of 4ply/fingering-weight yarn. The featured mittens were knitted with In the Wool Shed 4ply/fingering-weight yarn, 100-per-cent Bluefaced-Leicester wool, approx. 385m (421yd) per 110g skein, which is enough to make 2 pairs of mittens.
- Four 3.00mm (US 2.5) double-pointed needles
  Or
  Two 3.00mm × 60cm (US 2.5 × 24in) circular needles
  Or
  One 3.00mm × 80cm (US 2.5 × 32in) circular needle
- 30g (1oz) of size 7 or 8 seed beads. The featured mittens include Toho size 8 Metallic-Iris Green/Brown seed beads.
- Stitch/thread marker, for marking the beginning/end of the round

- 2 stitch markers of another colour, for marking the beaded pattern
- 2 stitch markers of a third colour, for marking the thumb gusset
- Stitch-holder thread, for holding stitches
- Tapestry needle
- Beading mat/container, for holding beads for threading
- Big Eye beading needle, or beading needle threaded with transition thread, for threading beads on to yarn

Tension

- 29sts and 42 rows in 10cm (4in) by using 3.00mm (US 2.5) needles, in stocking stitch worked in the round.

Knitting Notes

Thread the beads on to the yarn before you start to knit each mitten.

The mittens are worked in Beaded Stocking Stitch by using the slip-stitch technique. The placement of beads for the upper part of each mitten is presented in the Double-Diamond Chart. The mittens are knitted in the round, so every row of the chart is read from right to left.

Two versions of the pattern are provided: the first is for when you are working with double-pointed needles, and the second is for when you are working with two circular needles or, if the Magic-Loop technique is being used, one long circular needle.

These mittens require the Picot Cast-On, which is a decorative variation of the Cable Cast-On. Detailed instructions of how to work the Picot Cast-On can be found in Chapter 7.

When working the pattern version to be worked with double-pointed needles, 'N1' signifies the first needle of the round (to the left of the beginning/end-of-the-round marker), 'N2' signifies the second needle of the round and 'N3' signifies the third needle of the round (to the right of the beginning/end-of-the-round marker), and the remaining, fourth needle is held in the right hand, for working the stitches.

Beads are also placed within the cuff of each mitten.

Special Abbreviation
SB1 – slip up 1 bead next to the stitch just worked.

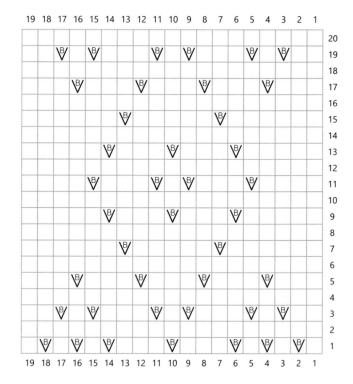

Double-Diamond Chart.

Mittens pattern worked with double-pointed needles

Right-Hand Mitten
Using 2 × 3.00mm (US 2.5) double-pointed needles, cast on 48[52: 56]sts with the Picot Cast-On as follows:

Cast on 5sts, *knit and cast off the next 2sts, slip the working stitch purlwise to the left-hand needle, cast on 4sts*; repeat from * to * until 47[51: 55]sts are present on the right-hand needle, cast on 1st.

Join the cast-on stitches into a circle, by slipping 16sts on to N1, 16sts on to N2 and leaving 16[20: 24]sts on N3.

When joining, take care not to twist the cast-on edge.

Cuff
Work in rib as follows: k1, *p2, k2*, repeat from * to * to the last 3sts, p2, k1.

Place a stitch marker/thread to mark the beginning/end of the round.

Work a second round in rib.

Beaded-Rib Pattern
Round 1: k1, *p1, SB1, p1, k2*, repeat from * to * to the last 3sts, p1, SB1, p1, k1.

Round 2: k1, *p2, k2*, repeat from * to * to the last 3sts, p2, k1.

Repeat Rounds 1 to 2, 10 times in total.

Repeat Round 2 once more.

Lower hand
Change to working in stocking stitch. Reorganize your stitches as follows: 11[12: 14]sts on N1, 12[13: 15]sts on N2 and 25[27: 27]sts on N3.

Work 1[1: 3] round(s) of stocking stitch.

Beaded-Stocking-Stitch section
Next round: knit over N1 and N2; on N3, k2, pm, start working the beaded pattern by following the Double-Diamond Chart over the next 19sts, pm and knit to the end of the round.

Thumb gusset

Increase to shape the thumb gusset, while continuing to place beads according to the Double-Diamond Chart, as follows:

Increase Round: k1, m1, pm for thumb, work to the last stitch of the round, pm for thumb, m1, k1.

Next 2 rounds: work the round, without increases, by following the chart for bead placement.

Increase Round: knit to thumb stitch marker, m1, sm, work to thumb stitch marker, sm, m1, knit to the end of the round.

Next 2 rounds: work the round, without increases, by following the chart for bead placement.

Repeat these last 3 rounds 5[5: 6] times in total – 60[64: 70]sts.

Work 8 rounds, without increases, by following the chart for bead placement.

Next round: k6[6: 7]sts and then slip these 6[6: 7]sts and the 6[6: 7]sts that were increased at the end of the round (on N3) on to a stitch-holder thread. Remove the thumb stitch markers as you continue knitting to the end of the round, and cast on 2sts with the Backward-Loop/Single-Thumb-Twist Cast-On to fill the gap above the thumb gusset and to join the mitten into the round again – 50[54: 58]sts.

Upper hand

Continue working straight on these stitches until you have completed 2 repeats of the charted bead pattern, plus Rows 1 and 2 of the chart again.

Work 1 round of stocking stitch, working a k2tog decrease on the 12th[13th: 13th]st and 37th[40th: 42nd]st, decreasing 1st in the middle of each side of the mitten – 48[52: 56]sts.

Change to working in rib pattern, without beads, as given for the cuff, and work 8 rounds of rib.

Cast off in rib pattern.

Thumb

With the RS and the 2sts that were cast on to fill the gap facing you knit pick up 1st from the ladder between the cast-on stitches and the stitches on the stitch holder (to the right), 2sts from the cast-on for the 2sts to fill the gap, and 1st between the ladder the cast-on stitches and the stitches on the stitch holder (to the left) on to N1, knit 6[6: 7]sts from the stitch holder on to N2 and knit the other 6[6: 7]sts from the stitch holder on to N3 – 16[16: 18]sts.

Work 4 rounds of stocking stitch.

Large size only: work one more round of stocking stitch, decreasing 1st at the centre of N2 and 1st at the centre of N3 – 16sts.

Change to working in k2, p2 rib as follows: k1, *p2, k2*, repeat from * to * to the last 3sts, p2, k1.

Work 4 rounds of rib in total.

Cast off in rib.

Left-Hand Mitten

Cast on 48[52: 56]sts by using the Picot Cast-On.

Join the cast-on stitches into a circle by slipping 16[20: 24] sts on to N1, 16sts on N2 and leaving 16sts on N3.

When joining, take care not to twist the cast-on edge.

Cuff

Work the cuff as for the Right-Hand Mitten.

Lower hand

Change to working in stocking stitch. Reorganize your stitches as follows: 25[27: 27]sts on N1, 12[13: 15]sts on N2 and 11[12: 14]sts on N3.

Work 1[1: 3] round(s) of stocking stitch.

Beaded-Stocking-Stitch section

Next round: k4[6: 6], pm, start working the beaded pattern by following the Double-Diamond Chart over the next 19sts, pm and knit over N2 and N3 to the end of the round.

Complete the lower hand of the Left-Hand Mitten as for the Right-Hand Mitten, but with the beaded pattern being worked at the beginning of the round (as established on the previous round) rather than at the end of the round over N2 and N3.

Thumb gusset

Work the thumb gusset as for the Right-Hand Mitten.

Upper hand

Work the upper hand as for the Right-Hand Mitten.

Thumb

Work the thumb as for the Right-Hand Mitten.

Finishing

Sew in the yarn ends on the WS of the fabric. Wash the mittens, and leave them lying flat to dry.

Mittens pattern worked with two circular needles or one long circular needle
Right-Hand Mitten

Using 3.00mm (US 2.5) circular needles, cast on 48[52: 56]sts with the Picot Cast-On as follows:

Cast on 5sts, *cast off 2sts, slip the working stitch purlwise to the left-hand needle, cast on 4sts*, repeat from * to * until 47[51: 55]sts are present on the right-hand needle, cast on 1st.

Join the cast-on stitches into a circle: if you are using 2 circular needles, slip the first 24[24: 28]sts that were cast on to N1, and leave the remaining 24[28: 28]sts on N2; if you are using the Magic-Loop technique, split the stitches so that 24[28: 28]sts are on the cord at the back and 24[24: 28]sts are on the needle, with the first stitch at the point of the needle, ready to be knitted.

When joining, take care not to twist the cast-on edge.

Cuff
Work in rib as follows: k1, *p2, k2*, repeat from * to * to the last 3sts, p2, k1.

Place a stitch marker/thread to mark the beginning/end of the round.

Work a second round in rib.

Beaded-Rib Pattern
Round 1: k1, *p1, SB1, p1, k2*, repeat from * to * to the last 3sts, p1, SB1, p1, k1.

Round 2: k1, *p2, k2*, repeat from * to * to the last 3sts, p2, k1.

Repeat Rounds 1 to 2, 10 times in total.

Repeat Round 2 once more.

Lower hand
Change to working in stocking stitch, and work 1[1:3] round(s).

Beaded-Stocking-Stitch section
Next round: k24[24: 28]sts on N1 or for the first group of stitches, k1[3: 3] on N2/for the second group, pm, start working the beaded pattern by following the Double-Diamond Chart over the next 19sts, pm and knit to the end of the round.

Thumb gusset
Increase to shape the thumb gusset, while continuing to place beads according to the Double-Diamond Chart, as follows:

Increase Round: k1, m1, pm for thumb, work to the last stitch of the round, pm for thumb, m1, k1.

Next 2 rounds: work the round, without increases, by following the chart for bead placement.

Increase Round: knit to thumb stitch marker, m1, sm, work to thumb stitch marker, sm, m1, knit to the end of the round.

Next 2 rounds: work the round, without increases, by following the chart for bead placement.

Repeat these last 3 rounds 5[5: 6] times in total – 60[64: 70]sts.

Work 8 rounds, without increases, by following the chart for bead placement.

Next round: k6[6: 7]sts and then slip these 6[6: 7]sts and the 6[6: 7]sts that were increased at the end of the round (on N2/for the second group) on to a stitch-holder thread. Remove thumb stitch markers as you continue knitting to the end of the round, and cast on 2sts with the Backward-Loop/Single-Thumb-Twist Cast-On to fill the gap above the thumb gusset and to join the mitten into the round again – 50[54: 58]sts.

Upper hand
Continue working straight on these stitches until you have completed 2 repeats of the charted bead pattern, plus Rows 1 and 2 of the chart again.

Work 1 round of stocking stitch, working a k2tog decrease on the 12th[13th: 13th]st and 37th[40th: 42nd]st, decreasing 1st in the middle of each side of the mitten – 48[52: 56]sts.

Change to working in rib pattern, without beads, as given for the cuff, and work 8 rounds of rib.

Cast off in rib pattern.

Thumb worked with two circular needles
With the RS and the 2sts that were cast on to fill the gap facing you, knit pick up 1st from the ladder between the cast-on stitches and the stitches on the stitch holder (to the right), 2sts from the cast-on for the 2sts to fill the gap, and 1st from the ladder between the cast-on stitches and the stitches from the stitch holder (to the left) and knit 4sts from the stitch holder on to the first circular needle. Knit the next 8[8: 10]sts from the stitch holder on to the second circular needle – 16[16: 18]sts.

Thumb worked with one long circular needle

With RS and the 2sts that were cast on to fill the gap facing you, knit pick up 1st from the ladder between the cast-on stitches and the stitches on the stitch holder (to the right), 2sts from the cast-on for the 2sts to fill the gap, and 1st from the ladder between the cast-on stitches and the stitches on the stitch holder (to the left) and knit 4sts from the stitch holder on to the circular needle, push these stitches on to the cord (forming the first group of stitches) and then knit 8[8: 10]sts from the stitch holder on to the circular needle (forming the second group of stitches) – 16[16: 18]sts.

Work 4 rounds of stocking stitch.

Large size only: work one more round of stocking stitch, decreasing 1st at the centre of each needle (group of stitches) – 16sts.

Change to working in k2, p2 rib as follows: k1, *p2, k2*, repeat from * to * to the last 3sts, p2, k1.

Work 4 rounds of rib in total.

Cast off in rib.

Left-Hand Mitten

Cast on 48[52: 56]sts by using the Picot Cast-On (as for the Right-Hand Mitten).

Join the cast-on stitches into a circle: if you are using 2 circular needles, slip the first 24[28: 28]sts that were cast on to N1, and leave the remaining 24[24: 28]sts on N2; if you are using the Magic-Loop technique, split the stitches so that 24[24: 28]sts are on the cord at the back and 24[28: 28]sts are on the needle, with the first stitch at the point of the needle, ready to be knitted.

When joining, take care not to twist the cast-on edge.

Cuff

Work the cuff as for the Right-Hand Mitten.

Lower hand

Change to working in stocking stitch, and work 1[1:3] round(s).

Beaded-Stocking-Stitch section

Next round: k4[6: 6], pm, start working the beaded pattern by following the Double-Diamond Chart over the next 19sts, pm, k1[2: 2] and knit to the end of the round.

Complete the lower hand of the Left-Hand Mitten as for the Right-Hand Mitten, but with the beaded pattern being worked at the beginning of the round (as established on the previous round) rather than at the end of the round.

Thumb gusset

Work the thumb gusset as for the Right-Hand Mitten.

Upper hand

Work the upper hand as for the Right-Hand Mitten.

Thumb

Work the thumb as for the Right-Hand Mitten.

Finishing

Sew in the yarn ends on the WS of the fabric. Wash the mittens, and leave them lying flat to dry.

Garter-and-Diamond Lace Shawl, knitted with Juniper Moon Farm Findley Dappled lace-weight yarn.

Garter-and-Diamond Lace Shawl, knitted with Katia Air Lux 4ply/fingering-weight yarn.

Garter-and-Diamond Lace Shawl

This shawl combines some simple garter-stitch and stocking-stitch panels with beaded Diamond-Lace panels and is finished with a beaded-lace edging. It is worked as a top-down triangular shawl, starting with a garter-stitch tab, with increases at the sides and centre of the shawl being worked on every other row. Once the main body of the shawl is completed, the shawl is cast off by knitting on a beaded edging.

The beads for the Diamond-Lace Pattern are added by using the crochet-hook method, as explained in Chapter 5. For the edging, the beads have to be threaded on to the yarn before you start to knit the edging, and the edging is worked according to the instructions for placing beads that are covered in Chapter 4. The edging as given in the pattern includes a beaded picot at the widest point of each pattern repeat. If you prefer to

work the shawl edging without the picot point, you just need to knit this stitch instead of making a picot.

The shawls have been blocked after knitting; information about blocking shawls is covered in Chapter 7. Because of the way that the lace pattern increases at the edges of the triangles, this shawl pattern makes a slightly crescent-shaped shawl rather than a triangle-shaped shawl.

The featured shawls were knitted with a variety of yarns and needle sizes. Tension gauges have been given for each of the variations, but, unlike a garment where size is very important, the finished size of the shawl can vary, depending on your personal taste. Thicker yarn and larger needles will make a larger shawl.

The finest and smallest shawl was knitted with a grey Juniper Moon Farm Findley Dappled lace-weight yarn, with three different colours of size 6 seed beads being included in the panels

Garter-and-Diamond Lace Shawl, knitted with Juniper Moon Farm Findley lace-weight yarn and Katia Concept Silk-Mohair lace-weight yarn held together.

The third and largest shawl was knitted with Juniper Moon Farm Findley lace-weight yarn and Katia Concept Silk-Mohair lace-weight yarn being held together as one yarn. The two yarns worked together create a warm and luxurious-feeling fabric, to make an ideal shawl to wrap up in on a cold winter's night. The beads included in this shawl are Toho size 6 seed beads.

Sizes

- The maximum width and depth (including the picot point) of each shawl, after washing and blocking, are given.
- Juniper Moon Farm Findley Dappled shawl approx. 142cm (56in) wide by 59cm (23¼in) deep
- Katia Air Lux shawl approx. 153cm (61in) wide by 61cm (24in) deep
- Juniper Moon Farm Findley and Katia Concept Silk-Mohair shawl approx. 182cm (71½in) wide by 83cm (32½in) deep

Materials

- 1 × 100g (3½oz) ball of Juniper Moon Findley Dappled lace-weight yarn, 50-per-cent wool, 50-per-cent silk, approx. 730m (798yd) per ball, in shade no. 101
- 3.25mm × 80cm (US 3 × 32in) circular needle
- 20g (¾oz) each of Toho size 6 Crystal Silver-Lined, Matubo™ size 6 Jet Labrador and Matubo™ size 6 Full Labrador seed beads
- 30g (1oz) of Matubo™ size 8 Full Labrador seed beads
  Or
  2 × 50g (1¾oz) balls of Katia Air Lux 4ply/fingering-weight yarn, 70-per-cent viscose, 30-per-cent virgin wool, approx. 300m (328yd) per ball, in shade no. 69
- 5.00mm × 80cm (US 8 × 32in) circular needle
- 50g (1¾oz) of Czech size 6 Metallic Purple Iris seed beads
  Or
  1 × 100g (3½oz) ball of Juniper Moon Farm Findley lace-weight yarn, 50-per-cent wool, 50-per-cent silk, approx. 730m (798yd) per ball, in shade no. 04
- 3 × 25g (1oz) balls of Katia Concept Silk-Mohair lace-weight yarn, 70-per-cent mohair, 30-per-cent silk, approx. 200m (219yd) per ball, in shade no 709
- 6.00mm × 80cm (US 10 × 32in) circular needle

of the Diamond-Lace Pattern, size 8 seed beads being used for the lace edging and size 6 seed beads on the picot points. The beads in the panels of the Diamond-Lace Pattern are placed by using the crochet-hook method, so it is quite easy to change the colours of the beads, but if you intend to use different colours and/or sizes of beads in the edging pattern, you do have to work out the knitting sequence of the beads, to get the beads threaded on to the yarn in the correct order before you start to knit the edging. An extra panel of the Diamond-Lace Pattern was worked for this shawl, making the shawl larger and with a longer edge.

The medium-size shawl was knitted with a mid-grey colour of Katia Air Lux 4ply/fingering-weight yarn and size 6 Czech seed beads. The same size of bead is used throughout the shawl, including the edging, but, for this shawl, the picot point was not worked as part of the edging. As a result, the edging forms a soft curve rather than a dramatic point.

- 50g (1¾oz) of Toho size 6 Gold-Lined Rainbow Crystal seed beads
- 0.60mm or 0.75mm (US steel hook 14) crochet hook
- Stitch markers
- Tapestry needle
- Beading mat/container, for holding beads for threading
- Container to hold beads when working the crochet-hook method
- Big Eye beading needle, or beading needle threaded with transition thread, for threading beads on to yarn

Tension

- The gauges for the three shawls were measured over the garter-stitch and stocking-stitch sections of the fabric, before washing and blocking.
- 27sts and 46 rows in 10cm (4in) using Juniper Moon Farm Findley Dappled lace-weight yarn with 3.25mm (US 3) needles.
- 22sts and 30 rows in 10cm (4in) using Katia Air Lux 4ply/fingering-weight yarn with 5.00mm (US 8) needles.
- 17sts and 25 rows in 10cm (4in) using Juniper Moon Farm Findley lace-weight yarn and Katia Concept Silk-Mohair, held together, with 6.00mm (US 10) needles.

Shawl

Using a circular needle, cast on 3sts with the Knit Cast-On.
Knit 7 rows.

Set-up Triangles Row (RS): k3, yo, pick up 3sts (1st for each garter ridge) along the side of the piece of garter-stitch fabric (the garter-stitch tab), yo, pick up 3sts from the cast-on row (the loops from the 3sts that were cast on) – 11sts.

Next row: k3, p1, pm, k3, pm, p1, k3.

Start working from the Diamond-Lace Chart, as follows:

Next row: k3, follow Row 1 of the Diamond-Lace Chart, sm, k3, sm, follow Row 1 of the Diamond-Lace Chart, k3.

Continue working both triangles by following the Diamond-Lace Chart, as established, until Row 48 has been completed.

Note: The Diamond-Lace Chart represents the increase triangles from Row 1 to Row 48. For those who prefer to work from written instructions, Rows 1 to 26 are presented below. However, for Rows 27 to 46 of the Diamond-Lace Pattern, you will have to follow the chart.

Row 1 (RS): k3, *yo, k1, yo*, k3, repeat from * to *, k3.
Row 2: k3, p3, k3, p3, k3.
Row 3: k3, *yo, k to marker, yo*, k3, repeat from * to *, k3.
Row 4: k3, *p to marker*, k3, repeat from * to *, k3.
Rows 5 to 8: (4 rows) repeat Rows 3 to 4, 2 times.
Row 9: k3, *yo, k to marker, yo*, k3, repeat from * to *, k3.

Knitting Notes

This shawl requires the Knit Cast-On.

This shawl is of a top-down construction that is started with a garter-stitch tab. The shawl has a three-stitch garter-stitch border at each side and down the centre of the shawl between the two triangles.

The Diamond-Lace Chart represents the increase triangles from Rows 1 to 48, but written instructions have also been provided for Rows 1 to 26. For Row 27 onwards, the shawl sections featuring the Diamond-Lace Pattern must be worked by following the chart, and then written instructions can be followed again for the stocking-stitch and garter-stitch sections. Note: Each row of the chart is worked twice for each row of the shawl.

The Diamond-Lace Chart *does not* includes the three-stitch garter-stitch border on each side of and down the centre of the shawl, between the two triangles.

The beads for the main body of the shawl are added by using the crochet-hook method, which is covered in Chapter 5. However, the beads for the edging need to be threaded on to the yarn before you start to knit the edging, which is worked according to the instructions for placing beads that are covered in Chapter 4.

The length of the shawl can be varied, depending on the weight of yarn to be used and the amount of yarn that you have. The shawl can be knitted exactly as written, it can be finished with four rows of garter stitch after a repeat of the lace panel or it can be finished after repeating the stocking-stitch and garter-stitch sections twice after the lace panel.

If the shawl is knitted as written in the instructions, the edging will require about 200m (218yd) of yarn. If the shawl has been worked with more repeats, such as for the sample Juniper Moon Farm Findley Dappled lace-weight shawl, there will be more stitches to cast off with the edging, so you will need more yarn for the edging than the amount quoted previously.

Diamond-Lace Chart for the Garter-and-Diamond Lace Shawl, for Rows 1 to 48. Note: The chart does not show the three-stitch garter-stitch edging on each side of and down the centre of the shawl, between the two triangles. Each row of the chart is worked twice for each row of the shawl. (See Resources at the end of this book for instructions to obtain a PDF version of this chart.)

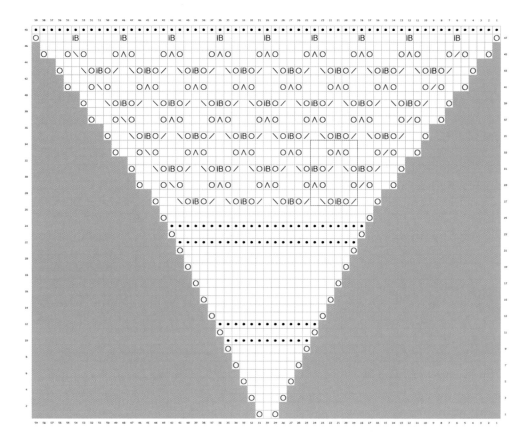

Row 10: knit.

Rows 11 to 12: (2 rows garter stitch) repeat Rows 9 to 10.

Rows 13 to 20: (8 rows stocking stitch) repeat Rows 3 to 4, 4 times.

Rows 21 to 24: (4 rows garter stitch) repeat Rows 9 to 10, 2 times.

Rows 25 to 26: (2 rows stocking stitch) repeat Rows 3 to 4.

Rows 27 to 46: (20 rows) work in the Diamond-Lace Pattern by following the Diamond-Lace Chart.

Work according to both the Diamond-Lace Chart and the written instructions.

Rows 47 to 50: (4 rows garter stitch) repeat Rows 9 to 10, 2 times.

Rows 51 to 58: (8 rows stocking stitch) repeat Rows 3 to 4, 4 times.

Rows 59 to 62: (4 rows garter stitch) repeat Rows 9 to 10, 2 times.

Rows 63 to 70: (8 rows stocking stitch) repeat Rows 3 to 4, 4 times.

Rows 71 to 74: (4 rows garter stitch) repeat Rows 9 to 10, 2 times.

Rows 75 to 76: (2 rows stocking stitch) repeat Rows 3 to 4.

Rows 77 to 96: (20 rows) work in Diamond-Lace Pattern by following the Diamond-Lace Chart again, as for Rows 27 to 46. Note: There will be more repeats of diamonds between the edges of the shawl (the red box on the chart identifies one diamond repeat).

Rows 97 to 100: (4 rows garter stitch) repeat Rows 9 to 10, 2 times.

Rows 101 to 108: (8 rows stocking stitch) repeat Rows 3 to 4, 4 times.

Rows 109 to 114: (6 rows garter stitch) repeat Rows 9 to 10, 3 times.

Leave the stitches on the needle, but cut the working yarn.

If you are working with lace-weight yarn and wish to make a larger shawl, after Row 96, you need to repeat Rows 47 to 96 again and then finish with 4 more rows of garter stitch.

Knitting the Chevron-Picot Edging on to the Shawl

Start of the Chevron-Picot Edging
With the WS of the shawl facing you, and working at the opposite end of the shawl to where the yarn for working the shawl body was cut, cast on 14sts to the needle holding all of the shawl stitches.

Row 1 (RS of edging): k13, skpo (worked with the last cast-on stitch and the first shawl-body stitch).
Row 2: sl1 wyb, k13.
Row 3: k1, k2tog, k10, skpo (worked with the last edging stitch and the next shawl-body stitch).
Row 4: sl1 wyb, k12.
Row 5: k1, k2tog, k9, skpo (worked with the last edging stitch and the next shawl-body stitch).
Row 6: sl1 wyb, k11.

Continue by following the Chevron-Picot-Edging Chart, starting with Row 17 of the chart, joining the edging to the shawl body on all odd-number rows with a skpo decrease, as established, until 3sts of the shawl body remain, ending after an even-number row. Note: This even-number row may not be at the end of a complete pattern repeat.

End of the Chevron-Picot-Edging Pattern
Rows 1, 3 and 5: k1, kfb, knit to 1st before the end of the edging stitches, skpo.
Rows 2 and 4: sl1, wyb, knit to the end of the row.
Row 6: work a knit cast off.

Finishing

Soak the shawl in hand-hot water for 15–20 minutes to make sure that the yarn has become thoroughly wet. Gently squeeze out the excess water, and either place the shawl in a laundry bag, to give it a short spin in the washing machine, or lay it on a clean towel and roll up the towel, to squeeze out more water. Lay out the shawl on a blocking board or large flat surface that can be pinned into. Stretch out the shawl, allowing the ends to curve slightly, and pin the fabric in place. Pin out the picot points. Leave the shawl to dry completely before unpinning.

If you used a yarn that is 30-per-cent acrylic, or more, in composition to knit your shawl, after washing, blocking and leaving it to dry, you can steam your shawl, to permanently fix its shape.

Knitting Notes

Thread the beads on to the yarn before you start to knit the edging.

The edging is started at the opposite end of the shawl to where the yarn for working the shawl body was cut. The lace rows (odd-number rows of the edging) are worked when the wrong side of the main shawl is facing you. The edging is worked in garter stitch; by working the edging in this way, the beads that are placed on yarn overs will appear on the right side of the finished shawl.

The Chevron-Picot-Edging Chart should be followed as for flat knitting, by reading odd-number rows from right to left and even-number rows from left to right.

The edging stitches are cast on to the circular needle that is holding all of the shawl stitches. You may prefer to use a short needle and the circular needle to knit the edging rather than use both ends of the circular needle to knit the edging.

There are twenty-one beads for each pattern repeat of the edging, but, if you knit the edging without the picot point, you will need twenty beads for each pattern repeat.

See the section 'Chevron-Picot Edging' in Chapter 6 for guidance about how to correctly centre the edging on your shawl and determine whether any partial pattern repeats of the edging should be worked.

Special Abbreviation
Beaded Picot (the corresponding symbol is included on the Chevron-Picot-Edging Chart) – cast on 2sts, knit and cast off the next 2sts, slip the working stitch to the left-hand needle, cast on 3sts, push up 1 bead next to the stitch on the right-hand needle, knit and cast off the next 3sts, slip the working stitch to the left-hand needle, cast on 2sts, knit and cast off the next 2sts.

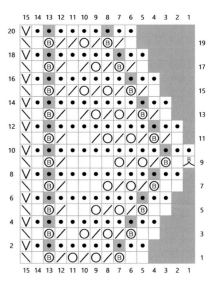

Chevron-Picot-Edging Chart.

Back view of the Rainbow-Storms Wing Shawl, knitted with Debbie Bliss Rialto Luxury Sock 4ply/fingering-weight yarn and Czech size 6 seed beads in the panel of the Diamond-Lace Pattern and size 8 seed beads in the edging, both in the colourway Rainbow Mix.

Rainbow-Storms Wing Shawl, knitted with Scheepjes Whirl 4ply/fingering-weight yarn and Miyuki size 6 beads in the panel of the Diamond-Lace Pattern and along the edge of the faggot lace of the edging and Toho size 8 beads for the strings of beads within the edging.

Rainbow-Storms Wing Shawl

The Rainbow-Storms Wing Shawl is very similar to the Garter-and-Diamond Lace Shawl, as it uses the same Diamond-Lace Pattern, but in this shawl the triangles are increased on every row at the outer edge and on every other row at the centre, making it a wide, crescent-shaped shawl. The shawl is finished with a different beaded-lace edging, the Butterfly-Lace Edging.

The shawl starts with a garter-stitch tab, but, as the edges are increased at a faster rate than the centre of the shawl, it is necessary to work a left- and a right-triangle pattern. The beads in the panel of the Diamond-Lace Pattern are added by using the crochet-hook method, as explained in Chapter 5.

The edging is worked in double-sided beaded lace, with the beads being threaded on to the yarn before the knitting of the edging is started. There are strings of beads across some of the yarn-over eyelet holes, so size 8 seed beads are used for this section of the shawl; size 6 or 8 beads can be used for the rest of the beads to be included in the edging. If size 6 beads are used, it is necessary to thread the beads in the correct order (in the reverse order to that which they will be knitted), to ensure that the beads are placed at the right places within the pattern. The section 'Edgings' in Chapter 6 gives more information about how to correctly thread two different types of bead in the Butterfly-Lace Edging.

Two samples of the shawl are featured, both knitted with 4ply/fingering-weight yarn. One was worked with Debbie Bliss Rialto Luxury Sock yarn, with Czech size 6 seed beads in the panel of the Diamond-Lace Pattern and matching size 8 seed beads in the edging. The other was knitted with Scheepjes Whirl yarn, with Miyuki size 6 beads in the panel of the Diamond-Lace Pattern and along the edge of the faggot lace in the edging and Toho size 8 beads in the edging strings.

Sizes

* The maximum width and depth of each shawl, after washing and blocking, are given.
* Debbie Bliss Rialto Luxury Sock shawl approx. 107cm (42in) wide by 46.5cm (18¼in) deep
* Scheepjes Whirl shawl approx. 101cm (39¾in) wide by 39cm (15½in) deep

Materials

* 1 × 100g (3½oz) ball of Debbie Bliss Rialto Luxury Sock 4ply/fingering-weight yarn, 75-per-cent wool, 25-per-cent polyamide, approx. 400m (437yd) per ball, in shade no. 5 Mutek
* 5.00mm × 80cm (US 8 × 32in) circular needle
  Or
  1 × 220g (7¾oz) cake of Scheepjes Whirl 4ply/fingering-weight yarn, 60-per-cent cotton, 40-per-cent acrylic, approx. 1,000m (1,093 yd) per cake, in shade no 754 Green Tea Tipple
* 4.50mm × 80cm (US 7 × 32in) circular needle
* 0.60mm or 0.75mm (US steel hook 14) crochet hook, for placing beads
* Approx. 140 × size 6 seed beads, for the Diamond-Lace Pattern
* 45g (1½oz) of size 8 seed beads, for the edging
* Stitch markers
* Tapestry needle
* Beading mat/container, for holding beads for threading
* Big Eye beading needle, or beading needle threaded with transition thread, for threading beads on to yarn
* Container to hold beads when working the crochet-hook method

Tension

* The gauges for the two shawls were measured over the garter-stitch and stocking-stitch sections of the fabric, before washing and blocking.
* 21.5sts and 32 rows in 10cm (4in) using Debbie Bliss Rialto Luxury Sock with 5.00mm (US 8) needles.
* 19.5sts and 33 rows in 10cm (4in) using Scheepjes Whirl with 4.5mm (US 7) needles.

Knitting Notes

This shawl requires the Knit Cast-On and is of a top-down construction that is started with a garter-stitch tab.

The increases on each side of the central 3st garter-stitch border are worked on every right-side row, but the increases at the edges are worked at the beginning and at the end of each row.

Note: When working the stocking-stitch sections on wrong-side rows, when you are purling, the end increase should be worked as a reverse yarn over. At the beginning of the next row, work that reverse yarn over through the back loop. This is to make the yarn overs the same size, as much as is possible.

Once the two triangles have been started, you will need to follow the Wing-Shawl Right-Triangle and Left-Triangle Charts, particularly for the Diamond-Lace Pattern.

The charts *do not* include the three-stitch garter-stitch border on each side of and down the centre of the shawl, between the two triangles.

Shawl

Using a circular needle, cast on 3sts, loosely, with the Knit Cast-On.

Knit 7 rows.

Set-up Triangles Row (RS): k3, yo, pick up 3sts (1st for each garter ridge) along the side of the piece of garter-stitch fabric (the garter-stitch tab), yo, pick up 3sts from the cast-on row (the loops from the 3sts that were cast on) – 11sts.

Next row: k3, p1, pm, k3, pm, p1, k3.

Start working from the Wing-Shawl Right-Triangle and Left-Triangle Charts, as follows:

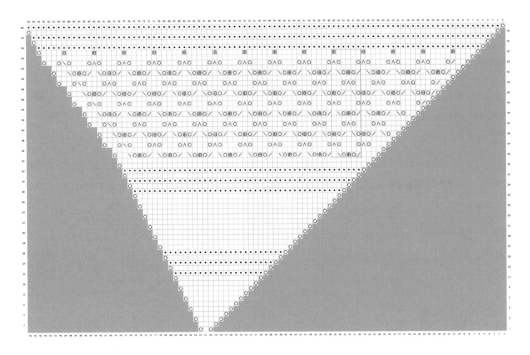

Wing-Shawl Right-Triangle Chart. (*See* Resources at the end of this book for instructions to obtain a PDF version of this chart.)

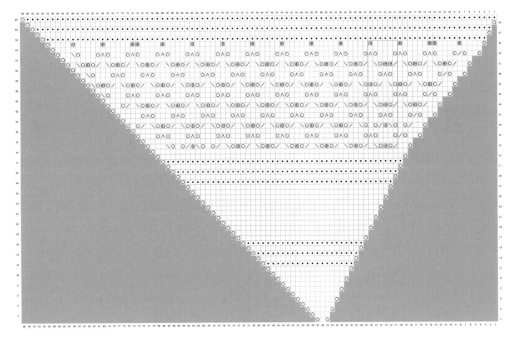

Wing-Shawl Left-Triangle Chart. (*See* Resources at the end of this book for instructions to obtain a PDF version of this chart.)

Row 1 (RS): k3, follow Row 1 of the Wing-Shawl Right-Triangle Chart, sm, k3, sm, follow Row 1 of the Wing-Shawl Left-Triangle Chart, k3.

Row 2: k3, follow Row 2 of the Wing-Shawl Left-Triangle Chart, sm, k3, sm, follow Row 2 of the Wing-Shawl Right-Triangle Chart, k3.

Continue working both triangles by following the Wing-Shawl Right-Triangle and Left-Triangle Charts as established, until Row 60 has been completed.

Work 10 rows of stocking stitch while continuing to increase on every row at the edges and on every other row on each side of the garter-stitch border at the centre of the shawl, as established – 231sts.

Work 6 rows of garter stitch while continuing to increase on every row at the edges and on every other row on each side of the garter-stitch border at centre of the shawl, as established – 249sts.

Leave the stitches on the needle, but cut the working yarn so that you can thread the size 8 seed beads on to the ball/cake of yarn.

Knitting the Butterfly-Lace Edging on to the Shawl

Knitting Notes

Thread the size 8 seed beads on to the yarn before you start to knit the edging.

The Butterfly-Lace Edging is knitted on to the shawl; this casts off one stitch of the shawl body at the end of every right-side row.

The edging stitches are cast on to the circular needle holding all of the shawl stitches. You may prefer to use a short needle and the circular needle to knit the edging rather than use both ends of the circular needle to knit the edging.

When knitting the Butterfly-Lace Edging, beads are placed on every row. On the Butterfly-Edging Chart, a coloured box indicates where the bead(s) need to be on the yarn-over stitch when you work into that stitch:

The yellow square is to remind you that each bead needs to be at the right-hand end of the yarn-over stitch, on the side of the fabric nearest to you, for both right-side and wrong-side rows.

The blue square is to remind you that each bead needs to be at the left-hand end of the yarn-over stitch, on the side of the fabric away from you, for both right-side and wrong-side rows.

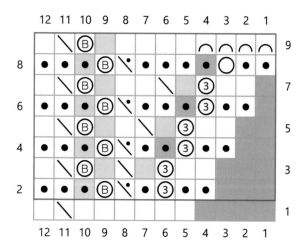

Butterfly-Lace Edging chart.

Start of the Butterfly-Lace Edging
With the RS of the shawl body facing you, cast on 11sts to the needle holding the shawl stitches.

Row 1 (RS): k8, ssk, ssk (worked with the last cast-on stitch and the first shawl-body stitch) – 10sts.
Row 2: knit.
Row 3: k7, ssk, ssk (worked with the last edging stitch and the next shawl-body stitch) – 9sts.
Row 4: knit.

Continue by following the Butterfly-Lace-Edging Chart from Row 1 (and then repeating the Butterfly-Lace-Edging Chart from Rows 2 to 9), joining the edging to the shawl body at the end of every RS row with a ssk decrease, as established, until 3sts of the shawl body remain, ending after a WS row.

End of the Butterfly-Lace Edging
Rows 1, 3 and 5: k1, kfb, knit to the last stitch, ssk.
Rows 2 and 4: knit.
Row 6: work a knit cast off.

Finishing
Soak the shawl in hand-hot water for 15–20 minutes to make sure that the yarn has become thoroughly wet. Gently squeeze out the excess water, and either place the shawl in a laundry bag, to give it a short spin in the washing machine, or lay it on a clean towel and roll up the towel, to squeeze out more water. Lay out the shawl on a blocking board or large flat surface that can be pinned into. Stretch out the shawl, allowing the ends to curve into a crescent-wing shape, and pin the fabric in place. Pin out the edging points. Leave the shawl to dry completely before unpinning.

If you use a yarn that is 30-per-cent acrylic, or more, in composition to knit your shawl, after washing, blocking and leaving it to dry, you can steam your shawl, to permanently fix its shape.

GARMENTS

To show how the following garment patterns can be knitted in a variety of yarns, the featured samples have been knitted in different yarns. The yarns used have been listed in the materials section of each pattern for reference, but, as long as you match the pattern gauges, you can use different yarns to knit these garments.

Forest Beaded Jacket

This classic edge-to-edge jacket that meets at the centre front with no closure/button has been worked in stocking stitch, with Beaded-Garter-Stitch edgings. The beading technique is covered in Chapter 3 and is based on traditional Norwegian Beaded Garter Stitch. The Beaded-Garter-Stitch bands for each piece are knitted first, and then stitches are picked up from one edge of each band from which the main part of each garment piece is then knitted.

The featured garments have been knitted in two different yarns. The purple-and-silver jacket was knitted with Fyberspates Scrumptious 4ply/fingering-weight yarn and Matubo™ size 8 seed beads. The turquoise-blue jacket was knitted with Garnstudio Drops Safran 4ply/fingering-weight, cotton yarn and Czech size 7 seed beads.

Forest Beaded Jacket, knitted with Fyberspates Scrumptious 4ply/ fingering-weight yarn and Matubo™ size 8 seed beads.

Materials

- 5[5: 5: 5: 5: 6: 6: 6] × 100g (3½oz) skeins of Fyberspates Scrumptious 4ply/fingering-weight yarn, 45-per-cent silk, 55-per-cent superwash merino, approx. 365m (399 yd) per skein, in shade no. 305 Purple
  Or
  9[10: 11: 12: 12: 13: 13: 14] × 50g (1¾oz) balls of Garnstudio Drops Safran 4ply/fingering-weight yarn, 100-per-cent cotton, approx. 160m (175yd) per ball, in shade no. 30 Turquoise
- Pair of 2.50mm (US 1.5) needles
- Pair of 3.25mm (US 3) needles
- At least 3,550[3,840: 3,930: 4,120: 4,210: 4,260: 4,520: 4,610] size 7 or 8 seed beads. Matubo™ size 8 Crystal Full Labrador seed beads were used for the purple jacket and Czech size 7 Silver-Lined Turquoise seed beads were used for the turquoise-blue jacket.
- Stitch holders
- Tapestry needle
- Beading mat/container, for holding beads for threading
- Big Eye beading needle, or beading needle theaded with transition thread, for threading beads on to yarn

Tension

- 27sts and 38 rows in 10cm (4in) with 3.25mm (US 3) needles over stocking-stitch fabric, after washing, blocking and leaving lying flat to dry.

Forest Beaded Jacket, knitted with Garnstudio Drops Safran 4ply/fingering-weight yarn and Czech size 7 seed beads.

Sizes

To fit bust/chest	86	91	96	102	106	112	116	122	cm
	34	36	38	40	42	44	46	48	in
Finished bust/chest	92	96	102	107	113	117	122	127	cm
measurement	36	38	40	42	44	46	48	50	in
Back length	55	57	57	58	58	59	59	60	cm
	21½	22¼	22¼	22¾	22¾	23¼	23¼	23½	in
Sleeve length to underarm	43.5	45.5	45.5	45.5	45.5	45.5	45.5	45.5	cm
	17	18	18	18	18	18	18	18	in

Knitting Notes

Thread the beads on to the yarn before you start to knit the Beaded Garter-Stitch bands. It is much easier to keep one ball of yarn for knitting the Beaded-Garter-Stitch bands and to use a new ball of yarn when starting to knit the main garment pieces.

If you are using a skeined yarn, rewind the yarn into balls before you start to knit.

This jacket requires the Knit Cast-On.

For details of how to knit Beaded Garter Stitch and how to follow charts for Beaded Garter Stitch, *see* Chapter 3.

To place the beaded pattern centrally in the Beaded-Garter-Stitch bands, extra repeats of Row 1 of the Forest-Beaded-Jacket Chart must be worked for the several pieces of the jacket for some sizes, before the main pattern repeat is started, and then Row 2 of the Forest-Beaded-Jacket Chart is followed by extra repeats of Row 1 to finish the band, as described within the pattern.

Beads are placed within the neckband, right-front band and left-front band.

Special Abbreviation
SB1 – slip up 1 bead next to the stitch just worked.

Shaping decreases are worked two stitches in from the edge of the fabric as follows:
k2, skpo, work to the last 4sts, k2tog, k2.

Shaping increases are worked two stitches in from the edge of the fabric as follows:
k2, m1, work to the last 2sts, m1, k2.

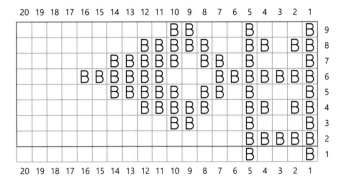

Forest-Beaded-Jacket Chart. Note: Every row of the chart is read from right to left. The row numbers on the chart refer to the ridge numbers of the garter-stitch fabric. The red box outlines one pattern repeat.

Repeat Row 2 of the Forest-Beaded-Jacket Chart 1[1: 1: 0: 0: 1: 1: 1] time(s), and then repeat Row 1 1[0: 0: 0: 0: 2: 1: 1] time(s) – 124[130: 138: 144: 152: 158: 164: 172] garter ridges completed.

Cast off.

Using 3.25mm (US 3) needles and with the RS of the band facing you (namely, with the beaded pattern visible and the trees pointing up towards the edge from which stitches will be picked up), knit pick up 1st for every garter ridge – 124[130: 138: 144: 152: 158: 164: 172]sts.

Continue working in stocking stitch until the Back measures 34[35: 35: 34: 33: 33: 31.5: 31.5]cm (13¼[13¾: 13¾: 13¼: 13: 13: 12¼: 12¼]in), including the beaded band, finishing after a WS row.

Armholes

Cast off 5[6: 7: 7: 8: 8: 8: 9]sts at the beginning of the next 2 rows.

Decrease 1st (see Knitting Notes) at each end of the next row and then at each end of every alternate row 10[11: 12: 13: 14: 15: 16: 18] times – 92[94: 98: 102: 106: 110: 114: 116]sts.

Continue working straight until the Back measures 52[54: 54: 55: 55: 56: 56: 57]cm (20½[21¼: 21¼: 21½: 21½: 22: 22: 22¼]in), including the beaded band, finishing after a RS row.

Back

Before you start to knit the Back, thread at least 941[999: 1,061: 1,116: 1,178: 1,193: 1,251: 1,313] seed beads on to 1 ball of the yarn.

Beaded-Garter-Stitch band

Using 2.50mm (US 1.5) needles, cast on 20sts with the Knit Cast-On.

Knit 1 row.

Work Row 1 of the Forest-Beaded-Jacket Chart 2[1: 1: 0: 0: 3: 2: 2] time(s), and then continue working from Row 2 of the Forest-Beaded-Jacket Chart, working the 8-row pattern 15[16: 17: 18: 19: 19: 20: 21] times.

Back neck and shoulders
P28[28: 29: 30: 31: 32: 34: 34]sts (forming the second group of stitches), cast off 36[38: 40: 42: 44: 46: 46: 48]sts and p28[28: 29: 30: 31: 32: 34: 34]sts (forming the first group of stitches).

Working over the first group of stitches only, decrease 1st at the neck edge on the next and then every alternate row 2 times (see Knitting Notes), and, *at the same time*, at the beginning of RS rows, cast off 5[5: 6: 6: 6: 6: 7: 7]sts 5[5: 1: 2: 3: 4: 1: 1] time(s) and then 0[0: 5: 5: 5: 5: 6: 6]sts 0[0: 4: 3: 2: 1: 4: 4] time(s). All the stitches on this shoulder are now cast off so there are no stitches on the working needle.

With the RS facing, rejoin the yarn at the neck edge, to work the second group of stitches. Decrease 1st at the neck edge on the next and then every alternate row 2 times (see Knitting Notes), and, *at the same time*, at the beginning of WS rows, cast off 5[5: 6: 6: 6: 6: 7: 7]sts 5[5: 1: 2: 3: 4: 1: 1] time(s) and then 0[0: 5: 5: 5: 5: 6: 6]sts 0[0: 4: 3: 2: 1: 4: 4] time(s). All the stitches are cast off on the second shoulder.

Left Front
Before you start to knit the Left Front, thread at least 449[501: 509: 558: 569: 575: 627: 635] seed beads on to 1 ball of the yarn.

Using 2.50mm (US 1.5) needles, cast on 20sts with the Knit Cast-On.

Knit 1 row.

Work Row 1 of the Forest-Beaded-Jacket Chart 5[0: 4: 0: 3: 6: 1: 5] time(s).

Size 102cm (40in) only: work Rows 3 to 9 of the Forest-Beaded-Jacket Chart, 1 time.

Continue working from Row 2 of the Forest-Beaded-Jacket Chart, working the 8-row pattern 7[8: 8: 8: 9: 9: 10: 10] times. Repeat Row 2 of the Forest-Beaded-Jacket Chart, 1 time – 62[65: 69: 72: 76: 79: 82: 86] garter ridges completed.

Leave the stitches on a stitch holder so that they can be picked up when knitting the Left-Front Band.

Using 3.25mm (US 3) needles and with the RS of the band facing you (namely, with the beaded pattern visible and the trees pointing up towards the edge from which stitches will be picked up), knit pick up 1st for every garter ridge – 62[65: 69: 72: 76: 79: 82: 86]sts.

Continue working in stocking stitch until the Left Front measures 34[35: 35: 34: 33: 33: 31.5: 31.5]cm (13¼[13¾: 13¾: 13¼: 13: 13: 12¼: 12¼]in), including the beaded band, finishing after a WS row.

Armhole
Cast off 5[6: 7: 7: 8: 8: 8: 9]sts at the beginning of the next row.

Purl 1 row.

Decrease 1st (see Knitting Notes) at the armhole edge of the next row and then every alternate row 10[11: 12: 13: 14: 15: 16: 18] times – 46[47: 49: 51: 53: 55: 57: 58]sts.

Continue working straight until the Left Front measures 45[47: 46: 47: 47: 47: 47: 48]cm (17¾[18½: 18: 18½: 18½: 18½: 18½: 18¾]in), including the beaded band, finishing after a WS row.

Front neck
K32[32: 33: 35: 36: 38: 40: 40]sts, k2tog, k2 and turn.

Put the remaining 10[11: 12: 12: 13: 13: 13: 14]sts at the neck edge on to a stitch holder.

Purl 1 row.

Decrease 1st as established at the neck edge on the next row and then every alternate row 9[9: 9: 10: 10: 11: 11: 11] times – 25[25: 26: 27: 28: 29: 31: 31]sts.

Continue working straight until the Left Front measures 52.5[54.5: 54.5: 55.5: 55.5: 56.5: 56.5: 57.5]cm (20½[21½: 21½: 21¾: 21¾: 22¼: 22¼: 22½]in), including the beaded band, finishing after a WS row.

Shoulder
At the beginning of RS rows, cast off 5[5: 6: 6: 6: 6: 7: 7]sts 5[5: 1: 2: 3: 4: 1: 1] time(s) and then 0[0: 5: 5: 5: 5: 6: 6]sts 0[0: 4: 3: 2: 1: 4: 4] time(s). All the stitches are cast off.

Right Front
Before you start to knit the Right Front, thread at least 449[501: 509: 558: 569: 575: 627: 635] beads on to 1 ball of the yarn.

Using 2.50mm (US 1.5) needles, cast on 20sts with the Knit Cast-On.

Knit 1 row.

Starting with Row 2 of the Forest-Beaded-Jacket Chart, work the 8-row pattern 7[8: 8: 9: 9: 9: 10: 10] times. Repeat Row 2 of the Forest-Beaded-Jacket Chart 1[1: 1: 0: 1: 1: 1: 1] time(s) and then Row 1 of the Forest-Beaded-Jacket Chart 5[0: 4: 0: 3: 6: 1: 5] time(s) – 62[65: 69: 72: 76: 79: 82: 86] garter ridges completed.

Cast off.

Using 3.25mm (US 3) needles and with the RS of the band facing you (namely, with the beaded pattern visible and the trees pointing up towards the edge from which stitches will be picked up), knit pick up 1st for every garter ridge – 62[65: 69: 72: 76: 79: 82: 86]sts.

Continue working in stocking stitch until the Right Front measures 34[35: 35: 34: 33: 33: 31.5: 31.5]cm (13¼[13¾: 13¾: 13¼: 13: 13: 12¼: 12¼]in), including the beaded band, finishing after a WS row.

Armhole
Knit 1 row.

Cast off 5[6: 7: 7: 8: 8: 8: 9]sts at the beginning of the next row.

Decrease 1st (see Knitting Notes) at the armhole edge of the next row and then every alternate row 10[11: 12: 13: 14: 15: 16: 18] times – 46[46: 49: 51: 53: 55: 57: 58]sts.

Continue working straight until the Right Front measures 45[47: 46: 47: 47: 47: 47: 48]cm (17¾[18½: 18: 18½: 18½: 18½: 18½: 18¾]in), including the beaded band, finishing after a WS row.

Front neck
K10[11: 12: 12: 13: 13: 13: 14]sts, slip these stitches on to a stitch holder, then k2, skpo and knit to the end of the row.

Purl 1 row.

Decrease 1st (as established) at the neck edge on the next row and then every alternate row 9[9: 9: 10: 10: 11: 11: 11] times – 25[25: 26: 27: 28: 29: 31: 31]sts.

Continue working straight until the Right Front measures 52.5[54.5: 54.5: 55.5: 55.5: 56.5: 56.5: 57.5]cm (20½[21½: 21½: 21¾: 21¾: 22¼: 22¼: 22½]in), including the beaded band, finishing after a RS row.

Shoulder
At the beginning of WS rows, cast off 5[5: 6: 6: 6: 6: 7: 7]sts 5[5: 1: 2: 3: 4: 1: 1] time(s) and then 0[0: 5: 5: 5: 5: 6: 6]sts 0[0: 4: 3: 2: 1: 4: 4] time(s) There should not be any open stitches at this point as all the shoulder stitches are cast off.

Sleeve (knit two)
Before you start to knit, thread at least 449[496: 496: 507: 507: 511: 558: 558] beads on to 1 ball of the yarn.

Using 2.50mm (US 1.5) needles, cast on 20sts with the Knit Cast-On.

Knit 1 row.

Work Row 1 of the Forest-Beaded-Jacket Chart 2[0: 0: 2: 2: 3: 0: 0] times, and then continue working from Row 2 of the Forest-Beaded-Jacket Chart, working the 8-row pattern 7[8: 8: 8: 8: 8: 9: 9] times. Repeat Row 2 of the Forest-Beaded-Jacket Chart 1[0: 0: 1: 1: 1: 0: 0] time(s), and then repeat Row 1 3[0: 0: 1: 1: 2: 0: 0] time(s) – 62[64: 64: 68: 68: 70: 72: 72] garter ridges completed.

Cast off.

Using 3.25mm (US 3) needles and with the RS of the band facing you (namely, with the beaded pattern visible and the trees pointing up towards the edge from which stitches will be picked up), knit pick up 1st for every garter ridge – 62[64: 64: 68: 68: 70: 72: 72]sts.

Purl 1 row.

Continue working in stocking stitch, increasing 1st (see Knitting Notes) at each end of the next row and then every 10th[10th: 8th: 8th: 8th: 8th: 6th: 6th] row 2[2: 11: 11: 5: 2: 20: 21] times and then every 8th[8th: 6th: 6th: 6th: 6th: 0: 0]row 11[12: 5: 5: 13: 17: 0: 0] times – 90[94: 98: 102: 106: 110: 114: 116]sts.

Continue working straight until the Sleeve measures 43.5[45.5: 45.5: 45.5: 45.5: 45.5: 45.5: 45.5]cm (17[18: 18: 18: 18: 18: 18: 18]in). including the beaded band, finishing after a WS row.

Sleeve cap
Cast off 5[6: 7: 7: 8: 8: 8: 9]sts at the beginning of the next 2 rows.

Sizes 86cm (34in) to 116cm (46in) only: cast off 2sts at the beginning of the next 2 rows 2[2: 2: 1: 1: 1: 0] time(s)

Decrease 1st (see Knitting Notes) at each end of the next row and then every alternate row 18[19: 22: 25: 25: 26: 30] times

Cast off 2sts at the beginning of the next 2 rows 2[2: 1: 1: 1: 1: 0] time(s) – 26[26: 26: 28: 30: 32: 36]sts.

Size 122cm (48in) only: decrease 1st (see Knitting Notes) at each end of the next row and then at each end of every alternate row 12 times, every 4th row 3 times and then every alternate row again 14 times – 38sts.

Cast off the remaining 26[26: 26: 28: 30: 32: 36: 38]sts.

Join shoulder seams with mattress stitch.

Neckband

Before you start to knit the Neckband, thread at least 254[262: 286: 294: 302: 314: 314: 322] beads on to 1 ball of the yarn.

Using 2.50mm (US 1.5) needles and with the RS of the garment facing you, starting with the Right Front, knit 10[11: 12: 12: 13: 13: 13: 14]sts from the Right-Front stitch holder, knit pick up 29[29: 33: 34: 34: 36: 36: 36]sts up the Right-Front neck edge, 7sts down the right-hand side of the Back neck edge, 36[38: 40: 42: 44: 46: 46: 48]sts from the cast-off at the Back neck, 7sts up the left-hand side of the Back neck edge, 29[29: 33: 34: 34: 36: 36: 36]sts down Left-Front neck edge and knit 10[11: 12: 12: 13: 13: 13: 14]sts from the Left-Front stitch holder – 128[132: 144: 148: 152: 158: 158: 162]sts.

Row 1 (WS): k1, *SB1, k1*, repeat from * to * to the end of the row.

Knit 7 rows.

Repeat Row 1.

Knit 1 row.

Cast off with the WS facing you.

Right-Front Band

Before you start to knit the Right-Front Band, thread at least 263[281: 275: 281: 281: 281: 281: 287] beads on to 1 ball of the yarn.

Using 2.50mm (US 1.5) needles and with the RS of the garment facing you, knit pick up 20sts across the band, 105[114: 111: 114: 114: 114: 114: 117]sts up the Right Front (approx. 3st for every 4 rows) and 6sts across the end of the Neckband – 131[140: 137: 140: 140: 140: 140: 143]sts.

Row 1 (WS): k1, SB1, k4, *SB1, k1*, repeat from * to * to the end of the row.

Row 2: knit.

Row 3: k1, SB1, knit to the last stitch, SB1, k1.

Repeat the last 2 rows 2 times and then Row 2 again – 5 rows.

Next row (WS): k1, *SB1, k1*, repeat from * to * to the end of the row.

Knit 1 row.

Cast off with the WS facing you.

Left-Front Band

Before you start to knit the Left-Front Band, thread at least 263[281: 275: 281: 281: 281: 281: 287] beads on to 1 ball of the yarn.

Using 2.50mm (US 1.5) needles and with the RS of the garment facing you, knit pick up 6sts across the end of the Neckband, 105[114: 111: 114: 114: 114: 114: 117]sts down the Left Front (approx. 3st for every 4 rows), and knit 20sts from the Left-Front-band stitch holder – 131[140: 137: 140: 140: 140: 140: 143]sts.

Row 1 (WS): *k1, SB1*, repeat from * to * to the last 5sts, k4, SB1, k1.

Row 2: knit.

Row 3: k1, SB1, knit to the last stitch, SB1, k1.

Repeat the last 2 rows 2 times and then Row 2 again – 5 rows.

Next row (WS): k1, *SB1, k1*, repeat from * to * to the end of the row.

Knit 1 row.

Cast off with the WS facing you.

Finishing

Wash and block all of the garment pieces, and leave them lying flat to dry before completing the making up. Sew each Sleeve into an armhole, making sure that the centre of each sleeve cap matches up with the corresponding shoulder seam and that the cast-off sections at each underarm align with the cast-off sections on each side of that sleeve cap. Sew both side seams and underarm seams. Weave in all yarn ends.

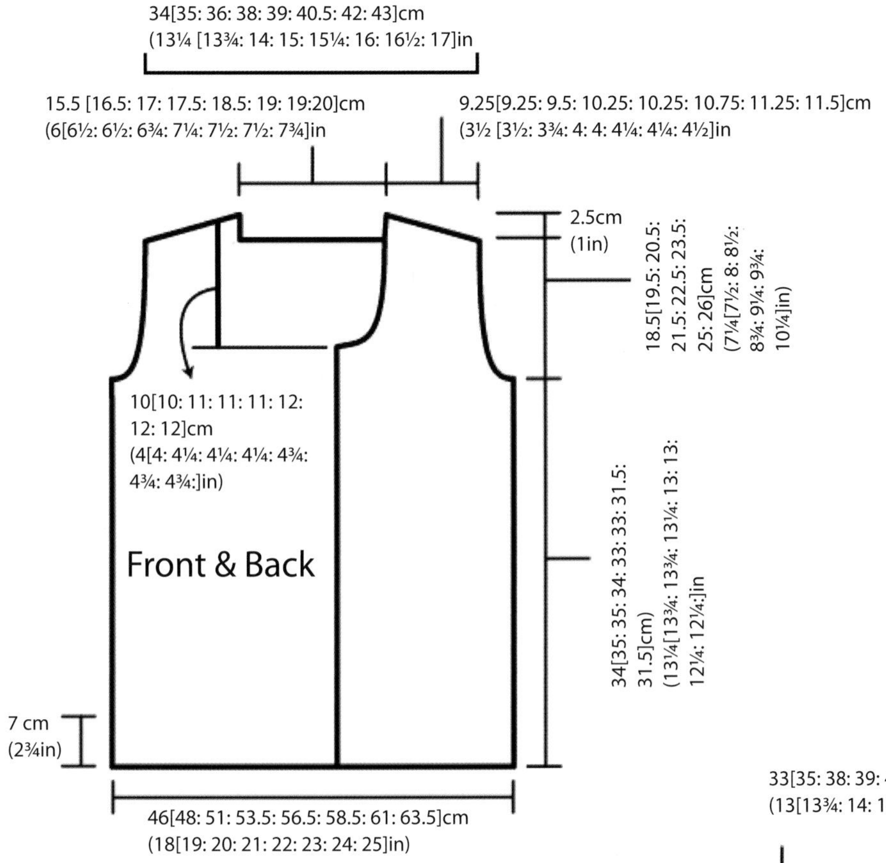
34[35: 36: 38: 39: 40.5: 42: 43]cm
(13¼ [13¾: 14: 15: 15¼: 16: 16½: 17]in
15.5 [16.5: 17: 17.5: 18.5: 19: 19:20]cm
(6[6½: 6½: 6¾: 7¼: 7½: 7½: 7¾]in
9.25[9.25: 9.5: 10.25: 10.25: 10.75: 11.25: 11.5]cm
(3½ [3½: 3¾: 4: 4: 4¼: 4¼: 4½]in
2.5cm
(1in)
18.5[19.5: 20.5: 21.5: 22.5: 23.5: 25: 26]cm
(7¼[7½: 8: 8½: 8¾: 9¼: 9¾: 10¼]in)
10[10: 11: 11: 11: 12: 12: 12]cm
(4[4: 4¼: 4¼: 4¼: 4¾: 4¾: 4¾:]in)
Front & Back
34[35: 35: 34: 33: 33: 31.5: 31.5]cm)
(13¼[13¾: 13¾: 13¼: 13: 13: 12¼: 12¼:]in
7 cm
(2¾in)
46[48: 51: 53.5: 56.5: 58.5: 61: 63.5]cm
(18[19: 20: 21: 22: 23: 24: 25]in)

Body schematic for the Forest Beaded Jacket.

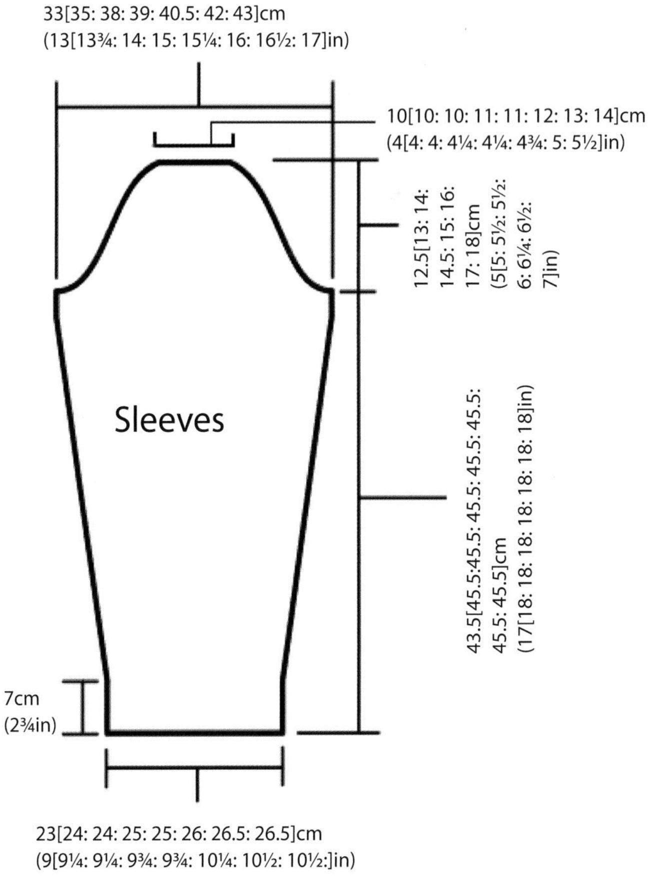
33[35: 38: 39: 40.5: 42: 43]cm
(13[13¾: 14: 15: 15¼: 16: 16½: 17]in)
10[10: 10: 11: 11: 12: 13: 14]cm
(4[4: 4: 4¼: 4¼: 4¾: 5: 5½]in)
12.5[13: 14: 14.5: 15: 16: 17: 18]cm
(5[5: 5½: 5½: 6: 6¼: 6½: 7]in)
Sleeves
43.5[45.5:45.5: 45.5: 45.5: 45.5: 45.5: 45.5]cm
(17[18: 18: 18: 18: 18: 18: 18]in)
7cm
(2¾in)
23[24: 24: 25: 25: 26: 26.5: 26.5]cm
(9[9¼: 9¼: 9¾: 9¾: 10¼: 10½: 10½:]in)

Sleeve schematic for the Forest Beaded Jacket.

Flying-V2 Cardigan, knitted with Bergère de France Coton Fifty 4ply/
fingering-weight yarn and Czech size 7 seed beads.

Flying-V2 Cardigan, knitted with Katia Concept Cotton-Cashmere 4ply/
fingering-weight yarn and Toho size 8 seed beads.

Flying-V2 Cardigan

The Flying-V2 Cardigan is knitted mainly in stocking stitch, and running up each front is a panel of Beaded Stocking Stitch, with the beads placed between purl stitches. The Beaded-Knitting technique is covered in Chapter 3.

The featured garments were knitted with two different yarns. The garment shape and style is basically the same for each garment, but the bands and cuffs are knitted differently. The light-green Rib Flying-V2 Cardigan was knitted with Bergère de France Coton Fifty 4ply/fingering-weight yarn and size 7 Czech seed beads, and the bottom bands and cuffs were worked in a rib of knit one stitch, purl one stitch, which draws in the edges, giving the garment a 1950s' look. The pale-blue Moss-Stitch Flying-V2 Cardigan was knitted with Katia Concept Cotton-Cashmere 4ply/fingering-weight yarn and size 8 Toho seed beads, and the bottom bands and cuffs were worked in moss (seed) stitch, to match the neckband and front bands.

Sizes

To fit bust/chest	86	91	96	102	106	112	116	122	cm
	34	36	38	40	42	44	46	48	in
Finished bust/chest	92	96	102	107	113	117	122	127	cm
measurement	36	38	40	42	44	46	48	50	in
Back length	55	57	57	58	58	59	59	60	cm
	21½	22¼	22¼	22¾	22¾	23¼	23¼	23½	in
Sleeve length to underarm	43.5	45.5	45.5	45.5	45.5	45.5	45.5	45.5	cm
	17	18	18	18	18	18	18	18	in

Materials

- 9[10: 10: 11: 11: 11: 12: 12] × 50g (1¾oz) balls of Bergère de France Coton Fifty 4ply/fingering-weight yarn, 50-per-cent cotton, 50-per-cent acrylic, approx. 140m (153 yd) per ball, in shade no. J9457
  Or
  8[9: 9: 10: 10: 11: 12: 12] × 50g (1¾oz) balls of Katia Concept Cotton-Cashmere 4ply/fingering-weight yarn, 90-per-cent cotton, 10-per-cent cashmere, approx. 155m (169yd) per ball, in shade no. 57
- Pair of 2.75mm (US 2) needles
- Pair of 3.25mm (US 3) needles
- Approx. 850 size 8 or 7 seed beads, for the Rib Cardigan
- Approx. 1,000 size 8 or 7 seed beads, for the Moss-Stitch Cardigan
- The pale-green Rib Cardigan was worked with Czech size 7 Turquoise Silver-Lined seed beads.
- The pale-blue Moss-Stitch Cardigan was worked with Toho size 8 Higher Metallic Dragonfly seed beads.
- 9 buttons
- Stitch holders
- 2 stitch markers
- Tapestry needle
- Beading mat/container, for holding beads for threading
- Big Eye beading needle or beading needle, threaded with transition thread, for threading beads on to yarn

Tension

- 27sts and 38 rows in 10cm (4in) with 3.25mm (US 3) needles over stocking-stitch fabric, after washing, blocking and leaving lying flat to dry.

Knitting Notes

Thread the beads on to the yarn before you start to knit the Beaded-Stocking-Stitch panels. The beads have to be pushed along the knitting yarn, which causes abrasion along the yarn, so when working the Rib Cardigan it is better to use a different ball of yarn to knit the front sections of rib and then join in the yarn with the beads threaded on to it to knit the rest of both front panels.

The beaded panels are worked by following the Flying-V2 Chart, which is a standard chart for flat knitting, reading odd-number rows from right to left and even-number rows from left to right. Each bead sits between two purl stitches on the right side of the knitted fabric.

Shaping decreases are worked two stitches in from the edge of the fabric as follows:
k2, skpo, work to the last 4sts, k2tog, k2.

Shaping increases are worked two stitches in from the edge of the fabric as follows:
k2, m1, work to 2sts before the end of the row, m1, k2.

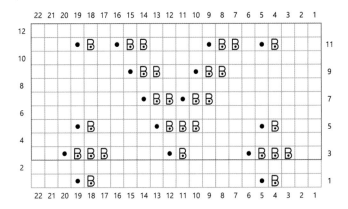

Flying-V2 Chart.

Back

For the Rib and Moss-Stitch Cardigans
Using 2.75mm (US 2) needles, cast on 123[129: 137: 143: 151: 157: 163: 171]sts.

For the Rib Cardigan
Row 1 (RS): k1, *p1, k1*, repeat from * to * to the end of the row.
Row 2: p1, *k1, p1*, repeat from * to * to the end of the row.
Repeat Rows 1 and 2 of k1, p1 rib until you have worked 40 rows in total – 10cm (4in).

For the Moss-Stitch Cardigan
Row 1: k1, *p1, k1*, repeat from * to * to the end of the row.
Repeat Row 1, 9 times – 2cm (¾in).

For the Rib and Moss-Stitch Cardigans
Change to working with 3.25mm (US 3) needles.
Next row (RS): continue by working in stocking stitch, and, at the beginning of the row, increase by 1st – 124[130: 138: 144: 152: 158: 164: 172]sts.
Continue working in stocking stitch until the Back measures 34[35: 35: 34: 33: 33: 31.5: 31.5]cm (13¼[13¾: 13¾: 13¼: 13: 13: 12¼: 12¼]in) from the cast-on, finishing after a WS row.

Armholes
Cast off 5[6: 7: 7: 8: 8: 8: 9]sts at the beginning of the next 2 rows.
Decrease 1st (see Knitting Notes) at each end of the next row and then every alternate row 10[11: 12: 13: 14: 15: 16: 18] times – 92[94: 98: 102: 106: 110: 114: 116]sts.
Continue working straight in stocking stitch until the Back measures 52[54: 54: 55: 55: 56: 56: 57]cm (20½[21¼: 21¼: 21½: 21½: 22: 22: 22¼]in) from the cast-on, finishing after a RS row.

Back neck and shoulders
P28[28: 29: 30: 31: 32: 34: 34]sts (forming the second group of stitches), cast off 36[38: 40: 42: 44: 46: 46: 48] sts and p28[28: 29: 30: 31: 32: 34: 34]sts (forming the first group of stitches).
Working over the first group of stitches only, decrease 1st (see Knitting Notes) at the neck edge on the next row and

then every alternate row 2 times, and, *at the same time*, at the beginning of RS rows, cast off 5[5: 6: 6: 6: 6: 7: 7]sts 5[5: 1: 2: 3: 4: 1: 1] time(s) and then 0[0: 5: 5: 5: 5: 6: 6]sts 0[0: 4: 3: 2: 1: 4: 4] time(s) –
With the RS facing, rejoin the yarn at the Back neck edge to work the second side of the neck and shoulder shaping with the second group of stitches. Decrease 1st (see Knitting Notes) at the neck edge on the next row and then every alternate row 2 times, and, *at the same time*, at the beginning of WS rows, cast off 5[5: 6: 6: 6: 6: 7: 7]sts 5[5: 1: 2: 3: 4: 1: 1] time(s) and then 0[0: 5: 5: 5: 5: 6: 6]sts 0[0: 4: 3: 2: 1: 4: 4] time(s). All stitches are cast off on the second shoulder.

Left Front

For the Rib Cardigan
Before you start to knit the Left Front, thread at least 380[400: 390: 400: 400: 400: 400: 410] beads on to 1 ball of the yarn. As the rib is 10cm (4in) deep, you may prefer to knit the rib with a different ball of yarn, without any beads on it.

For the Moss-Stitch Cardigan
Before you start to knit the Left Front, thread at least 460[480: 470: 480: 480: 480: 480: 490] beads on to 1 ball of the yarn.

For the Rib and Moss-Stitch Cardigans
Using 2.75mm (US 2) needles, cast on 61[65: 69: 71: 75: 79: 81: 85]sts, and work in rib or moss stitch, as given for the Back.
Change to working with 3.25mm (US 3) needles.
Next row (RS): continue by working in stocking stitch, increasing 1[0: 0: 1: 1: 0: 1: 1]st(s) at the beginning of the next row – 62[65: 69: 72: 76: 79: 82: 86]sts.
Work 2 rows of stocking stitch.

Rib Cardigan only: if you knitted the rib with a ball of yarn without threaded beads, you need to change to working with the ball of yarn threaded with beads.
Work the Beaded-Stocking-Stitch pattern as follows:
Row 1 (RS): k36[39: 43: 46: 50: 53: 56: 60], pm, work from the Flying-V2 Chart for 22sts, pm, k4.
Row 2: purl.

Continue working in stocking stitch and Beaded Stocking Stitch, as established, by following the Flying-V2 Chart for the beaded pattern over the 22sts between the stitch markers as set in Row 1 but working the Flying-V2 Chart between Rows 3 and 12 only (the pattern repeat) until the Left Front measures 34[35: 35: 34: 33: 33: 31.5: 31.5]cm (13¼[13¾: 13¾: 13¼: 13: 13: 12¼: 12¼]in) from the cast-on, finishing after a WS row.

Armhole

Continue working in stocking stitch and Beaded Stocking Stitch, as established, and *at the same time*:

Cast off 5[6: 7: 7: 8: 8: 8: 9]sts at the beginning of the next row.

Purl 1 row.

Decrease 1st (see Knitting Notes) at the beginning of the next row and then every alternate row 10[11: 12: 13: 14: 15: 16: 18] times – 46[47: 49: 51: 53: 55: 57: 58]sts.

Continue working straight in stocking stitch and Beaded Stocking Stitch, as established, until the Left Front measures 45[47: 46: 47: 47: 47: 47: 48]cm (17¾[18½: 18: 18½: 18½: 18½: 18½: 18¾]in) from the cast-on, finishing after a WS row.

Front neck

Work 32[32: 33: 35: 36: 38: 40: 40]sts in pattern, k2tog, k2, and slip the remaining 10[11: 12: 12: 13: 13: 13: 14]sts to a stitch holder.

Purl 1 row

Decrease 1st at the neck edge as established on the next row and then every alternate row 9[9: 9: 10: 10: 11: 11: 11] times, and continue including the Beaded-Stocking-Stitch pattern where possible to the end of the current pattern repeat.

Continue working straight in stocking stitch until the Left Front measures 52.5[54.5: 54.5: 55.5: 55.5: 56.5: 56.5: 57.5]cm (20½[21½: 21½: 21¾: 21¾: 22¼: 22¼: 22½]in) from the cast-on, finishing after a WS row.

Shoulder

At the beginning of RS rows, cast off 5[5: 6: 6: 6: 6: 7: 7]sts 5[5: 1: 2: 3: 4: 1: 1] time(s) and then 0[0: 5: 5: 5: 5: 6: 6]sts 0[0: 4: 3: 2: 1: 4: 4] time(s). All the shoulder stitches are cast off at this point.

Right Front

For the Rib Cardigan

Before you start to knit the Right Front, thread at least 380[400: 390: 400: 400: 400: 400: 410] beads on to 1 ball of the yarn. As the rib is 10cm (4in) deep, you may prefer to knit the rib with a different ball of yarn, without any beads on it.

For the Moss-Stitch Cardigan

Before you start to knit the Right Front, thread at least 460[480: 470: 480: 480: 480: 480: 490] beads on to 1 ball of the yarn.

For the Rib and Moss-Stitch Cardigans

Using 2.75mm (US 2) needles, cast on 61[65: 69: 71: 75: 79: 81: 85]sts, and work in rib or moss stitch as given for the Back.

Change to working with 3.25mm (US 3) needles.

Next row (RS): continue by working in stocking stitch, increasing 1[0: 0: 1: 1: 0: 1: 1]st(s) at the beginning of the next row – 62[65: 69: 72: 76: 79: 82: 86]sts.

Work 2 rows of stocking stitch.

Rib Cardigan only: if you knitted the rib with a ball of yarn without threaded beads, you need to change to working with the ball of yarn threaded with beads.

Work the Beaded-Stocking-Stitch pattern as follows:

Row 1 (RS): k4, pm, work from the Flying-V2 Chart for 22sts, pm, knit to the end of the row.

Row 2: purl.

Continue working in stocking stitch and Beaded Stocking Stitch as established, by following the Flying-V2 Chart for the beaded pattern over the 22sts between the stitch markers as set in Row 1 but working the Flying-V2 Chart between Rows 3 and 12 only (the pattern repeat) until the Right Front measures 34[35: 35: 34: 33: 33: 31.5: 31.5]cm (13¼[13¾: 13¾: 13¼: 13: 13: 12¼: 12¼]in) from the cast-on, finishing after a WS row.

Armhole

Continue working in stocking stitch and Beaded Stocking Stitch, as established, and *at the same time*:

Knit 1 row.

Cast off 5[6: 7: 7: 8: 8: 8: 9]sts at the beginning of the next row.

Decrease 1st (see Knitting Notes) at the end of next row and then every alternate row 10[11: 12: 13: 14: 15: 16: 18] times – 46[47: 49: 51: 53: 55: 57: 58]sts.

Continue working straight in stocking stitch and Beaded Stocking Stitch, as established, until the Right Front measures 45[47: 46: 47: 47: 47: 47: 48]cm (17¾[18½: 18: 18½: 18½: 18½: 18½: 18¾]in) from the cast-on, finishing after a WS row.

Front neck
K10[11: 12: 12: 13: 13: 13: 14]sts, slip these stitches on to a stitch holder, then k2, ssk and work in pattern to the end of the row.

Purl 1 row.

Decrease 1st at the neck edge as established on the next row and then every alternate row 9[9: 9: 10: 10: 11: 11: 11] times, and continue including the Beaded-Stocking-Stitch pattern where possible to the end of the current pattern repeat.

Continue working straight in stocking stitch until the Right Front measures 52.5[54.5: 54.5: 55.5: 55.5: 56.5: 56.5: 57.5] cm (20½[21½: 21½: 21¾: 21¾: 22¼: 22¼: 22½]in) from the cast-on, finishing after a RS row.

Shoulder
At the beginning of WS rows, cast off 5[5: 6: 6: 6: 6: 7: 7]sts 5[5: 1: 2: 3: 4: 1: 1] time(s) and then 0[0: 5: 5: 5: 5: 6: 6]sts 0[0: 4: 3: 2: 1: 4: 4] time(s).

Sleeve (knit two)

For the Rib Cardigan
Using 2.75mm (US 2) needles, cast on 61[63: 63: 67: 67: 69: 71: 71]sts and work in rib (as for the Back) for 7cm (2¾in).

Change to working with 3.25mm (US 3) needles.

Working in stocking stitch, increase 1st at the beginning of the next row – 62[64: 64: 68: 68: 70: 72: 72]sts.

Purl 1 row.

Increase 1st (see Knitting Notes) at each end of the next row and every 10th[10th: 8th: 8th: 8th: 8th: 6th: 6th] row 2[2: 11: 11: 5: 2: 20: 21] times and then every 8th[8th: 6th: 6th: 6th: 6th: 0:0] row 11[12: 5: 5: 13: 17: 0: 0] times – 90[94: 98: 102: 106: 110: 114: 116]sts.

For the Moss-Stitch Cardigan
Using 2.75mm (US 2) needles, cast on 61[63: 63: 67: 67: 69: 71: 71]sts and work in moss stitch (as for the Back) for 2cm (¾in).

Change to working with 3.25mm (US 3) needles.

Working in stocking stitch, increase 1st at the beginning of the next row – 62[64: 64: 68: 68: 70: 72: 72]sts.

Purl 1 row.

Increase 1st (see Knitting Notes) at each end of the next row and every 10th[10th: 10th: 10th: 8th: 8th: 8th: 8th] row 13[12: 4: 4: 15: 12: 9: 6] times and then every 0[8th: 8th: 8th: 6th: 6th: 6th: 6th] row 0[2: 12: 12: 3: 7: 11: 15] times – 90[94: 98: 102: 106: 110: 114: 116]sts.

For the Rib and Moss-Stitch Cardigans
Continue working straight in stocking stitch until the Sleeve measures 43.5[45.5: 45.5: 45.5: 45.5: 45.5: 45.5: 45.5]cm (17[18: 18: 18: 18: 18: 18: 18]in) from the cast-on, finishing after a WS row.

Sleeve cap
Cast off 5[6: 7: 7: 8: 8: 8: 9]sts at the beginning of the next 2 rows.

Sizes 86cm (34in) to 116cm (46in) only: cast off 2sts at the beginning of the next 2 rows 2[2: 2: 1: 1: 1: 0] time(s).

Decrease 1st (see Knitting Notes) at each end of the next row and then every alternate row 18[19: 22: 25: 25: 26: 30] times.

Cast off 2sts at the beginning of the next 2 rows 2[2: 1: 1: 1: 1: 0] time(s) – 26[26: 26: 28: 30: 32: 36]sts.

Size 122cm (48in) only: decrease 1st (see Knitting Notes) at each end of the next row and then every alternate row 12 times, every 4th row 3 times and then every alternate row again 14 times – 38sts.

Cast off the remaining 26[26: 26: 28: 30: 32: 36: 38]sts.
Join shoulder seams.

Neckband

For the Rib and Moss-Stitch Cardigans
Using 2.75mm (US 2) needles and with the RS of the garment facing you, starting with the Right Front, knit 10[11: 12: 12: 13: 13: 13: 14]sts from the Right-Front stitch holder, knit pick up 29[29: 33: 34: 34: 36: 36: 36]sts up the Right-Front neck edge, 7sts down the right-hand side of the Back neck edge, 36[38: 40: 42: 44: 46: 46: 48]sts from the cast-off at the Back neck, 7sts up the left-hand side of the Back neck edge, 29[29: 33: 34: 34: 36: 36: 36]sts down the Left-Front neck edge and knit 10[11: 12: 12: 13: 13: 13: 14]sts from the Left-Front stitch holder – 128[132: 144: 148: 152: 158: 158: 162]sts.

Knit 1 row, decreasing 1st at the centre of the Back.

Next row: k1, *p1, k1*, repeat from * to * to the end of the row.

Repeat this row, 6 times.

Cast off with the Knit Cast-Off on a WS row.

Button Band (Left Front)

For the Rib Cardigan
Using 2.75mm (US 2) needles and with the RS of the Left Front facing you, knit pick up 99[105: 101: 105: 105: 105: 105: 107]sts from the neck edge (not including the Neckband) to the top of the rib and 30sts across the rib – 129[135: 131: 135: 135: 135: 135: 137]sts.

For the Moss-Stitch Cardigan
Using 2.75mm (US 2) needles and with the RS of the Left Front facing you, knit pick up 123[129: 125: 129: 129: 129: 129: 131]sts from the neck edge (not including the Neckband) to the top of the moss stitch and 6sts across the moss stitch – 129[135: 131: 135: 135: 135: 135: 137]sts.

For the Rib and Moss-Stitch Cardigans
Knit 1 row.

Next row: k1, *p1, k1*, repeat from * to * to the end of the row.

Repeat this row, 6 times.

Cast off with the Knit Cast-Off on a WS row.

Buttonhole Band (Right Front)

For the Rib Cardigan
Using 2.75mm (US 2) needles and with the RS of the Right Front facing you, knit pick up 30sts from the bottom edge to the top of the rib and 99[105: 101: 105: 105: 105: 105: 107]sts from the top of the rib to the neck edge (not including the Neckband) – 129[135: 131: 135: 135: 135: 135: 137]sts.

For the Moss-Stitch Cardigan
Using 2.75mm (US 2) needles and with the RS of the Right Front facing you, knit pick up 6sts from the bottom edge to the top of the moss stitch and 123[129: 125: 129: 129: 129: 129: 131]sts from the top of the moss stitch to the neck edge (not including the Neckband) – 129[135: 131: 135: 135: 135: 135: 137]sts.

For the Rib and Moss-Stitch Cardigans
Knit 1 row.

Next row: k1, *p1, k1*, repeat from * to * to the end of the row.

Repeat this row, 1 time.

Buttonhole Row: continuing in pattern as set, work 4sts, cast off 2sts, *work 13sts in pattern as set, cast off 2sts*, repeat from * to * 6[2: 6: 2: 2: 2: 2: 0] times and then **work 12[14: 14: 14: 14: 14: 14]sts in pattern as set, cast off 2sts**, repeat from ** to ** 0[4: 0: 4: 4: 4: 4: 6] times, k4.

Next row: keeping in pattern, work the row by casting on 2sts over every 2sts that were cast off in the previous row.

Work 3 more rows of moss stitch.

Cast off with the Knit Cast-Off on a WS row.

Finishing

Wash and block all of the garment pieces, and leave them lying flat to dry before completing the making up. Sew each Sleeve into an armhole, making sure that the centre of each sleeve cap matches up with the corresponding shoulder seam and that the cast-off sections at each underarm align with the cast-off sections on each side of that sleeve cap. Sew the side and underarm seams. Sew on the buttons. Weave in all yarn ends.

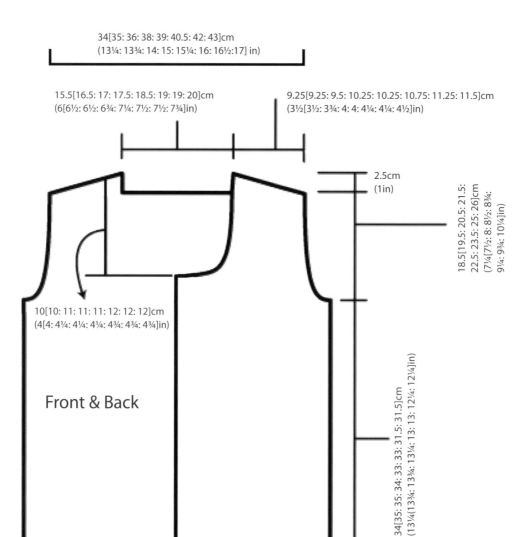

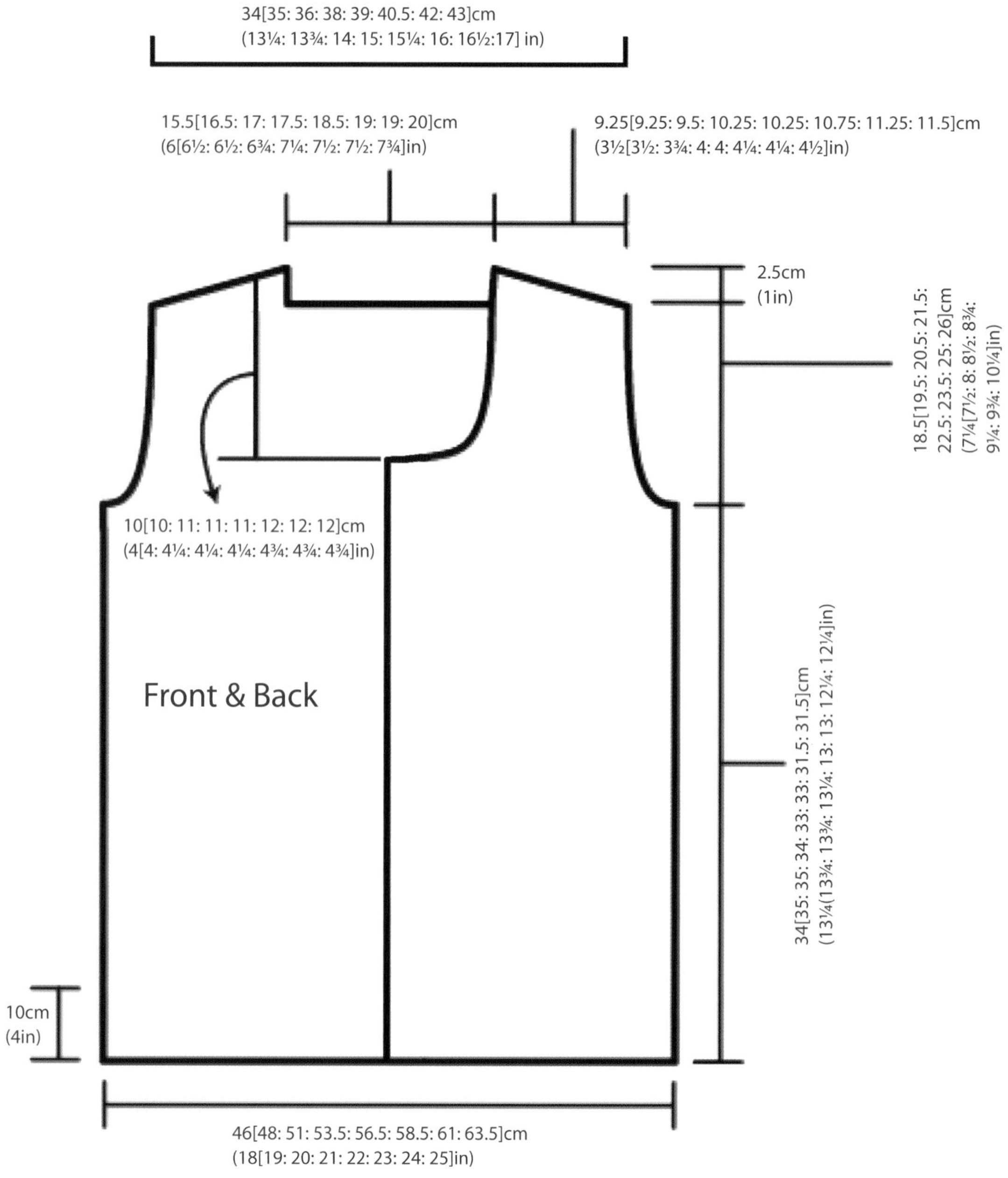

34[35: 36: 38: 39: 40.5: 42: 43]cm
(13¼[13¾: 14: 15: 15¼: 16: 16½:17] in)

15.5[16.5: 17: 17.5: 18.5: 19: 19: 20]cm
(6[6½: 6½: 6¾: 7¼: 7½: 7½: 7¾]in)

9.25[9.25: 9.5: 10.25: 10.25: 10.75: 11.25: 11.5]cm
(3½[3½: 3¾: 4: 4: 4¼: 4¼: 4½]in)

2.5cm
(1in)

18.5[19.5: 20.5: 21.5: 22.5: 23.5: 25: 26]cm
(7¼[7½: 8: 8½: 8¾: 9¼: 9¾: 10¼]in)

10[10: 11: 11: 11: 12: 12: 12]cm
(4[4: 4¼: 4¼: 4¼: 4¾: 4¾: 4¾]in)

Front & Back

34[35: 35: 34: 33: 33: 31.5: 31.5]cm
(13¼[13¾: 13¾: 13¼: 13: 13: 12¼: 12¼]in)

10cm
(4in)

46[48: 51: 53.5: 56.5: 58.5: 61: 63.5]cm
(18[19: 20: 21: 22: 23: 24: 25]in)

Body schematic for the Rib Flying-V2 Cardigan, with rib cuffs and bands.

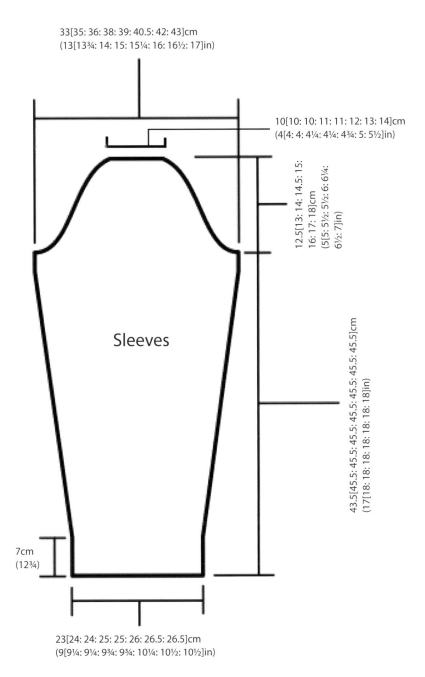

33[35: 36: 38: 39: 40.5: 42: 43]cm
(13[13¾: 14: 15: 15¼: 16: 16½: 17]in)

10[10: 10: 11: 11: 12: 13: 14]cm
(4[4: 4: 4¼: 4¼: 4¾: 5: 5½]in)

12.5[13: 14: 14.5: 15: 16: 17: 18]cm
(5[5: 5½: 5½: 6: 6¼: 6½: 7]in)

43.5[45.5: 45.5: 45.5: 45.5: 45.5: 45.5: 45.5]cm
(17[18: 18: 18: 18: 18: 18: 18]in)

Sleeves

7cm
(12¾)

23[24: 24: 25: 25: 26: 26.5: 26.5]cm
(9[9¼: 9¼: 9¾: 9¾: 10¼: 10½: 10½]in)

Sleeve schematic for the Rib Flying-V2 Cardigan, with rib cuffs and bands.

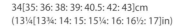

34[35: 36: 38: 39: 40.5: 42: 43]cm
(13¼[13¾: 14: 15: 15¼: 16: 16½: 17]in)

15.5[16.5: 17: 17.5: 18.5: 19: 19: 20]cm)
(6[6½: 6½: 6¾: 7¼: 7½: 7½: 7¾]in)

9.25[9.25: 9.5: 10.25: 10.25: 10.75: 11.25: 11.5]cm
3½[3½: 3¾: 4: 4: 4¼: 4¼: 4½]in)

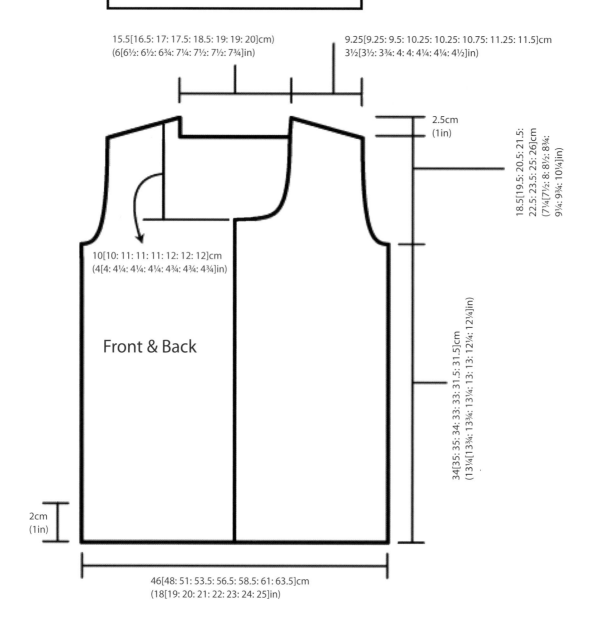

2.5cm
(1in)

18.5[19.5: 20.5: 21.5: 22.5: 23.5: 25: 26]cm
(7¼[7½: 8: 8½: 8¾: 9¼: 9¾: 10¼]in)

10[10: 11: 11: 11: 12: 12: 12]cm
(4[4: 4¼: 4¼: 4¼: 4¾: 4¾: 4¾]in)

Front & Back

34[35: 35: 34: 33: 33: 31.5: 31.5]cm
(13¼[13¾: 13¾: 13¼: 13: 13: 12¼: 12¼]in)

2cm
(1in)

46[48: 51: 53.5: 56.5: 58.5: 61: 63.5]cm
(18[19: 20: 21: 22: 23: 24: 25]in)

Body schematic for the Moss-Stitch Flying-V2 Cardigan, with moss-stitch edges.

33[35: 36: 38: 39: 40.5: 42: 43]cm
(13[13¾: 14: 15: 15¼ 16: 16½: 17]in)

10[10: 10: 11: 11: 12: 13: 14]cm
(4[4: 4: 4¼: 4¼: 4¾: 5: 5½]in)

12.5[13: 14: 14.5: 15:
16: 17: 18]cm
(5[5: 5½: 5½: 6: 6¼:
6½: 7]in)

Sleeves

43.5[45.5: 45.5: 45.5: 45.5: 45.5: 45.5: 45.5]cm
(17[18: 18: 18: 18: 18: 18: 18]in)

2cm
(¾in)

23[24: 24: 25: 25: 26: 26.5: 26.5]cm
(9[9¼: 9¼: 9¾: 9¾: 10¼: 10½: 10½]in)

Sleeve schematic for the Moss-Stitch Flying-V2 Cardigan, with moss-stitch edges.

Abbreviations and Chart Symbols

Abbreviations

General abbreviations

AB – aurora borealis

approx. – approximately

cm – centimetre(s)

DK – double knit (yarn weight)

g – gram(s)

in – inch(es)

k – knit

k1tbl – knit 1st through the back loop

m – metre(s)

mm – millimetre(s)

oz – ounce(s)

p – purl

p1tbl – purl 1st through the back loop

p2tbl – purl 2sts through the back loop

pm – place stitch marker

RS – right side of fabric (the public side)

sl1 – slip 1st purlwise

sl1 wyb – slip 1st purlwise with the yarn at the back (away from you)

sm – slip the stitch marker

st(s) – stitch(es)

w&t – wrap and turn. Slip the next stitch purlwise from the left-hand needle to the right-hand needle, bring yarn forward between the points of the needles and slip the slipped stitch back to the left-hand needle. Turn the work, to start the next row.

WS – wrong side of fabric (side not visible to the public)

yb – take yarn back between the points of the needles

yd – yard(s)

yf – bring yarn forward between the points of the needles

Instructions for working with beads

BP – Beaded Picot. Cast on 2sts, knit and cast off the next 2sts, slip the working stitch to the left-hand needle, cast on 3sts, push up 1 bead next to the stitch on the right-hand needle, knit and cast off the next 3sts, slip the working stitch to the left-hand needle, cast on 2sts, knit and cast off the next 2sts.

hB – place 1 bead on the crochet hook, slip the next stitch on the left-hand needle on to the crochet hook, push the bead off of the crochet hook and over the stitch and re-place the stitch on to the left-hand needle. Work the stitch as a knit stitch on RS rows and as a purl stitch on WS rows.

k1Btbl – push 1 bead through the stitch to the right side as you work a knit-1st-through-the-back-loop stitch.

K1, SB1 – knit 1st and push up 1 bead next to the stitch just knitted.

p1Btbl – push 1 bead through the stitch to the right side as you work a purl-1st-through-the-back-loop stitch.

P1, SB1 – purl 1st and push up 1 bead next to the stitch just purled.

SB1 – slip up 1 bead next to the stitch just worked.

SB(number) – slip up the number of beads stated next to the stitch just worked.

slB (RS) – bring yarn forward with the bead, slip the next stitch purlwise from the left-hand needle to the right-hand needle, take yarn back while making sure that the bead is in front of the slipped stitch.

slB (WS) – take yarn back with the bead, slip the next stitch purlwise from the left-hand needle to the right-hand needle, bring yarn forward while making sure that the bead is behind the slipped stitch.

yoB – work a yarn over with 1 bead on the yarn-over loop.

yoB3 – work a yarn over with 3 beads on the yarn-over loop.

Increases

kfb – increase by knitting into the front and back of the stitch.

m1 – make one. From the front to the back, lift the strand running between the stitch closest to the point of the left-hand needle and the stitch closest to the point of the right-hand needle on to the left-hand needle (the lifted strand will look like a yarn-over loop) and then knit this strand by working it through the back of the loop, to twist the loop shut as the new stitch is made.

pfb – increase by purling into the front and back of the stitch.

yo – yarn over. For a yarn over that is to sit between two knit stitches, from the back, bring the yarn between the points of the needles and over the right-hand needle; for a yarn over that is to sit between a knit stitch and a purl stitch, from the back, bring the yarn between the points of the needles, over the right-hand needle and back between the points of the needles; for a yarn over that is to sit between two purl stitches, from the front, take the yarn over the right-hand needle and forward between the points of the needles; and for a yarn over that is to sit between a purl stitch and a knit stitch, from the front, take the yarn over the right-hand needle to the back.

yrn – yarn around the needle. With the yarn at the front, take the yarn over the right-hand needle and forward between the points of the needles, ready to work a purl stitch.

Decreases

k2tog – knit 2sts together.

p2tog – purl 2sts together.

p3tog – purl 3sts together.

p4tog – purl 4sts together.

p7tog – purl 7sts together.

sk2po – slip 1st, knit 2sts together, pass the slipped stitch over. Slip the next stitch on the left-hand needle to the right-hand needle knitwise, knit 2sts together (k2tog) on the left-hand needle and pass the slipped stitch over the stitch that was just knitted and off of the right-hand needle.

skpo – slip 1st, knit 1st, pass the slipped stitch over. Slip the next stitch on the left-hand needle to the right-hand needle knitwise, knit 1st on the left-hand needle and pass the slipped stitch over the stitch that was just knitted and off of the right-hand needle.

ssk – slip the next 2sts, one at a time, knitwise, from the left-hand needle to the right-hand needle, put the left-hand needle through these 2 slipped stitches from left to right, in front of the right-hand needle (as if you were going to work a k2tog through the back loops), and knit these 2sts together.

ssp – slip next 2sts, one at a time, knitwise, to the right-hand needle, slip these 2sts back to the left-hand needle and purl the 2sts together through their back loops.

Cables

1/1LC or C2F – 1-over-1 left-cross cable (RS): Slip the next stitch purlwise from the left-hand needle to the cable needle and hold the cable needle at the front of the knitting, knit 1st through the back loop from the left-hand needle, knit 1st through the back loop from the cable needle. 1-over-1 left-cross cable (WS): Slip the next stitch purlwise from the left-hand needle to the cable needle and hold the cable needle at the front of the knitting, purl 1st through the back loop from the left-hand needle, purl 1st through the back loop from the cable needle.

1/1RC or C2B – 1-over-1 right-cross cable (RS): Slip the next stitch purlwise from the left-hand needle to the cable needle and hold the cable needle at the back of the knitting (away from you), knit 1st through the back loop from the left-hand needle, knit 1st through the back loop from the cable needle. 1-over-1 right-cross cable (WS): Slip the next stitch purlwise from the left-hand needle to the cable needle and hold the cable needle at the back of the knitting (away from you), purl 1st through the back loop from the left-hand needle, purl 1st through the back loop from the cable needle.

1k/1pLC – 1-knit-over-1-purl left-cross cable (RS): Slip the next stitch purlwise from the left-hand needle to the cable needle and hold the cable needle at the front of the knitting, purl 1st from the left-hand needle, knit 1st through the back loop from the cable needle. 1-knit-over-1-purl left-cross cable (WS): Slip the next stitch purlwise from the left-hand needle to the cable needle and hold the cable needle at the front of the knitting, purl 1st through the back loop from the left-hand needle, knit 1st from the cable needle.

1k/1pRC – 1-knit-over-1-purl right-cross cable (RS): Slip the next stitch purlwise from the left-hand needle to the cable needle and hold the cable needle at the back of the knitting (away from you), knit 1st through the back loop from the left-hand needle, purl 1st from the cable needle. 1-knit-over-1-purl right-cross cable (WS): Slip the next stitch purlwise from the left-hand needle to the cable needle and hold the cable needle at the back of the knitting (away from you), knit 1st from the left-hand needle, purl 1st through the back loop from the cable needle.

Bavarian Twisted-Stitch Cables – the knit stitches are worked through the back loop and the purl stitches are worked normally on right-side rows. The purl stitches are worked through the back loop and the knit stitches are worked normally on wrong-side rows.

C6B or 3/3RCC – 3-over-3 right-cross cable. Slip the next 3sts purlwise from the left-hand needle to the cable needle and hold the cable needle at the back of the knitting (away from you), knit the next 3sts from the left-hand needle, k3 from the cable needle.

C6F or 3/3LCC – 3-over-3 left-cross cable. Slip the next 3sts purlwise from the left-hand needle to the cable needle and hold the cable needle at the front of the knitting, knit the next 3sts from the left-hand needle, k3 from the cable needle.

Chart symbols

☐	**Knit** on RS rows **Purl** on WS rows
⬤	**Purl** on RS rows **Knit** on WS rows
B	**Place a bead** In **Beaded Garter Stitch**, knit the stitch and then push up 1 bead next to this stitch. In **Bead Knitting**, work 1 bead through the stitch as you work the stitch, working a knit stitch on RS rows and a purl stitch through the back loop on WS rows.
B.	**Beaded purl stitch (RS):** Purl the stitch and then push up 1 bead next to this stitch. **Beaded purl stitch (WS):** Knit the stitch and then push up 1 bead next to this stitch.
B∨	**Beaded slip stitch (RS):** Bring the yarn between the points of the needles, push up 1 bead, slip the next stitch on the left-hand needle to the right-hand needle purlwise and take the yarn back between the points of the needles. The bead sits on the yarn in front of the slipped stitch. **Beaded Slip Stitch (WS):** Take the yarn back between the points of the needles, push up 1 bead, slip the next stitch on the left-hand needle to the right-hand needle purlwise and bring the yarn forward between the points of the needles, leaving the bead on the yarn in front of the slipped stitch as viewed from the RS.
Ⓑ	**Beaded yarn over with 1 bead:** Push up 1 bead next to the stitch just worked, on the right-hand needle, as you make the yarn over.
③	**Beaded yarn over with 3 beads:** Push up 3 beads (or the number in the centre of the circle) next to the stitch just worked, on the right-hand needle, as you make the yarn over.
▦	**How to work the yarn over with beads of the previous row** The bead(s) from the previous row should be at the right-hand end of the yarn over, on the side of the fabric nearest to you, as you work the yarn over.
▦	**How to work the yarn over with beads of the previous row** The bead(s) from the previous row should be at the left-hand end of the yarn over, on the side of the fabric away from you, as you work the yarn over.

B⌄	**Beaded Picot:** Cast on 2sts, knit and cast off the next 2sts, slip the working stitch to the left-hand needle, cast on 3sts, push up 1 bead next to the stitch on the right-hand needle, knit and cast off the next 3sts, slip the working stitch to the left-hand needle, cast on 2sts, knit and cast off the next 2sts. (BP)
⎮B	**Hook Bead:** Place 1 bead on the crochet hook, slip the next stitch on the left-hand needle on to the crochet hook, push the bead off of the crochet hook and over the stitch and re-place the stitch on to the left-hand needle. Work the stitch as a knit stitch on RS rows and as a purl stitch on WS rows.
⌒	**Cast off** in stitch pattern.
○	**Yarn over:** The yarn should always pass over the right-hand needle from the side nearest you to the side away from you. For a yarn over that is to sit between two knit stitches, the yarn must first come from the back between the points of the needles and go over the right-hand needle. For a yarn over that is to sit between two purl stitches, the yarn must go from the front over the right-hand needle and then come back between the points of the needles to the front. For a yarn over that is to sit between a knit stitch and a purl stitch, the yarn must first come from the back between the points of the needles, go over the right-hand needle and then come back between the points of the needles again. For a yarn over that is to sit between a purl stitch and a knit stitch, the yarn must go from the front over the right-hand needle to the back.
ᴓ	**Make one:** From the front to the back, lift the strand running between the stitch closest to the point of the left-hand needle and the stitch closest to the point of the right-hand needle on to the left-hand needle (the lifted strand will look like a yarn-over loop) and then knit this strand by working it through the back of the loop, to twist the loop shut as the new stitch is made.
Ω	**k1tbl** on RS rows **p1tbl** on WS rows

⊙	**p1tbl** on RS rows **k1tbl** on WS rows
＼	**Left-leaning decrease** on RS rows Either ssk or skpo
／	**Right-leaning decrease** on RS rows k2tog
＼•	**Decrease to match left-leaning decrease** (on WS rows) Either ssp or p2togtbl Or, in garter stitch, ssk or skpo
•／	**Decrease to match right-leaning decrease** (on WS rows) p2tog Or, in garter stitch, k2tog
∧	**Centred double decrease:** Slip the next 2sts on the left-hand needle together knitwise to the right-hand needle, knit 1st on the left-hand needle, pass the 2sts that were slipped together over the stitch that was just knitted and off of the right-hand needle. (s2kpo)
∨	**Slip stitch** purlwise with the yarn at the back (away from you).
⊠	**3-over-3 right-cross cable:** Slip the next 3sts to a cable needle and hold at the back of the knitting (away from you), k3 from the left-hand needle and then k3 from the cable needle. (C6B)
⊠	**3-over-3 left-cross cable:** Slip the next 3sts to a cable needle and hold at the front of the knitting, k3 from the left-hand needle and then k3 from the cable needle. (C6F)

1-over-1 right-cross cable with twisted stitches (RS): Slip the next stitch to a cable needle and hold at the back of the knitting (away from you), k1tbl from the left-hand needle and then k1tbl from the cable needle. (C2Btbl)

1-over-1 right-cross cable with twisted stitches (WS): Slip the next stitch to a cable needle and hold at the back of the knitting (away from you), p1tbl from the left-hand needle and then p1tbl from the cable needle. (C2Btbl)

1-over-1 left-cross cable with twisted stitches (RS): Slip the next stitch purlwise from the left-hand needle to the cable needle and hold at the front of the knitting, k1tbl from the left-hand needle and then k1tbl from the cable needle. (C2Ftbl)

1-over-1 left-cross cable with twisted stitches (WS): Slip the next stitch purlwise from the left-hand needle to the cable needle and hold at the front of the knitting, p1tbl from the left-hand needle and then p1tbl from the cable needle. (C2Ftbl)

1-knit-over-1-purl right-cross cable (RS): Slip the next stitch purlwise from the left-hand needle to the cable needle and hold at the back of the knitting (away from you), k1tbl from the left-hand needle and then p1 from the cable needle. (1k/1pRC)

1-knit-over-1-purl right-cross cable (WS): Slip the next stitch purlwise from the left-hand needle to the cable needle and hold at the back of the knitting (away from you), k1 from the left-hand needle and then p1tbl from the cable needle. (1k/1pRC)

1-knit-over-1-purl left-cross cable (RS): Slip the next stitch purlwise from the left-hand needle to the cable needle and hold at the front of the knitting, p1 from the left-hand needle and then k1tbl from the cable needle. (1k/1pLC)

1-knit-over-1-purl left-cross cable (WS): Slip the next stitch purlwise from the left-hand needle to the cable needle and hold at the front of the knitting, p1tbl from the left-hand needle and then k1 from the cable needle. (1k/1pLC)

☐	**Background colour** (colour 1) in Fair Isle patterns
■	**Contrast colour** (colour 2) in Fair Isle patterns
☐	**Outline of pattern repeat**

Resources

Resources of the author

Website

www.fionamorrisdesigns.co.uk
The pattern for the wire-knitted and beaded flower is available for direct download from the following link to Fiona's website: http://www.fionamorrisdesigns.co.uk/wordpress/wp-content/uploads/Diamond_-Jewellery.pdf

YouTube channel, Fiona Morris Designs

https://www.youtube.com/channel/UC3qO1Wa9Jr0goc428bkgahw?view_as=subscriber
The techniques described in this book are demonstrated by Fiona on her YouTube channel.

Charts

Each of the following charts can be obtained as a PDF, by writing to Fiona at fiknits@gmail.com with the relevant codes.
Diamond-Lace Chart: Code DLC1
Wing-Shawl Right-Triangle Chart: Code WSRT2
Wing-Shawl Left-Triangle Chart: Code WSLT3

Suppliers of materials used for samples and projects

Beads

Creative Beadcraft https://www.creativebeadcraft.co.uk
CJ Beaders http://www.cjbeaders.com
Beads Direct https://www.beadsdirect.co.uk

Wires

Scientific Wire Company https://www.wires.co.uk/

Manufacturers of yarns used for samples and projects

Adriafil
Anchor
Baa ram ewe
Bergère de France
Debbie Bliss
Fyberspates
Garnstudio Drops Design®
In the Wool Shed
Jenny Watson
Juniper Moon Farm
Katia
King Cole
Lang Yarns
Patons
Sirdar
Rico® Design
Rowan
Stylecraft
West Yorkshire Spinners

Charting software

Stitchmastery https://www.stitchmastery.com/

Further Reading

Chin, L.M., *Knit and Crochet with Beads* (Interweave Press, Inc., 2004)

Durant, J., *Knit One Bead Too* (Storey Publishing, 2009)

Nelkin, L., *Knockout Knits* (Potter Craft, 2014)

Thomas, M., *Mary Thomas's Knitting Book* (Dover Publications Inc., 1972)

Index

Other Knitting Titles from Crowood

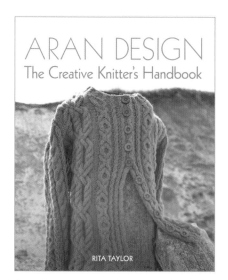

978 1 78500 407 0

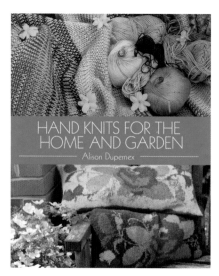

978 1 78500 455 1

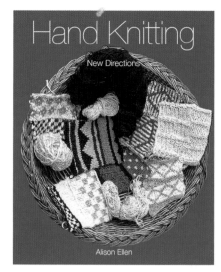

978 1 84797 217 0

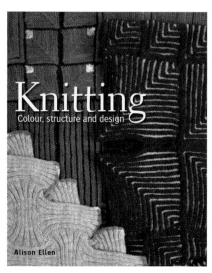

978 1 84797 284 2

987 1 78500 029 4

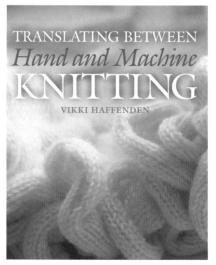

978 1 78500 431 5